D0484986

AN
INCLUSIVE-LANGUAGE
LECTIONARY

AN
INCLUSIVE-LANGUAGE
LECTIONARY

Readings for Year B
Revised Edition

*Prepared for voluntary use in churches by
the Inclusive-Language Lectionary Committee
appointed by the Division of Education and
Ministry, National Council of the Churches of
Christ in the U.S.A.*

· Published for
The Cooperative Publication Association
by
John Knox Press, *Atlanta*
The Pilgrim Press, *New York*
The Westminster Press, *Philadelphia*

Copyright © 1987 Division of Education and Ministry, National Council of the Churches of Christ in the U.S.A.

All rights reserved—no part of this book may be reproduced in any form without permission in writing from the publisher, except by a reviewer who wishes to quote brief passages in connection with a review in magazine or newspaper.

Lectionary texts are based on the Revised Standard Version of the Bible, copyrighted 1946, 1952, © 1971, 1973, and the Apocrypha, copyrighted © 1957, by the Division of Christian Education of the National Council of the Churches of Christ in the U.S.A.

BOOK DESIGN BY ALICE DERR

PRINTED IN THE UNITED STATES OF AMERICA
9 8 7 6 5 4 3 2 1

Library of Congress Cataloging-in-Publication Data

An Inclusive-language lectionary. Readings for year B.

  Includes index.
  1. Bible—Liturgical lessons, English.
2. Lectionaries—Texts. I. National Council
of the Churches of Christ in the United States
of America. Inclusive Language Lectionary
Committee. II. Title.
BS391.2.I522   1987   264′.34   87-8164
ISBN 0-664-24059-3 (Westminster Press : pbk.)

Preface

All persons are equally loved, judged, and accepted by God. This belief has been promoted by the church and has its roots in the origins of the Judeo-Christian tradition. Young and old, male and female, and persons of every racial, cultural, and national background are included in the faith community. Basic to a sense of equality and inclusiveness is the recognition that God by nature transcends all human categories. God is more than male or female, and is more than can be described in historically and culturally limiting terms. Words and language, though inadequate and limited, are means by which we convey God's holiness and mystery. Seeking faithful expression about God and about God's inclusive love for all people, the Division of Education and Ministry of the National Council of the Churches of Christ authorized the preparation of *An Inclusive-Language Lectionary.*

A Task Force on Biblical Translation was appointed by the Division of Education and Ministry to investigate the way in which the language of the Bible presents the characteristics of God and of human beings. In 1980, after almost three years of study and discussion, the Task Force recommended to the Division the creation of an Inclusive-Language Lectionary Committee, which was then appointed. Members bring not only their personal commitment to the Christian faith and involvement in particular congregations but also their experience as pastors, teachers, and leaders who have relied on the Bible as their source of inspiration and basis for understanding God's word for the church today. They bring expertise in Hebrew, Greek, linguistics, English, worship, Old and New Testaments, theology, and education. In addition, the members come from a variety of denominations and liturgical traditions. The Inclusive-Language Lectionary Committee consists of Robert A. Bennett, Dianne Bergant, Victor Roland Gold (Chair), Thomas Hoyt, Jr., Kellie C. Jones, Patrick D. Miller, Jr., Virginia Ramey Mollenkott, Sharon H. Ringe (Vice-Chair), Susan Thistlethwaite, Burton H. Throckmorton, Jr., and Barbara A. Withers (Editor). David Ng is the National Council of the Churches of Christ liaison to the Committee.

The Inclusive-Language Lectionary Committee followed the general guidelines provided by the Division of Education and Ministry to prepare lectionary readings for use in services of worship. These readings are based on the Revised Standard Version of the Bible, with the text revised primarily in those places where gender-specific or other exclusive language could be modified to reflect in English an inclusiveness of all persons. All modifications are supportable by the original Greek and Hebrew texts. The Committee worked on lectionary passages first in subcommittees, each committee consulting not only the original texts but also various translations and commentaries. All subcommittee work was submitted to an Editorial Committee which reviewed the texts for consistency of changes and agreement with guiding principles. The Editorial Committee consists of Barbara A. Withers (Editor), Burton H. Throckmorton, Jr. (Associate Editor), Patrick D. Miller, Jr., and Sharon H. Ringe. As the last step, the full Committee reviewed all work and made all final decisions.

Like most other lectionaries in use today, this lectionary follows the pattern of a three-year cycle beginning with the first Sunday in Advent. The readings for Year A were originally published in October of 1983 and followed the table of readings prepared by the Consultation on Church Union. The second and third volumes contained the readings from the Table of Readings and Psalms prepared for trial use by the North American Committee on Calendar and Lectionary. This revised edition of Year B follows the latter table of readings. A few additions and substitutions were made, consistent with the Committee's mandate (see Appendix, p. 255).

The Introduction which follows offers an explanation of what a lectionary is and discusses the need for inclusive language and how the Committee approached the gender-specific language of the Revised Standard Version. The lectionary passages, along with explanatory footnotes, form the major portion of this volume. An appendix stating a rationale for the major alternative words and phrases and an index of the biblical passages that appear in this lectionary complete this volume.

An Inclusive-Language Lectionary is offered to the church as a responsible attempt to represent the biblical writings in an inclusive manner. Respecting its commitment to be responsive to the interests and needs of the church for which the lectionary has been prepared, the Committee has included the term "Lord" in addition to its formal equivalent, "Sovereign," in the text. This revision was first made in Year C (1985) in an attempt to meet a concern of many persons throughout the church who had used original editions of Years A and B in which "Lord" does not appear. For example, "Give thanks to the SOVEREIGN [*or* LORD], call upon God's name" (Isa. 12:3). "Lord" is printed in this manner as an *alternate* or *substitute* for the word immediately preceding it. "Lord" is *not* to be read aloud *with* the word that precedes it.

An Inclusive-Language Lectionary is a major attempt to recast the language of scripture so that it addresses women and men equally. The church has never believed that God is male or that God speaks to the church in male-oriented language more relevant to men than to women. So the Committee submits this lectionary to the church, remembering the words of the apostle Paul: "There is neither Jew nor Greek, there is neither slave nor free, there is neither male nor female; for you are all one in Christ Jesus" (Gal. 3:28).

Introduction

A lectionary is a fixed selection of readings, taken from both the Old and the New Testament, to be read and heard in the churches' services of worship. Most lectionaries are simply tables or lists of readings to be used in weekly worship; some include daily readings. They cite the biblical book from which the reading is taken, as well as the chapter and verses: for example, Christmas Day: *Luke 2:1–20.* By contrast, this lectionary contains the full text of each reading.

Recent History of Lectionary Development. The International Commission on English in the Liturgy created an ecumenical group known as the Consultation on Common Texts. One of the tasks of this Consultation was to explore the possibilities of creating a lectionary that would be acceptable to most English-speaking Christians: Anglican, Protestant, and Roman Catholic. To that end, a small working group known as the North American Committee on Calendar and Lectionary was formed. Over a period of five years a revised table of lections, or readings, was developed that took into account critiques of the Vatican II lectionary (early 1960s) and its subsequent adaptations by the major Protestant denominations. The report of the North American Committee was approved by the Consultation on Common Texts in 1982, and this "common texts" lectionary was recommended for trial use in the churches beginning with Advent 1983. It is this Table of Readings and Psalms which this lectionary follows, using the Revised Standard Version as its text.

Function of the Lectionary in Congregational Worship. In churches that use the lectionary every Sunday, congregations hear the same scriptures read. Thus the wider church, within denominations and across denominational lines, is united in its hearing, thinking, and praying. A lectionary provides a way for Christians to live out the church year, which begins on the first Sunday of Advent and proceeds through Christmas, Epiphany, Ash Wednesday, Lent, Passion (Palm) Sunday, Maundy Thursday, Good Friday,

Easter, Ascension, and Pentecost. At least four readings are prescribed for each Sunday as well as for special days such as Christmas, Easter, All Saints, and Thanksgiving. The lectionary attempts to provide comprehensive and balanced coverage of the entire Bible. Over a three-year period about 95 percent of the New Testament is heard, as well as about 60 percent of the Old Testament.

It is apparent that any selection of scripture read in a service of worship has been lifted from its biblical context. In the study of the Bible, the context in which a biblical passage occurs is crucial to its interpretation. When passages are read in a service of worship, however, they are read in a new context, in relation to one another and to the church year. This radical change in the context of selections is a major fact that differentiates a lectionary from the Bible.

A lectionary thus has a special function in the worship of the church. It does not supplant the Bible. The Bible is the church's book—created by and for the church. A lectionary is also the church's book, being a prescribed set of readings selected by the church from its scripture for its own special use in worship. The unique feature of *An Inclusive-Language Lectionary* is that it recasts some of the wording of the Revised Standard Version in order to provide both to reader and to hearer a sense of belonging to a Christian faith community in which truly all are one in Christ.

Why Inclusive Language? The lectionary readings are based on the Revised Standard Version and original Greek and Hebrew texts, with the intent of reflecting the full humanity of women and men in the light of the gospel. A growing number of people feel they have been denied full humanity by a pattern of exclusion in English usage. Consider, for example, the traditional English use of the word "man." A man is a male human being, as opposed to a female human being. But in common usage "man" has also meant "human being," as opposed to "animal." On the other hand, "woman" means female, but never *human being.* No word that refers to a female person identifies her with humanity. So, in common English idiom, "man" has been defined by his humanity, but "woman" by her sex, by her relationship to man. "Woman" becomes a subgroup under "human." "Man" is the human race; "woman" is man's sexual partner, in traditional English usage.

This is but one example of how language *reflects* the way in which we think but also *informs* the way in which we think. The mandate to the Lectionary Committee is to seek "language which expresses inclusiveness with regard to human beings and which attempts to expand the range of images beyond the masculine to assist the church in understanding the full nature of God." In the Appendix the reader will find specific examples of how these kinds of excluding language and imagery have been dealt with in this lectionary.

10

The RSV is highly respected by biblical scholars and is widely used in this country. However, in this lectionary the wording of the RSV has been recast to minimize the gender-specific language and other excluding imagery reflected in its language in reference to human beings, Christ, and God. Except for these changes the text of the RSV, for the most part, has been retained.

Gender-specific language, however, is not unique to English translations of the Bible; it is characteristic of the languages in which the Bible was written. Both the Old Testament and the New Testament were written in languages and in cultures that were basically patriarchal; and as the English language is also patriarchal, the patriarchal character of both Testaments has slipped easily into the great English versions of the Bible.

Language About Human Beings. In a few instances the RSV Bible committee has already avoided male-specific language in reference to human beings. For example, in Rom. 7:1 the RSV has used "person" ("the law is binding on a *person*") as a translation of the Greek word *anthropos* (meaning "man" or "person"). But most of the time *anthropos* is translated "man," or, in the plural, "men." For example, Matt. 5:16 in the RSV reads, "Let your light so shine before *men*" where the meaning of "men" is obviously "people," but not male people exclusively. This verse can be rendered: "Let your light so shine before *others*"—that is, men and women, which represents the clear intention of the words.

Excluding language also appears when masculine pronoun subjects are supplied with third person singular verbs when the context does not require them. Compare, for example, the RSV of John 6:35–37: "Jesus said to them, 'I am the bread of life; *he* who comes to me shall not hunger, and *he* who believes in me shall never thirst . . . ; and *him* who comes to me I will not cast out." What is the intention of this passage? It surely is not that only *men* come to Jesus and believe in Jesus. Why, then, does the RSV read "he" and "him"? It is because of the assumption that "he" also means "she," though we know that it does not.

In this lectionary all readings have been recast so that no masculine word pretends to include a woman. For example, the word "brethren" has been rendered in a variety of ways, including "sisters and brothers." Formal equivalents have been adopted for other male-specific words and phrases. For example, "kingdom" is usually rendered "realm" but also by other terms such as "reign" or "dominion"; "king" in reference to God or a messianic figure is rendered "ruler" and "monarch."

In a few instances, references to women have been added—for example, "Abraham [*and Sarah*]." Where the name of a person or details in the narrative make the gender clear, no change has been made. Thus, David is referred to as a "king," the wounded traveler in the parable of the Samaritan

11

is a "man," and Jesus meets a "woman" by the well in Samaria. Where the gender of the person is not specified, the character is referred to as a "person" (e.g., John 9). Also, contemporary English usage suggests that we refer to a person as having a disabling condition, such as polio, rather than to a "cripple" or a "crippled person." So the biblical reference to "the blind and the lame" is rendered "those who are blind and those who are lame" (see Jer. 31:8). Where "darkness" is set in contrast with "light" and has a moral connotation, a substitute word for darkness is supplied—for example, "The light shines in the *deepest night*" (John 1:5).

Language About Jesus Christ. Jesus was a male human being. But when the Gospel of John says, "The Word became flesh" (John 1:14), it does not say or imply that the Word became *male* flesh, but simply *flesh.* Of course, to "become flesh," the one from God had to become male or female, but the language used in this lectionary tries to overcome the implication that in the incarnation Jesus' *maleness* is decisive—or even relevant—for the salvation of women and men who believe, or for matters in which the imitation or model of Christ is a concern.

In this lectionary the fact of Jesus' maleness is taken for granted. The historical Jesus is referred to as a man, and the pronouns "he," "his," and "him" are used when the reference is to that historical person. These male-specific pronouns, however, are not used to refer to the preexistent or post-crucifixion Jesus. They are replaced by proper names such as "Jesus," "Christ," and other words appropriate in the context, so that in hearing the gospel the church may recognize the inclusiveness of all humankind in the incarnation.

Formal equivalents adopted in this lectionary for "the Son of man," "Son," and "Son of God" are, respectively, "the Human One," "Child," and "Child of God." (For a discussion of these terms, see the Appendix.)

Language About God. The God worshiped by the biblical authors and worshiped in the church today cannot be regarded as having gender, race, or color. Such attributes are used metaphorically or analogically. Father is only one metaphor for God in the Bible; other personal metaphors include mother, midwife, and breadmaker. Less familiar, but equally appropriate, are such impersonal images for God as love, rock, and light. Images for God in this lectionary are expressed in inclusive language so that when the church hears its scripture read, it is not overwhelmed by the male metaphors but is also enabled to hear female metaphors for God.

In the RSV Old Testament, the major names for God are "God" *(Elohim),* "Lᴏʀᴅ" *(Yahweh),* and "Lord" *(Adonai),* and several variations of these nouns—for example, "the Lᴏʀᴅ God" and "the Lord Gᴏᴅ." In this lectionary, "Lᴏʀᴅ" *(Yahweh)* is rendered "Gᴏᴅ" or "Sᴏᴠᴇʀᴇɪɢɴ," using an initial capital letter and small capitals, and "Lord" *(Adonai)* is rendered "God" or "Sovereign," using an initial capital letter and lowercase letters. (For a discussion of these terms, see the Appendix.)

In the New Testament lections, the formal equivalent adopted in this lectionary for "God the Father" or "the Father" is "God the Father [*and Mother*]" or "God the [*Mother and*] Father." The words that have been added to the text are italicized and in brackets. If the reader chooses to omit the bracketed words, the sentence will read exactly as rendered in the RSV. Where God is called "Father" several times in a single passage, as is often the case in the Gospel of John, the word "Father" is frequently rendered "God." (For an explanation of metaphor, and of specific ways in which this lectionary has recast scriptural language about God and images for God, see the Appendix.)

The terms "Sovereign" and "God" are used in this lectionary in place of the term "Lord"; but "Lord" appears in brackets as an *alternate* or *substitute reading.* So if one prefers, one may always read "Lord." "Lord" is not to be read aloud with the word that precedes it. See Appendix, pages 249–250.

ADVENT 1

Lesson 1 ～ Isaiah 63:16–64:8

Hear the prophet's intercessory prayer.

¹⁶ For you, O God, are our Father [*and Mother**],
    though Abraham [*and Sarah***] do not know us
    and Israel does not acknowledge us;
  you, O SOVEREIGN [[*or* LORD]], are our Father [*and Mother**],
    our Redeemer from of old is your name.
¹⁷ O SOVEREIGN [[*or* LORD]], why do you make us err from your ways
    and harden our heart, so that we do not fear you?
  Return for the sake of your servants,
    the tribes of your heritage.
¹⁸ Your holy people possessed your sanctuary a little while;
    our adversaries have trodden it down.
¹⁹ We have become like those over whom you have never ruled,
    like those who are not called by your name.
⁶⁴:¹ O that you would rend the heavens and come down,
    that the mountains might quake at your presence—
² as when fire kindles brushwood
    and the fire causes water to boil—
  to make your name known to your adversaries,
    and that the nations might tremble at your presence!
³ When you did terrible things which we looked not for,
    you came down, the mountains quaked at your presence.
⁴ From of old no one has heard
    or perceived by the ear,
  no eye has seen a God besides you,
    who works for those who wait for God.
⁵ You meet the one that joyfully works righteousness,
    those that remember you in your ways.
  Behold, you were angry, and we sinned;
    in our sins we have been a long time, and shall we be saved?
⁶ We have all become like one who is unclean,
    and all our righteous deeds are like a polluted garment.
  We all fade like a leaf,
    and our iniquities, like the wind, take us away.
⁷ There is no one that calls upon your name,
    that bestirs oneself to take hold of you;

---

*Addition to the text. See "Metaphor" and "God the Father and Mother" in the Appendix.
**Addition to the text. RSV *Abraham does.* See Appendix.

15

for you have hidden your face from us,
  and have delivered us into the hand of our iniquities.
⁸ Yet, O SOVEREIGN [*or* LORD], you are our Father [*and Mother**];
  we are the clay, and you are our potter;
  we are all the work of your hand.

Psalm 80:1–7

¹ Give ear, O Shepherd of Israel,
  you who lead Joseph like a flock!
You who are enthroned upon the cherubim, shine forth
² before Ephraim and Benjamin and Manasseh!
 Stir up your might,
  and come to save us!
³ Restore us, O God;
  let your face shine, that we may be saved!
⁴ O SOVEREIGN [*or* LORD] God of hosts,
  how long will you be angry with your people's prayers?
⁵ You have fed them with the bread of tears,
  and given them tears to drink in full measure.
⁶ You make us the scorn of our neighbors;
  and our enemies laugh among themselves.
⁷ Restore us, O God of hosts;
  let your face shine, that we may be saved!

Lesson 2 ～ 1 Corinthians 1:3–9

Paul thanks the Corinthians because of the grace of God given them.

³ Grace to you and peace from God our Father [*and Mother**] and from
the Sovereign [*or* Lord] Jesus Christ.
  ⁴ I give thanks to God always for you because of the grace of God which
was given you in Christ Jesus, ⁵ that in every way you were enriched in Christ
with all speech and all knowledge—⁶ even as the testimony to Christ was
confirmed among you—⁷ so that you are not lacking in any spiritual gift, as
you wait for the revealing of our Sovereign [*or* Lord] Jesus Christ, ⁸ who will
sustain you to the end, guiltless in the day of our Sovereign [*or* Lord] Jesus
Christ. ⁹ God is faithful, by whom you were called into the community of
God's Child,◇ Jesus Christ our Sovereign [*or* Lord].

---

*Addition to the text. See "Metaphor" and "God the Father and Mother" in the Appendix.
◇RSV *his Son.* See Appendix.

16

The disciples are told they are to be on the watch, for they do not know when the Sovereign will come.

³² But of that day or that hour no one knows, not even the angels in heaven, nor God's Child,◇ but only God.⊗ ³³ Take heed, watch; for you do not know when the time will come. ³⁴ It is like someone going on a journey, who, upon leaving home, puts the servants in charge, each with a particular task, and commands the doorkeeper to be on the watch. ³⁵ Watch therefore—for you do not know when the sovereign□ will come, in the evening or at midnight, or at cockcrow, or in the morning—³⁶ lest the sovereign come suddenly and find you asleep. ³⁷ And what I say to you I say to all: Watch.

◇RSV *the Son.* See Appendix.
⊗RSV *the Father.* See Appendix.
□RSV *master of the house.* See Appendix.

ADVENT 2

Lesson 1 ～ Isaiah 40:1-11

The prophet announces the coming of God.

¹ Comfort, comfort my people,
  says your God.
² Speak tenderly to Jerusalem,
  and cry to it
that its warfare is ended,
  that its iniquity is pardoned,
that it has received from GOD's [[*or* the LORD's]] hand
  double for all its sins.
³ A voice cries:
  "In the wilderness prepare the way of the SOVEREIGN [[*or* LORD]],
  make straight in the desert a highway for our God.
⁴ Every valley shall be lifted up,
  and every mountain and hill be made low;
the uneven ground shall become level,
  and the rough places a plain.
⁵ And the glory of GOD [[*or* the LORD]] shall be revealed,
  and all flesh shall see it together,
  for the mouth of GOD [[*or* the LORD]] has spoken."
⁶ A voice says, "Cry!"
  And I said, "What shall I cry?"
All flesh is grass,
  and all its beauty is like the flower of the field.
⁷ The grass withers, the flower fades,
  when the breath of GOD [[*or* the LORD]] blows upon it;
  surely the people is grass.
⁸ The grass withers, the flower fades;
  but the word of our God will stand forever.
⁹ Get you up to a high mountain,
  O Zion, herald of good tidings;
lift up your voice with strength,
  O Jerusalem, herald of good tidings,
  lift it up, fear not;
say to the cities of Judah,
  "Behold your God!"
¹⁰ The Sovereign [[*or* Lord]] GOD comes with might,
  and rules with a mighty arm;
God's reward is with God,
  and God's recompense before God.

¹¹ God will feed the flock like a shepherd,
  gather the lambs in God's arms,
 carry them in God's bosom,
  and gently lead those that are with young.

Psalm 85:8–13

⁸ Let me hear what God the SOVEREIGN [*or* LORD] will speak,
  for God will speak peace to God's people,
  to God's saints, to those who turn to God in their hearts.
⁹ Surely salvation is at hand for those who fear God,
  that glory may dwell in our land.
¹⁰ Steadfast love and faithfulness will meet;
  righteousness and peace will kiss each other.
¹¹ Faithfulness will spring up from the ground,
  and righteousness will look down from the sky.
¹² The SOVEREIGN [*or* LORD] will give what is good,
  and our land will yield its increase.
¹³ Righteousness will go before God,
  and make God's footsteps a way.

Lesson 2 ～ 2 Peter 3:8–15a

The author tells Christians they are to wait for the day of God and the coming of the Sovereign.

⁸ But do not ignore this one fact, beloved, that with the Sovereign [*or* Lord] one day is as a thousand years, and a thousand years as one day. ⁹ The Sovereign [*or* Lord] is not slow in fulfilling the promise as some count slowness, but is forbearing toward you, not wishing that any should perish, but that all should reach repentance. ¹⁰ But the day of the Sovereign [*or* Lord] will come like a thief, and then the heavens will pass away with a loud noise, and the elements will be dissolved with fire, and the earth and the works that are upon it will be burned up.

¹¹ Since all these things are thus to be dissolved, what sort of persons ought you to be in lives of holiness and godliness, ¹² waiting for and hastening the coming of the day of God, because of which the heavens will be kindled and dissolved, and the elements will melt with fire! ¹³ But according to the Sovereign's [*or* Lord's] promise we wait for new heavens and a new earth in which righteousness dwells.

¹⁴ Therefore, beloved, since you wait for these, be zealous to be found by the Sovereign ⟦*or* Lord⟧ without spot or blemish, and at peace. ¹⁵ And count the forbearance of our Sovereign ⟦*or* Lord⟧ as salvation.

Gospel ⁓ Mark 1:1–8

Mark begins the Gospel with the announcement of the coming of John the Baptist.

¹ The beginning of the gospel of Jesus Christ, the Child◊ of God.
² As it is written in Isaiah the prophet,

"I send my messenger before your face,
who shall prepare your way;
³ the voice of one crying in the wilderness:
Prepare the way of the Sovereign ⟦*or* Lord⟧,
make the paths of the Sovereign ⟦*or* Lord⟧ straight—"

⁴ John the baptizer appeared in the wilderness, preaching a baptism of repentance for the forgiveness of sins. ⁵ And there went out to John all the country of Judea, and all the people of Jerusalem; and they were baptized by him in the river Jordan, confessing their sins. ⁶ Now John was clothed with camel's hair, and had a leather girdle around his waist, and ate locusts and wild honey. ⁷ And he preached, saying, "After me comes the one who is mightier than I, the thong of whose sandals I am not worthy to stoop down and untie. ⁸ I have baptized you with water; but the one who comes will baptize you with the Holy Spirit."

◊RSV *Son.* See Appendix.

ADVENT 3

Lesson 1 ～ Isaiah 61:1–4, 8–11

The one whom God has anointed proclaims good news.

¹ The Spirit of the Sovereign [[*or* Lord]] GOD is upon me,
　　because GOD [[*or* the LORD]] has anointed me
　to bring good tidings to those who are afflicted;
　　God has sent me to bind up the brokenhearted,
　to proclaim liberty to the captives,
　　and the opening of the prison to those who are bound;
² to proclaim the year of GOD's [[*or* the LORD's]] favor,
　　and the day of vengeance of our God;
　　to comfort all who mourn;
³ to grant to those who mourn in Zion—
　　to give them a garland instead of ashes,
　the oil of gladness instead of mourning,
　　the mantle of praise instead of a faint spirit;
　that they may be called oaks of righteousness,
　　the planting of GOD [[*or* the LORD]], that God may be glorified.
⁴ They shall build up the ancient ruins,
　　they shall raise up the former devastations;
　they shall repair the ruined cities,
　　the devastations of many generations.
⁸ For I the SOVEREIGN [[*or* LORD]] love justice,
　　I hate robbery and wrong;
　I will faithfully give them their recompense,
　　and I will make an everlasting covenant with them.
⁹ Their descendants shall be known among the nations,
　　and their offspring in the midst of the peoples;
　all who see them shall acknowledge them,
　　that they are a people whom GOD [[*or* the LORD]] has blessed.
¹⁰ I will greatly rejoice in the SOVEREIGN [[*or* LORD]],
　　my soul shall exult in my God,
　who has clothed me with the garments of salvation,
　　and covered me with the robe of righteousness,
　as a bridegroom decks himself with a garland,
　　and as a bride adorns herself with her jewels.
¹¹ For as the earth brings forth its shoots,
　　and as a garden causes what is sown in it to spring up,
　so the Sovereign [[*or* Lord]] GOD will cause righteousness and praise
　　to spring forth before all the nations.

Canticle ∼ Luke 1:46b–55

⁴⁶ My soul magnifies the Sovereign [[or Lord]],
⁴⁷ and my spirit rejoices in God my Savior,
⁴⁸ who has regarded the low estate of God's servant.
   For henceforth all generations will call me blessed;
⁴⁹ for the one who is mighty has done great things for me,
   and holy is God's name.
⁵⁰ And God's mercy is on those who fear God
   from generation to generation.
⁵¹ God has shown strength with God's arm,
   and has scattered the proud in the imagination of their hearts,
⁵² God has put down the mighty from their thrones,
   and exalted those of low degree;
⁵³ God has filled the hungry with good things,
   and has sent the rich empty away.
⁵⁴ God has helped God's servant Israel,
   in remembrance of God's mercy,
⁵⁵ as God spoke to our ancestors,
   to Abraham [and Sarah*] and to their posterity forever.

Lesson 2 ∼ 1 Thessalonians 5:16–24

Paul admonishes the church at Thessalonica.

¹⁶ Rejoice always, ¹⁷ pray constantly, ¹⁸ give thanks in all circumstances; for this is the will of God in Christ Jesus for you. ¹⁹ Do not quench the Spirit, ²⁰ do not despise prophesying, ²¹ but test everything; hold fast what is good, ²² abstain from every form of evil.
²³ May the God of peace sanctify you wholly; and may your spirit and soul and body be kept sound and blameless at the coming of our Sovereign [[or Lord]] Jesus Christ. ²⁴ The one who calls you is faithful, and will do it.

---

*Addition to the text. RSV *to Abraham and to his posterity.* See "Addition of Women's Names to the Text" in the Appendix.

Gospel ~ John 1:6–8, 19–28

John the Baptist, sent from God, proclaims that he is not the Christ, but is the voice of the one who announces the Christ.

⁶ There was a man sent from God, whose name was John. ⁷ John came for testimony, to bear witness to the light, that all might believe through him. ⁸ John was not the light, but came to bear witness to the light.

¹⁹ And this is the testimony of John, when the Jews sent priests and Levites from Jerusalem to ask him, "Who are you?" ²⁰ John confessed, he did not deny, but confessed, "I am not the Christ." ²¹ And they asked, "What then? Are you Elijah?" John said, "I am not." "Are you the prophet?" And he answered, "No." ²² They said then, "Who are you? Let us have an answer for those who sent us. What do you say about yourself?" ²³ John said, "I am the voice of one crying in the wilderness, 'Make straight the way of the Sovereign ⟦*or* Lord⟧,' as the prophet Isaiah said."

²⁴ Now they had been sent from the Pharisees. ²⁵ They asked John, "Then why are you baptizing, if you are neither the Christ, nor Elijah, nor the prophet?" ²⁶ John answered them, "I baptize with water; but among you stands one whom you do not know, ²⁷ even the one who comes after me, the thong of whose sandal I am not worthy to untie." ²⁸ This took place in Bethany beyond the Jordan, where John was baptizing.

ADVENT 4

Lesson 1 ~ 2 Samuel 7:8–16

The word of God, sent to Nathan, announces a kingdom—not for the whole family of David but for Solomon.

⁸ Now therefore thus you shall say to my servant David, "Thus says the GOD [or LORD] of hosts, I took you from the pasture, from following the sheep, that you should be prince over my people Israel; ⁹ and I have been with you wherever you went, and have cut off all your enemies from before you; and I will make for you a great name, like the name of the great ones of the earth. ¹⁰ And I will appoint a place for my people Israel, and will plant them, that they may dwell in their own place, and be disturbed no more; and the violent shall afflict them no more, as formerly, ¹¹ from the time that I appointed judges over my people Israel; and I will give you rest from all your enemies. Moreover GOD [or the LORD] declares to you that GOD [or the LORD] will make you a house. ¹² When your days are fulfilled and you lie down with your ancestors, I will raise up your offspring after you, who shall come forth from your body, and I will establish a kingdom for that offspring, ¹³ who shall build a house for my name, and I will establish the throne of that kingdom forever. ¹⁴ I will be parent to your child, and your child shall be my child. When your child commits iniquity, I will chasten that one with a rod of human discipline, with stripes of human hands; ¹⁵ but I will not take away my steadfast love as I took it from Saul, whom I put away from before you. ¹⁶ And your house and your kingdom shall be made sure forever before me; your throne shall be established forever."

Psalm 89:1–4, 19–24

¹ I will sing of your steadfast love, O GOD [or LORD], forever;
　　with my mouth I will proclaim your faithfulness to all generations.
² For your steadfast love was established forever,
　　your faithfulness is firm as the heavens.
³ You have said, "I have made a covenant with my chosen one,
　　I have sworn to David my servant:
⁴ 'I will establish your descendants forever,
　　and build your throne for all generations.'"
¹⁹ Of old you spoke in a vision
　　to your faithful one, and said:
　　"I have set the crown upon one who is mighty,
　　　I have exalted one chosen from the people.

²⁰ I have found David, my servant;
    with my holy oil I have anointed him;
²¹ so that my hand shall ever abide with David,
    my arm also shall strengthen him.
²² The enemy shall not outwit him,
    the wicked shall not humble him.
²³ I will crush David's foes before him
    and strike down those who hate him.
²⁴ My faithfulness and my steadfast love shall be with him,
    and in my name shall David's horn be exalted."

Lesson 2 ～ Romans 16:25–27

Paul's letter to the Romans closes with this ascription.

²⁵ Now to the one who is able to strengthen you according to my gospel and the preaching of Jesus Christ, according to the revelation of the mystery which was kept secret for long ages, ²⁶ but is now disclosed and through the prophetic writings is made known to all nations, according to the command of the eternal God, to bring about the obedience of faith—²⁷ to the only wise God be glory forevermore through Jesus Christ! Amen.

Gospel ～ Luke 1:26–38

The angel Gabriel announces to Mary that she will bear the child of God.

²⁶ In the sixth month the angel Gabriel was sent from God to a city of Galilee named Nazareth, ²⁷ to a virgin betrothed to a man whose name was Joseph, of the house of David; and her name was Mary. ²⁸ And the angel came to her and said, "Hail, O favored one, God [[*or* the Lord]] is with you!" ²⁹ But she was greatly troubled at the saying, and considered in her mind what sort of greeting this might be. ³⁰ And the angel said to her, "Do not be afraid, Mary, for you have found favor with God. ³¹ You will conceive in your womb and bear a child, whose name you shall call Jesus.

³² This one will be great, and will be called the Child◇ of the Most
 High;
 and the Sovereign [[*or* Lord]] God will give to that Child the throne
 of David, the ancestor of the Child,
³³ to reign over the house of Jacob forever;
 and of that reign☆ there will be no end."

³⁴ And Mary said to the angel, "How shall this be, since I have no husband?" ³⁵ And the angel said to her,

 "The Holy Spirit will come upon you,
 and the power of the Most High will overshadow you;
 therefore the child to be born will be called holy,
 the Child◇ of God.

³⁶ And your kinswoman Elizabeth in her old age has also conceived a child; and this is the sixth month with her who was called barren. ³⁷ For with God nothing will be impossible." ³⁸ And Mary said, "I am the servant of God [[*or* the Lord]]; let it be to me according to your word." And the angel departed from her.

◇RSV *Son.* See Appendix.
☆RSV *his kingdom.* See Appendix.

CHRISTMAS EVE/DAY

Lesson 1 ~ Isaiah 9:2–7

An oracle points to the coming of one who brings a new age of peace and justice.

² The people who walked without light
    have seen a great light;
  those who dwelt in a land of deep shadows,
    on them has light shined.
³ You have multiplied the nation,
    you have increased its joy;
  they rejoice before you
    as with joy at the harvest,
    as victors rejoice when they divide the spoil.
⁴ For the yoke of Israel's burden,
    and the staff for its shoulder,
    the rod of its oppressor,
    you have broken as on the day of Midian.
⁵ For every boot of the tramping warrior in battle tumult
    and every garment rolled in blood
    will be burned as fuel for the fire.
⁶ For to us a child is born,
    to us an heir is given;
  and the government will be upon the shoulder
    of that one whose name will be called
  "Wonderful Counselor, Mighty God,
    Everlasting Father [*and Mother**], Prince of Peace."
⁷ Of the increase of that government and of peace
    there will be no end,
  upon the throne of David, and over David's kingdom,
    to establish it, and to uphold it
  with justice and with righteousness
    from this time forth and forevermore.
The zeal of the GOD [*or* LORD] of hosts will do this.

---

*Addition to the text. See "Metaphor" and "God the Father and Mother" in the Appendix.

Psalm 96

¹ O sing to GOD [*or* the LORD] a new song;
    sing to GOD [*or* the LORD], all the earth!
² Sing to GOD [*or* the LORD]; bless God's name.
    Tell of God's salvation from day to day.
³ Declare God's glory among the nations,
    God's marvelous works among all people!
⁴ For great is GOD [*or* the LORD], and greatly to be praised,
    indeed, to be feared above all gods.
⁵ For all the gods of the nations are idols;
    but the SOVEREIGN [*or* LORD] made the heavens.
⁶ Honor and majesty are before God;
    strength and beauty are in God's sanctuary.
⁷ Ascribe to GOD [*or* the LORD], O families of nations,
    ascribe to GOD [*or* the LORD] glory and strength!
⁸ Ascribe to GOD [*or* the LORD] the glory due God's name;
    bring an offering, and come into God's courts!
⁹ Worship GOD [*or* the LORD] in holy array;
    tremble before God, all the earth!
¹⁰ Say among the nations, "GOD [*or* The LORD] reigns!
    The world is established; it shall never be moved.
    God will judge the nations with equity."
¹¹ Let the heavens be glad, and let the earth rejoice;
    let the sea roar, and all that fills it;
¹²   let the field exult, and everything in it!
  Then shall all the trees of the wood sing for joy
¹³   before GOD [*or* the LORD], who comes,
    who comes to judge the earth,
  who will judge the world with righteousness,
    and the nations with truth.

Lesson 2 ∽ Titus 2:11–14

The letter to Titus points to the meaning of Christ's appearance.

¹¹ For the grace of God has appeared for the salvation of all, ¹² training us to renounce irreligion and worldly passions, and to live sober, upright, and godly lives in this world, ¹³ awaiting our blessed hope, the appearing of the glory of our great God and Savior Jesus Christ, ¹⁴ who gave up Christ's self for us to redeem us from all iniquity and to purify for Christ's self a chosen people who are zealous for good deeds.

Gospel ~ Luke 2:1–20

Luke describes the birth of Jesus.

¹ In those days a decree went out from Caesar Augustus that all the world should be enrolled. ² This was the first enrollment, when Quirinius was governor of Syria. ³ And all went to be enrolled, each to their own city. ⁴ And Joseph also went up from Galilee, from the city of Nazareth, to Judea, to the city of David, which is called Bethlehem, because he was of the house and lineage of David, ⁵ to be enrolled with Mary, his betrothed, who was with child. ⁶ And while they were there, the time came for her to be delivered. ⁷ And she gave birth to her firstborn son, whom she wrapped in swaddling clothes and laid in a manger, because there was no place for them in the inn.

⁸ And in that region there were shepherds out in the field, keeping watch over their flock by night. ⁹ And an angel of God [[*or* the Lord]] appeared to them, and the glory of God [[*or* the Lord]] shone around them, and they were filled with fear. ¹⁰ And the angel said to them, "Be not afraid; for I bring you good news of a great joy which will come to all the people; ¹¹ for to you is born this day in the city of David a Savior, who is Christ the Sovereign [[*or* Lord]]. ¹² And this will be a sign for you: you will find a baby wrapped in swaddling clothes and lying in a manger." ¹³ And suddenly there was with the angel a multitude of the heavenly host praising God and saying,

¹⁴ "Glory to God in the highest,
  and on earth peace among those with whom God is pleased!"

¹⁵ When the angels went away from them into heaven, the shepherds said to one another, "Let us go over to Bethlehem and see this thing that has happened, which God [[*or* the Lord]] has made known to us." ¹⁶ And they went with haste, and found Mary and Joseph, and the baby lying in a manger. ¹⁷ And when they saw it they made known the saying which had been told them concerning this child; ¹⁸ and all who heard it wondered at what the shepherds told them. ¹⁹ But Mary kept all these things, pondering them in her heart. ²⁰ And the shepherds returned, glorifying and praising God for all they had heard and seen, as it had been told them.

CHRISTMAS DAY, Additional Lections, First Set

Lesson 1 ~ Isaiah 62:6–7, 10–12

*God sets watchers on the walls of Zion to contemplate the return of the exiles
to the holy city.*

6 Upon your walls, O Jerusalem,
    I have set watchers;
  all the day and all the night
    they shall never be silent.
You who put GOD [or the LORD] in remembrance,
    take no rest,
7 and give God no rest
    until Jerusalem is established
    and is made an object of praise on the earth.
10 Go through, go through the gates,
    prepare the way for the people;
  build up, build up the highway,
    clear it of stones,
    lift up an ensign over the peoples.
11 GOD [or The LORD] has proclaimed
    to the end of the earth:
Say to the children of Zion,
    "Your salvation comes;
God's reward is with God,
    and God's recompense goes before God."
12 And they shall be called The holy people,
    The redeemed of GOD [or the LORD];
  and you shall be called Sought out,
    a city not forsaken.

Psalm 97

¹ GOD [*or* The LORD] reigns; let the earth rejoice;
   let the many coastlands be glad!
² Clouds and thick darkness are round about God;
   righteousness and justice are the foundation of God's throne.
³ Fire goes before God,
   and burns up God's adversaries round about.
⁴ God's lightnings lighten the world;
   the earth sees and trembles.
⁵ The mountains melt like wax before the SOVEREIGN [*or* LORD],
   before the God [*or* Lord] of all the earth.
⁶ The heavens proclaim God's righteousness;
   and all people behold God's glory.
⁷ All worshipers of images are put to shame,
   who make their boast in worthless idols;
   all gods bow down before God.
⁸ Zion hears and is glad,
   and the daughters of Judah rejoice,
   because of your judgments, O GOD [*or* LORD].
⁹ For you, O GOD [*or* LORD], are most high over all the earth;
   you are exalted far above all gods.
¹⁰ GOD [*or* The LORD] loves those who hate evil,
   preserves the lives of the saints,
   and delivers them from the hand of the wicked.
¹¹ Light dawns for the righteous,
   and joy for the upright in heart.
¹² Rejoice in GOD [*or* the LORD], O you righteous,
   and give thanks to God's holy name!

Lesson 2 ~ Titus 3:4–7

In the letter to Titus we are told that all things are changed because of the mercy of God.

⁴ When the goodness and loving kindness of God our Savior appeared, ⁵ we were saved, not because of deeds done by us in righteousness, but in virtue of God's own mercy, by the washing of regeneration and renewal in the Holy Spirit, ⁶ which God poured out upon us richly through Jesus Christ our Savior, ⁷ so that we might be justified by God's grace and become heirs in hope of eternal life.

Gospel ～ Luke 2:8–20

Luke describes the birth of Jesus.

⁸ And in that region there were shepherds out in the field, keeping watch over their flock by night. ⁹ And an angel of God [[*or* the Lord]] appeared to them, and the glory of God [[*or* the Lord]] shone around them, and they were filled with fear. ¹⁰ And the angel said to them, "Be not afraid; for I bring you good news of a great joy which will come to all the people; ¹¹ for to you is born this day in the city of David a Savior, who is Christ the Sovereign [[*or* Lord]]. ¹² And this will be a sign for you: you will find a baby wrapped in swaddling clothes and lying in a manger." ¹³ And suddenly there was with the angel a multitude of the heavenly host praising God and saying,

¹⁴ "Glory to God in the highest,
 and on earth peace among those with whom God is pleased!"

¹⁵ When the angels went away from them into heaven, the shepherds said to one another, "Let us go over to Bethlehem and see this thing that has happened, which God [[*or* the Lord]] has made known to us." ¹⁶ And they went with haste, and found Mary and Joseph, and the baby lying in a manger. ¹⁷ And when they saw it they made known the saying which had been told them concerning this child; ¹⁸ and all who heard it wondered at what the shepherds told them. ¹⁹ But Mary kept all these things, pondering them in her heart. ²⁰ And the shepherds returned, glorifying and praising God for all they had heard and seen, as it had been told them.

CHRISTMAS DAY, Additional Lections, Second Set

Lesson 1 ~ Isaiah 52:7–10

Isaiah proclaims God's word of comfort.

⁷ How beautiful upon the mountains
 are the feet of the one who brings good tidings,
who publishes peace, who brings good tidings of good,
 who publishes salvation,
 who says to Zion, "Your God reigns."
⁸ Hark, your watchers lift up their voice,
 together they sing for joy;
for eye to eye they see
 the return of GOD [*or* the LORD] to Zion.
⁹ Break forth together into singing,
 you waste places of Jerusalem;
for GOD [*or* the LORD] has comforted God's people,
 and has redeemed Jerusalem.
¹⁰ GOD [*or* The LORD] has bared God's holy arm
 before the eyes of all the nations;
and all the ends of the earth shall see
 the salvation of our God.

Psalm 98

¹ O sing a new song to GOD [*or* the LORD],
 who has done marvelous things,
whose right hand and holy arm
 have gained the victory!
² GOD [*or* The LORD] has made known the victory,
 and has revealed God's vindication in the sight of the nations.
³ God has remembered God's steadfast love and faithfulness
 to the house of Israel.
All the ends of the earth have seen
 the victory of our God.
⁴ Make a joyful noise to GOD [*or* the LORD], all the earth;
 break forth into joyous song and sing praises!
⁵ Sing praises to GOD [*or* the LORD] with the lyre,
 with the lyre and the sound of melody!
⁶ With trumpets and the sound of the horn
 make a joyful noise before the Ruler,⌑ the SOVEREIGN [*or* LORD]!

⌑RSV *King.* See Appendix.

⁷ Let the sea roar, and all that fills it;
 the world and those who dwell in it!
⁸ Let the floods clap their hands;
 let the hills sing together for joy
⁹ before GOD [[*or* the LORD]], who comes
 to judge the earth,
  to judge the world with righteousness,
  and the nations with equity.

Lesson 2 ~ Hebrews 1:1–12

The letter to the Hebrews begins by emphasizing that Jesus Christ is greater than the prophets and the angels.

¹ In many and various ways God spoke of old to our forebears by the prophets; ² but in these last days God has spoken to us by a Child,[◇] whom God appointed the heir of all things, through whom also God created the world. ³ This Child, by whose word of power the universe is upheld, reflects the glory of God and bears the very stamp of God's nature. Having made purification for sins, the Child sat down at the right hand of the Majesty on high, ⁴ having become as much superior to angels as the name the Child has obtained is more excellent than theirs.

⁵ For to what angel did God ever say,

"You are my Child,[◇]
today I have begotten you"?

Or again,

"I will be to the Child a parent,
and the Child shall be my very own"?

⁶ And again, when bringing the firstborn into the world, God says,

"Let all the angels of God worship this Child."

⁷ Of the angels it is said,

"God makes the angels into winds,
and the servants of God into flames of fire."

⁸ But of the Child[◇] it is said,

"Your throne, O God, is forever and ever,
the righteous scepter is the scepter of your dominion.[☆]

[◇]RSV *Son.* See Appendix.
[☆]RSV *kingdom.* See Appendix.

⁹ You have loved righteousness and hated lawlessness;
    therefore God, your God, has anointed you
    with the oil of gladness beyond your comrades."

¹⁰ And,

    "You, Sovereign [[or Lord]], founded the earth in the beginning,
    and the heavens are the work of your hands;
    ¹¹ they will perish, but you remain;
    they will all grow old like a garment,
    ¹² like a mantle you will roll them up,
    and they will be changed.
    But you are the same,
    and your years will never end."

Gospel ~ John 1:1–14

The author of the Gospel of John unfolds the mystery of the incarnation.

¹ In the beginning was the Word, and the Word was with God, and the Word was God. ² The Word was in the beginning with God; ³ all things were made through the Word, and without the Word was not anything made that was made. ⁴ In the Word was life, and the life was the light of all. ⁵ The light shines in the deepest night, and the night has not overcome it.

⁶ There was a man sent from God, whose name was John. ⁷ John came for testimony, to bear witness to the light, that all might believe through him. ⁸ John was not the light, but came to bear witness to the light.

⁹ The true light that enlightens everyone was coming into the world. ¹⁰ The Word was in the world, and the world was made through the Word, yet the world did not know the Word. ¹¹ The Word came to the Word's own home, but those to whom the Word came did not receive the Word. ¹² But to all who received the Word, who believed in the name of the Word, power was given to become children of God; ¹³ who were born, not of blood nor of the will of the flesh nor of human will, but of God.

¹⁴ And the Word became flesh and dwelt among us, full of grace and truth; we have beheld the Word's glory, glory as of the only Child[◊] from [*God*] the Father [*and Mother**]*.

◊RSV *Son.* See Appendix.
*Addition to the text. See "Metaphor" and "God the Father and Mother" in the Appendix.

CHRISTMAS 1
(Or the lections for Epiphany)

Lesson 1 ~ Isaiah 61:10–62:3

Isaiah extols the glory of God.

¹⁰ I will greatly rejoice in the SOVEREIGN [or LORD],
    my soul shall exult in my God,
who has clothed me with the garments of salvation,
    and covered me with the robe of righteousness,
as a bridegroom decks himself with a garland,
    and as a bride adorns herself with her jewels.
¹¹ For as the earth brings forth its shoots,
    and as a garden causes what is sown in it to spring up,
so the Sovereign [or Lord] GOD will cause righteousness and praise
    to spring forth before all the nations.
⁶²:¹ For Zion's sake I will not keep silent,
    and for Jerusalem's sake I will not rest,
until its vindication goes forth as brightness,
    and its salvation as a burning torch.
² The nations shall see your vindication,
    and all the rulers□ your glory;
and you shall be called by a new name
    which the mouth of GOD [or the LORD] will give.
³ You shall be a crown of beauty in the hand of the SOVEREIGN [or
    LORD],
    and a royal diadem in the hand of your God.

□RSV *kings.* See Appendix.

Psalm 111

¹ Praise GOD ⟦*or* the LORD⟧!
  I will give thanks to GOD ⟦*or* the LORD⟧ with my whole heart,
    in the company of the upright, in the congregation.
² Great are the works of GOD ⟦*or* the LORD⟧,
    studied by all who have pleasure in them.
³ Full of honor and majesty is God's work,
    and God's righteousness endures forever.
⁴ God has caused God's wonderful works to be remembered,
    and is gracious and merciful,
⁵ providing food for those who fear God
    and being ever mindful of the covenant.
⁶ God has shown God's people the power of God's works,
    in giving them the heritage of the nations.
⁷ The works of God's hands are faithful and just;
    all God's precepts are trustworthy,
⁸ they are established forever and ever,
    to be performed with faithfulness and uprightness.
⁹ God sent redemption to God's people
    and has commanded the covenant forever.
  Holy and terrible is God's name!
¹⁰ The fear of GOD ⟦*or* the LORD⟧ is the beginning of wisdom;
    a good understanding have all those who practice it.
  God's praise endures forever!

Lesson 2 ～ Galatians 4:4–7

Paul writes to the Galatians about the time of Christ's coming.

⁴ But when the time had fully come, God sent forth God's Child,◇ born of woman, born under the law, ⁵ to redeem those who were under the law, so that we might receive adoption as children of God. ⁶ And because you are children, God has sent the Spirit of the Child◇ into our hearts, crying, "[*God! my Mother and* *] Father!" ⁷ So through God you are no longer a slave but a child, and if a child then an heir.

◇RSV *his Son.* See Appendix.
*Addition to the text. RSV *"Abba!"* See "Metaphor" and "God the Father and Mother" in the Appendix.

Gospel ⁓ Luke 2:22–40

Mary and Joseph take the infant Jesus to the temple in Jerusalem, and the child is met there by Simeon and Anna.

22 And when the time came for their purification according to the law of Moses, they brought the child Jesus up to Jerusalem to be presented to God [or the Lord] 23 (as it is written in the law of God [or the Lord], "Every male that opens the womb shall be called holy to God [or the Lord]"), 24 and to offer a sacrifice according to what is said in the law of God [or the Lord], "a pair of turtledoves, or two young pigeons." 25 Now there was a man in Jerusalem, whose name was Simeon, who was righteous and devout, looking for the consolation of Israel, and the Holy Spirit was upon him. 26 And it had been revealed to Simeon by the Holy Spirit that he should not see death before he had seen the Christ of God [or the Lord]. 27 And inspired by the Spirit, Simeon came into the temple; and when the parents brought in the child Jesus, to do for him according to the custom of the law, 28 Simeon took the child in his arms and blessed God and said,

29 "Sovereign [or Lord], now let your servant depart in peace,
   according to your word;
30 for my eyes have seen your salvation
31 which you have prepared in the presence of all people,
32 a light for revelation to the Gentiles,
   and for glory to your people Israel."

33 And the father and mother of Jesus marveled at what was said about their child; 34 and Simeon blessed them and said to Mary, Jesus' mother,

"This child is set for the fall and rising of many in Israel,
   and for a sign that is spoken against
35 (and a sword will pierce through your own soul also),
   that thoughts out of many hearts may be revealed."

36 And there was a prophet, Anna, the daughter of Phanuel, of the tribe of Asher; she was of a great age, having lived with her husband seven years, 37 and as a widow till she was eighty-four. She did not depart from the temple, worshiping with fasting and prayer night and day. 38 And coming up at that very hour she gave thanks to God, and spoke about the child to all who were looking for the redemption of Jerusalem.

39 And when Mary and Joseph had performed everything according to the law of God [or the Lord], they returned into Galilee, to their own city, Nazareth. 40 And the child grew and became strong, filled with wisdom; and the favor of God was upon the child.

JANUARY 1 (New Year)

Lesson 1 ~ Ecclesiastes 3:1–13

The Preacher speaks of times and seasons.

¹ For everything there is a season, and a time for every matter under heaven:

² a time to be born, and a time to die;
  a time to plant, and a time to pluck up what is planted;
³ a time to kill, and a time to heal;
  a time to break down, and a time to build up;
⁴ a time to weep, and a time to laugh;
  a time to mourn, and a time to dance;
⁵ a time to cast away stones, and a time to gather stones together;
  a time to embrace, and a time to refrain from embracing;
⁶ a time to seek, and a time to lose;
  a time to keep, and a time to cast away;
⁷ a time to rend, and a time to sew;
  a time to keep silence, and a time to speak;
⁸ a time to love, and a time to hate;
  a time for war, and a time for peace.
⁹ What gain have the workers from their toil?

¹⁰ I have seen the business that God has given to the human race to be busy with. ¹¹ God has made everything beautiful in its time, and has put eternity into human minds, yet they cannot find out what God has done from the beginning to the end. ¹² I know that there is nothing better for them than to be happy and enjoy themselves as long as they live; ¹³ also that it is God's gift to humanity that all should eat and drink and take pleasure in all their toil.

Psalm 8

¹ O SOVEREIGN [*or* LORD], our God,
    how majestic is your name in all the earth!
  You whose glory above the heavens is chanted
²   by the mouth of babies and infants,
  you have founded a bulwark because of your foes,
    to still the enemy and the avenger.
³ When I look at your heavens, the work of your fingers,
    the moon and the stars which you have established;
⁴ what are human beings that you are mindful of them,
    and mortals that you care for them?

⁵ Yet you have made them little less than God,
  and crowned them with glory and honor.
⁶ You have given them dominion over the works of your hands;
  you have put all things under their feet,
⁷ all sheep and oxen,
  and also the beasts of the field,
⁸ the birds of the air, and the fish of the sea,
  whatever passes along the paths of the sea.
⁹ O SOVEREIGN [or LORD], our God,
  how majestic is your name in all the earth!

Lesson 2 ～ Colossians 2:1–7

Paul sends a message of encouragement to the church at Colossae.

¹ For I want you to know how greatly I strive for you, and for those at Laodicea, and for all who have not seen my face, ² that their hearts may be encouraged as they are knit together in love, to have all the riches of assured understanding and the knowledge of God's mystery, of Christ, ³ in whom are hid all the treasures of wisdom and knowledge. ⁴ I say this in order that no one may delude you with beguiling speech. ⁵ For though I am absent in body, yet I am with you in spirit, rejoicing to see your good order and the firmness of your faith in Christ.

⁶ As therefore you received Christ Jesus the Sovereign [or Lord], so live in Christ, ⁷ rooted and built up in Christ and established in the faith, just as you were taught, abounding in thanksgiving.

Gospel ～ Matthew 9:14–17

Jesus teaches John's disciples about the radically new age that has begun.

¹⁴ Then the disciples of John came to Jesus, saying, "Why do we and the Pharisees fast, but your disciples do not fast?" ¹⁵ And Jesus said to them, "Can the wedding guests mourn as long as the bridegroom is with them? The days will come, when the bridegroom is taken away from them, and then they will fast. ¹⁶ And no one puts a piece of unshrunk cloth on an old garment, for the patch tears away from the garment, and a worse tear is made. ¹⁷ Neither is new wine put into old wineskins; if it is, the skins burst, and the wine is spilled, and the skins are destroyed; but new wine is put into fresh wineskins, and so both are preserved."

JANUARY 1 Holy Name of Jesus; Solemnity of Mary, Mother of God

Lesson 1 ∽ Numbers 6:22–27

Moses learns how Aaron is to bless the people of Israel.

²² GOD [*or* The LORD] said to Moses, ²³ "Say to Aaron and his offspring, Thus you shall bless the people of Israel: you shall say to them,

²⁴ GOD [*or* The LORD] bless you and keep you:

²⁵ GOD [*or* The LORD] make God's face to shine upon you, and be gracious to you:

²⁶ GOD [*or* The LORD] lift up God's countenance upon you, and give you peace.

²⁷ "So shall they put my name upon the people of Israel, and I will bless them."

Psalm 67

¹ May God be gracious to us and bless us
and make God's face to shine upon us,
² that your way may be known upon earth,
and your saving power among all nations.
³ Let the people praise you, O God;
let all the people praise you!
⁴ Let the nations be glad and sing for joy,
for you judge the people with equity
and guide the nations upon earth.
⁵ Let the people praise you, O God;
let all the people praise you!
⁶ The earth has yielded its increase;
God, our God, has blessed us.
⁷ God has blessed us;
let all the ends of the earth fear God!

Lesson 2 ～ Galatians 4:4–7

Paul writes to the Galatians about the time of Christ's coming.

⁴ But when the time had fully come, God sent forth God's Child,◇ born of woman, born under the law, ⁵ to redeem those who were under the law, so that we might receive adoption as children of God. ⁶ And because you are children, God has sent the Spirit of the Child◇ into our hearts, crying, "[*God! my Mother and**] Father!" ⁷ So through God you are no longer a slave but a child, and if a child then an heir.

Lesson 2 (alternate) ～ Philippians 2:9–13

Paul reflects on Christ's example of humility.

⁹ Therefore God has highly exalted Jesus and bestowed on Jesus the name which is above every name, ¹⁰ that at the name of Jesus every knee should bow, in heaven and on earth and under the earth, ¹¹ and every tongue confess that Jesus Christ is Sovereign ⟦*or* Lord⟧, to the glory of God the Father [*and Mother**].

¹² Therefore, my beloved, as you have always obeyed, so now, not only as in my presence but much more in my absence, work out your own salvation with fear and trembling; ¹³ for God is at work in you, both to will and to work for God's good pleasure.

◇RSV *his Son*. See Appendix.
*Addition to the text. RSV Gal. 4:6 *"Abba!"*; Phil. 2:11 *God the Father*. See "Metaphor" and "God the Father and Mother" in the Appendix.

Gospel ~ Luke 2:15-21

Luke describes the shepherds' visit to Bethlehem.

[15] When the angels went away from them into heaven, the shepherds said to one another, "Let us go over to Bethlehem and see this thing that has happened, which God [*or* the Lord] has made known to us." [16] And they went with haste, and found Mary and Joseph, and the baby lying in a manger. [17] And when they saw it they made known the saying which had been told them concerning this child; [18] and all who heard it wondered at what the shepherds told them. [19] But Mary kept all these things, pondering them in her heart. [20] And the shepherds returned, glorifying and praising God for all they had heard and seen, as it has been told them.

[21] And at the end of eight days, the child was circumcised and was called Jesus, the name given by the angel before the child was conceived in the womb.

CHRISTMAS 2
(Or the lections for Epiphany if not otherwise used)

Lesson 1 ～ Jeremiah 31:7–14

The prophet Jeremiah assures Israel that their despair shall be turned to joy.

7 For thus says the SOVEREIGN [[or LORD]]:
   "Sing aloud with gladness for Jacob,
      and raise shouts for the chief of the nations;
   proclaim, give praise, and say,
      'GOD [[or The LORD]] has saved the people,
      the remnant of Israel.'
8 I will bring them from the north country,
      and gather them from the farthest parts of the earth,
   among them those who are blind and those who are lame,
      the woman with child and the woman in travail, together;
      a great company, they shall return here.
9 With weeping they shall come,
      and with consolations I will lead them back,
   I will make them walk by brooks of water,
      in a straight path in which they shall not stumble;
   for I am a father [*and a mother**] to Israel,
      and Ephraim is my firstborn.
10 Hear the word of GOD [[or the LORD]], O nations,
      and declare it in the coastlands afar off;
   say, 'The one who scattered Israel will gather them,
      and will keep them as a shepherd keeps a flock.'
11 For GOD [[or the LORD]] has ransomed Jacob,
      and has redeemed them from hands too strong for them.
12 They shall come and sing aloud on the height of Zion,
      and they shall be radiant over the goodness of GOD [[or the LORD]],
   over the grain, the wine, and the oil,
      and over the young of the flock and the herd;
   their life shall be like a watered garden,
      and they shall languish no more.
13 Then shall the women rejoice in the dance,
      and the young men and the old shall be merry.
   I will turn their mourning into joy,
      I will comfort them, and give them gladness for sorrow.
14 I will feast the soul of the priests with abundance,
      and my people shall be satisfied with my goodness,
                    says the SOVEREIGN [[or LORD]]."

---

*Addition to the text. See "Metaphor" and "God the Father and Mother" in the Appendix.

Lesson 1 (alternate) ~ Ecclesiasticus (Sirach) 24:1–4, 12–16

Sirach sings the praises of Wisdom.

¹ Wisdom will praise herself,
  and will glory in the midst of her people.
² In the assembly of the Most High she will open her mouth,
  and in the presence of the host of the Most High she will glory:
³ "I came forth from the mouth of the Most High,
  and covered the earth like a mist.
⁴ I dwelt in high places,
  and my throne was in a pillar of cloud.
¹² So I took root in an honored people,
  in the portion of God [[*or* the Lord]], who is their inheritance.
¹³ I grew tall like a cedar in Lebanon,
  and like a cypress on the heights of Hermon.
¹⁴ I grew tall like a palm tree in En-gedi,
  and like rose plants in Jericho;
 like a beautiful olive tree in the field,
  and like a plane tree I grew tall.
¹⁵ Like cassia and camel's thorn I gave forth the aroma of spices,
  and like choice myrrh I spread a pleasant odor,
 like galbanum, onycha, and stacte,
  and like the fragrance of frankincense in the tabernacle.
¹⁶ Like a terebinth I spread out my branches,
  and my branches are glorious and graceful."

¹² Praise GOD [[or the LORD]], O Jerusalem!
　　Praise your God, O Zion,
¹³ for God strengthens the bars of your gates,
　　and blesses your children within you,
¹⁴ making peace in your borders,
　　and filling you with the finest of the wheat.
¹⁵ God sends forth a command to the earth;
　　God's word runs swiftly.
¹⁶ God gives snow like wool,
　　scattering hoarfrost like ashes,
¹⁷ and casting forth ice like morsels;
　　who can stand before God's cold?
¹⁸ God sends forth God's word, and melts them,
　　making the wind blow, and the waters flow.
¹⁹ God declares God's word to Jacob,
　　God's statutes and ordinances to Israel.
²⁰ God has not dealt thus with any other nation;
　　they do not know the ordinances.
　　Praise GOD [[or the LORD]]!

Lesson 2 ～ Ephesians 1:3–6, 15–18

The writer of the letter to the Ephesians begins by praising God's grace in Jesus Christ.

³ Blessed be God the Father [*and Mother**] of our Sovereign [[or Lord]] Jesus Christ, who has blessed us in Christ with every spiritual blessing in the heavenly places, ⁴ even as God chose us in Christ before the foundation of the world, that we should be holy and blameless before God, ⁵ who destined us in love to be God's children through Jesus Christ, according to the purpose of God's will, ⁶ to the praise of God's glorious grace freely bestowed on us in the Beloved.

¹⁵ For this reason, because I have heard of your faith in the Sovereign [[or Lord]] Jesus and your love toward all the saints, ¹⁶ I do not cease to give thanks for you, remembering you in my prayers, ¹⁷ that the God of our Sovereign [[or Lord]] Jesus Christ, the Father [*and Mother**] of glory, may give you a spirit of wisdom and of revelation in the knowledge of God, ¹⁸ having the eyes of your hearts enlightened, that you may know what is the hope to which you have been called, what are the riches of God's glorious inheritance in the saints.

---

*Addition to the text. RSV v. 3 *the God and Father;* v. 17 *the Father of glory.* See "Metaphor" and "God the Father and Mother" in the Appendix.

Gospel ~ John 1:1–18

The author of the Gospel of John unfolds the mystery of the incarnation.

¹ In the beginning was the Word, and the Word was with God, and the Word was God. ² The Word was in the beginning with God; ³ all things were made through the Word, and without the Word was not anything made that was made. ⁴ In the Word was life, and the life was the light of all. ⁵ The light shines in the deepest night, and the night has not overcome it.

⁶ There was a man sent from God, whose name was John. ⁷ John came for testimony, to bear witness to the light, that all might believe through him. ⁸ John was not the light, but came to bear witness to the light.

⁹ The true light that enlightens everyone was coming into the world. ¹⁰ The Word was in the world, and the world was made through the Word, yet the world did not know the Word. ¹¹ The Word came to the Word's own home, but those to whom the Word came did not receive the Word. ¹² But to all who received the Word, who believed in the name of the Word, power was given to become children of God; ¹³ who were born, not of blood nor of the will of the flesh nor of human will, but of God.

¹⁴ And the Word became flesh and dwelt among us, full of grace and truth; we have beheld the Word's glory, glory as of the only Child° from [*God*] the Father [*and Mother**]. ¹⁵ (John bore witness to the Child, and cried, "This was the person of whom I said, 'The one who comes after me ranks before me, for that one was before me.' ") ¹⁶ And from the fullness of the Child have we all received, grace upon grace. ¹⁷ For the law was given through Moses; grace and truth came through Jesus Christ. ¹⁸ No one has ever seen God; the only Child,° who is in the bosom of [*God*] the [*Mother and**] Father, that one has made God known.

°RSV *Son.* See Appendix.
*Addition to the text. See "Metaphor" and "God the Father and Mother" in the Appendix.

EPIPHANY

Lesson 1 ~ Isaiah 60:1–6

Isaiah tells of the coming of God's glory to the people.

¹ Arise, shine; for your light has come,
  and the glory of GOD [*or* the LORD] has risen upon you.
² For shadows shall cover the earth,
  and thick shadow the nations;
 but GOD [*or* the LORD] will arise upon you,
  and the glory of God will be seen upon you.
³ And nations shall come to your light,
  and rulers⬚ to the brightness of your rising.
⁴ Lift up your eyes round about, and see;
  they all gather together, they come to you;
 your sons shall come from afar,
  and your daughters shall be carried in the arms.
⁵ Then you shall see and be radiant,
  your heart shall thrill and rejoice;
 because the abundance of the sea shall be turned to you,
  the wealth of the nations shall come to you.
⁶ A multitude of camels shall cover you,
  the young camels of Midian and Ephah;
 all those from Sheba shall come.
 They shall bring gold and frankincense,
  and shall proclaim the praise of GOD [*or* the LORD].

Psalm 72:1–14

¹ Give the ruler⬚ your justice, O God,
  and your righteousness to the royal heir!
² May the ruler judge your people with righteousness,
  and your poor with justice!
³ Let the mountains bear prosperity for the people,
  and the hills, in righteousness!
⁴ May the ruler defend the cause of the poor of the people,
  give deliverance to the needy,
  and crush the oppressor!
⁵ May the ruler live while the sun endures,
  and as long as the moon, throughout all generations!
⁶ May the ruler be like rain that falls on the mown grass,
  like showers that water the earth!

⬚RSV Isa. 60:3 *kings;* Ps. 72:1 *king.* See Appendix.

⁷ In the ruler's days may righteousness flourish,
and peace abound, till the moon be no more!
⁸ May the ruler have dominion from sea to sea,
and from the River to the ends of the earth!
⁹ May the foes of the ruler bow down,
and the enemies lick the dust!
¹⁰ May the kings of Tarshish and of the isles
render tribute,
may the kings of Sheba and Seba
bring gifts!
¹¹ May all kings bow down
and all nations serve the ruler!
¹² For the ruler delivers the needy when they call,
the poor and those who have no helper,
¹³ and has pity on the weak and the needy,
and saves the lives of the needy.
¹⁴ The ruler redeems their lives from oppression and violence,
and their blood is precious in the ruler's sight.

Lesson 2 ∽ Ephesians 3:1–12

The Ephesians learn about ministry that is rooted in Christ.

¹ For this reason I, Paul, a prisoner for Christ Jesus on behalf of you Gentiles—² assuming that you have heard of the stewardship of God's grace that was given to me for you, ³ how the mystery was made known to me by revelation, as I have written briefly. ⁴ When you read this you can perceive my insight into the mystery of Christ, ⁵ which was not made known to the human race in other generations as it has now been revealed to Christ's holy apostles and prophets by the Spirit; ⁶ that is, how the Gentiles are joint heirs, members of the same body, and partakers of the promise in Christ Jesus through the gospel.

⁷ Of this gospel I was made a minister according to the gift of God's grace which was given me by the working of God's power. ⁸ To me, though I am the very least of all the saints, this grace was given, to preach to the Gentiles the unsearchable riches of Christ, ⁹ and to make everyone see what is the plan of the mystery hidden for ages in God who created all things; ¹⁰ that through the church the manifold wisdom of God might now be made known to the principalities and powers in the heavenly places. ¹¹ This was according to the eternal purpose which God has realized in Christ Jesus our Sovereign [*or* Lord], ¹² in whom we have boldness and confidence of access through our faith in Christ.

Matthew describes the visit of the magi to the child.

¹ Now when Jesus was born in Bethlehem of Judea in the days of Herod the king, magi from the East came to Jerusalem, saying, ² "Where is the one who has been born king of the Jews? For we have seen his star in the East, and have come to worship him." ³ And hearing this, Herod the king was troubled, and all Jerusalem as well; ⁴ and assembling all the chief priests and scribes of the people, he inquired of them where the Christ was to be born. ⁵ They told Herod, "In Bethlehem of Judea; for so it is written by the prophet:

⁶ 'And you, O Bethlehem, in the land of Judah,
are by no means least among the rulers of Judah;
for from you shall come a ruler
who will govern my people Israel.' "

⁷ Then Herod summoned the magi secretly, ascertained from them what time the star appeared, and ⁸ sent them to Bethlehem, saying, "Go and search diligently for the child, and when you have found him bring me word, that I too may come and worship him." ⁹ When they had heard the king they went their way; and the star which they had seen in the East went before them, till it came to rest over the place where the child was. ¹⁰ When they saw the star, they rejoiced exceedingly with great joy; ¹¹ and going into the house they saw the child with Mary his mother, and they fell down and worshiped him. Then, opening their treasures, they offered the child gifts, gold and frankincense and myrrh. ¹² And being warned in a dream not to return to Herod, they departed to their own country by another way.

BAPTISM OF JESUS

Lesson 1 ～ Genesis 1:1–5

This is the account of God's creation of the world.

¹ In the beginning God created the heavens and the earth. ² The earth was without form and void, and darkness was upon the face of the deep; and the Spirit of God was moving over the face of the waters.

³ And God said, "Let there be light"; and there was light. ⁴ And God saw that the light was good; and God distinguished between the light and the darkness. ⁵ God called the light Day, and the darkness Night. And there was evening and there was morning, one day.

Psalm 29

¹ Ascribe to GOD [or the LORD], O heavenly beings,
    ascribe to GOD [or the LORD] glory and strength.
² Ascribe to GOD [or the LORD] the glory of God's name;
    worship GOD [or the LORD] in holy array.
³ The voice of GOD [or the LORD] is upon the waters;
    the God of glory thunders,
    GOD [or the LORD], upon many waters.
⁴ The voice of GOD [or the LORD] is powerful,
    the voice of GOD [or the LORD] is full of majesty.
⁵ The voice of GOD [or the LORD] breaks the cedars,
    GOD [or the LORD] breaks the cedars of Lebanon,
⁶ making Lebanon to skip like a calf,
    and Sirion like a young wild ox.
⁷ The voice of GOD [or the LORD] flashes forth flames of fire.
⁸ The voice of GOD [or the LORD] shakes the wilderness,
    GOD [or the LORD] shakes the wilderness of Kadesh.
⁹ The voice of GOD [or the LORD] makes the oaks to whirl,
    and strips the forests bare;
    and in God's temple all cry, "Glory!"
¹⁰ GOD [or The LORD] sits enthroned over the flood;
    GOD [or the LORD] sits enthroned as ruler□ forever.
¹¹ May GOD [or the LORD] give strength to God's people!
    May GOD [or the LORD] bless the people with peace!

□RSV *king.* See Appendix.

Lesson 2 ~ Acts 19:1–7

Paul baptizes in the name of the Sovereign Jesus.

[1] While Apollos was at Corinth, Paul passed through the upper country and came to Ephesus. There Paul found some disciples, [2] and said to them, "Did you receive the Holy Spirit when you believed?" And they said, "No, we have never even heard that there is a Holy Spirit." [3] And Paul said, "Into what then were you baptized?" They said, "Into John's baptism." [4] And Paul said, "John baptized with the baptism of repentance, telling the people to believe in the one who was to come after him, that is, Jesus." [5] On hearing this, they were baptized in the name of the Sovereign [[or Lord]] Jesus. [6] And when Paul had laid his hands upon them, the Holy Spirit came on them; and they spoke with tongues and prophesied. [7] There were about twelve of them in all.

Gospel ~ Mark 1:4–11

Mark tells of Jesus' baptism by John.

[4] John the baptizer appeared in the wilderness, preaching a baptism of repentance for the forgiveness of sins. [5] And there went out to him all the country of Judea, and all the people of Jerusalem; and they were baptized by him in the river Jordan, confessing their sins. [6] Now John was clothed with camel's hair, and had a leather girdle around his waist, and ate locusts and wild honey. [7] And he preached, saying, "After me comes the one who is mightier than I, the thong of whose sandals I am not worthy to stoop down and untie. [8] I have baptized you with water; but the one who comes will baptize you with the Holy Spirit."

[9] In those days Jesus came from Nazareth of Galilee and was baptized by John in the Jordan. [10] And having come up out of the water, immediately Jesus saw the heavens opened and the Spirit descending upon him like a dove; [11] and a voice came from heaven, "You are my beloved Child;◇ with you I am well pleased."

◇RSV *Son.* See Appendix.

EPIPHANY 2

Lesson 1 ~ 1 Samuel 3:1–10 (11–20 optional)

The boy Samuel is called by God and established as a prophet.

¹ Now the boy Samuel was ministering to GOD [*or* the LORD] under Eli. And the word of GOD [*or* the LORD] was rare in those days; there was no frequent vision.

² At that time Eli, whose eyesight had begun to grow dim, so that he could not see, was lying down in his own place; ³ the lamp of God had not yet gone out, and Samuel was lying down within the temple of GOD [*or* the LORD], where the ark of God was. ⁴ Then GOD [*or* the LORD] called, "Samuel! Samuel!" and Samuel said, "Here I am!" ⁵ and ran to Eli, and said, "Here I am, for you called me." But Eli said, "I did not call; lie down again." So Samuel went and lay down. ⁶ And GOD [*or* the LORD] called again, "Samuel!" And Samuel arose and went to Eli, and said, "Here I am, for you called me." But Eli said, "I did not call, my son; lie down again." ⁷ Now Samuel did not yet know GOD [*or* the LORD], and the word of GOD [*or* the LORD] had not yet been revealed to Samuel. ⁸ And GOD [*or* the LORD] called Samuel again the third time. And Samuel arose and went to Eli, and said, "Here I am, for you called me." Then Eli perceived that GOD [*or* the LORD] was calling the boy. ⁹ Therefore Eli said to Samuel, "Go, lie down; and if GOD [*or* the LORD] calls you, you shall say, 'Speak, O SOVEREIGN [*or* LORD], for your servant hears.'" So Samuel went and lay down in his place.

¹⁰ And GOD [*or* the LORD] came and stood forth, calling as at other times, "Samuel! Samuel!" And Samuel said, "Speak, for your servant hears." ¹¹ Then GOD [*or* the LORD] said to Samuel, "I am about to do a thing in Israel, at which the two ears of everyone that hears it will tingle. ¹² On that day I will fulfill against Eli all that I have spoken concerning his house, from beginning to end. ¹³ And I tell Eli that I am about to punish his house forever, for the iniquity which he knew, because his sons were blaspheming God, and Eli did not restrain them. ¹⁴ Therefore I swear to the house of Eli that the iniquity of Eli's house shall not be expiated by sacrifice or offering forever."

¹⁵ Samuel lay until morning; then he opened the doors of the house of GOD [*or* the LORD]. And Samuel was afraid to tell the vision to Eli. ¹⁶ But Eli called Samuel and said, "Samuel, my son." And Samuel said, "Here I am." ¹⁷ And Eli said, "What was it that God told you? Do not hide it from me. May God do so to you and more also, if you hide anything from me of all that God told you." ¹⁸ So Samuel told Eli everything and hid nothing from him. And Eli said, "It is the SOVEREIGN [*or* LORD]; let God do what seems good."

¹⁹ And Samuel grew, and GOD [*or* the LORD] was with him and let none of Samuel's words fall to the ground. ²⁰ And all Israel from Dan to Beersheba knew that Samuel was established as a prophet of GOD [*or* the LORD].

Psalm 63:1–8

[1] O God, you are my God, I seek you,
 my soul thirsts for you;
 my flesh faints for you,
  as in a dry and weary land where no water is.
[2] So I have looked upon you in the sanctuary,
 beholding your power and glory.
[3] Because your steadfast love is better than life,
 my lips will praise you.
[4] So I will bless you as long as I live;
 I will lift up my hands and call on your name.
[5] My soul is feasted as with marrow and fat,
 and my mouth praises you with joyful lips,
[6] when I think of you upon my bed,
 and meditate on you in the watches of the night;
[7] for you have been my help,
 and in the shadow of your wings I sing for joy.
[8] My soul clings to you;
 your right hand upholds me.

Lesson 2 (alternate) ~ Romans 16:1–7[+]

Paul commends Phoebe and greets other co-workers in the church at Rome.

[1] I commend to you our sister Phoebe, a deacon of the church at Cenchreae, [2] that you may receive her in the Sovereign [[or Lord]] as befits the saints, and help her in whatever she may require from you, for she has been a helper of many and of myself as well.

[3] Greet Prisca and Aquila, my co-workers in Christ Jesus, [4] who risked their necks for my life, to whom not only I but also all the churches of the Gentiles give thanks; [5] greet also the church in their house. Greet my beloved Epaenetus, who was the first convert in Asia for Christ. [6] Greet Mary, who has worked hard among you. [7] Greet Andronicus and Junia,[‡] my kinsfolk and prisoners with me; they are noteworthy among the apostles, and they were in Christ before me.

[+]Lection added. See Appendix, p. 255.
[‡]RSV *Junias.*

Lesson 2 ~ 1 Corinthians 6:12–15a, 19–20[+]

Paul writes to the Corinthians that they are members of Christ.

[12] "All things are lawful for me," but not all things are helpful. "All things are lawful for me," but I will not be enslaved by anything. [13] "Food is meant for the stomach and the stomach for food"—and God will destroy both one and the other. The body is not meant for immorality, but for the Sovereign [*or* Lord], and the Sovereign [*or* Lord] for the body. [14] And God raised the Sovereign [*or* Lord] and will also raise us up by God's power. [15] Do you not know that your bodies are members of Christ? [19] Do you not know that your body is a temple of the Holy Spirit within you, which you have from God? You are not your own; [20] you were bought with a price. So glorify God in your body.

Gospel ~ John 1:35–42

Two of John's disciples follow Jesus, testifying that Jesus is the Messiah.

[35] The next day again John was standing with two of his disciples, [36] and looking at Jesus walking by, he said, "Behold, the Lamb of God!" [37] The two disciples heard John say this, and they followed Jesus. [38] Jesus turned, and saw them following, and said to them, "What do you seek?" And they said, "Rabbi" (which means Teacher), "where are you staying?" [39] Jesus said to them, "Come and see." They came and saw where Jesus was staying; and they stayed with him that day, for it was about the tenth hour. [40] One of the two who heard John speak, and followed Jesus, was Andrew, Simon Peter's brother. [41] Andrew first found his brother Simon, and said to him, "We have found the Messiah" (which means Christ). [42] Andrew brought Simon to Jesus. Jesus looked at him, and said, "So you are Simon the son of John? You shall be called Cephas" (which means Peter).

[+]The NACCL reads 1 Cor. 6:12–20. See Appendix, p. 255.

EPIPHANY 3

Lesson 1 ~ Jonah 3:1–5, 10

Jonah's second call to preach to Nineveh results in the conversion of its inhabitants.

¹ Then the word of GOD [*or* the LORD] came to Jonah the second time, saying, ² "Arise, go to Nineveh, that great city, and proclaim to it the message that I tell you." ³ So Jonah arose and went to Nineveh, according to the word of GOD [*or* the LORD]. Now Nineveh was an exceedingly great city, three days' journey in breadth. ⁴ Jonah began to go into the city, going a day's journey. And he cried, "Yet forty days, and Nineveh shall be overthrown!" ⁵ And the people of Nineveh believed God; they proclaimed a fast, and put on sackcloth, from the greatest of them to the least of them.

¹⁰ When God saw what they did, how they turned from their evil way, God repented of the evil which God had vowed to do to them, and did not do it.

Psalm 62:5–12

⁵ For God alone my soul waits in silence,
    for my hope is from God,
⁶ who alone is my rock and my salvation,
    my fortress; I shall not be shaken.
⁷ On God rests my deliverance and my honor;
    my mighty rock, my refuge is God.
⁸ Trust in God at all times, O people;
    pour out your heart before God,
    who is a refuge for us.
⁹ Those of low estate are but a breath,
    those of high estate are a delusion;
  in the balances they go up;
    they are together lighter than a breath.
¹⁰ Put no confidence in extortion,
    set no vain hopes on robbery;
    if riches increase, set not your heart on them.
¹¹ Once God has spoken;
    twice have I heard this:
  that power belongs to God;
¹²   and that to you, O God [*or* Lord], belongs steadfast love.
    For you repay all people
        according to their work.

Lesson 2 ~ 1 Corinthians 7:29–31 (32–35 optional)

Paul writes to the Corinthians about living in the time when the form of this world is passing away.

²⁹ I mean, sisters and brothers, the appointed time has grown very short; from now on, let those who are married live as though they were not, ³⁰ and those who mourn as though they were not mourning, and those who rejoice as though they were not rejoicing, and those who buy as though they had no goods, ³¹ and those who deal with the world as though they had no dealings with it. For the form of this world is passing away.

³² I want you to be free from anxieties. The unmarried man is anxious about the affairs of the Sovereign [or Lord], how to please the Sovereign [or Lord]; ³³ but the married man is anxious about worldly affairs, how to please his wife, ³⁴ and his interests are divided. And the unmarried woman or young girl is anxious about the affairs of the Sovereign [or Lord], how to be holy in body and spirit; but the married woman is anxious about worldly affairs, how to please her husband. ³⁵ I say this for your own benefit, not to lay any restraint upon you, but to promote good order and to secure your undivided devotion to the Sovereign [or Lord].

Gospel ~ Mark 1:14–20

Jesus calls Simon and Andrew.

¹⁴ Now after John was arrested, Jesus came into Galilee, preaching the gospel of God, ¹⁵ and saying, "The time is fulfilled, and the realm☆ of God is at hand; repent, and believe in the gospel."

¹⁶ And passing along by the Sea of Galilee, Jesus saw Simon, and Andrew the brother of Simon, casting a net in the sea; for they were fishers. ¹⁷ And Jesus said to them, "Follow me and I will make you become fishers of people." ¹⁸ And immediately they left their nets and followed him. ¹⁹ And going on a little farther, Jesus saw James the son of Zebedee and John his brother, who were in their boat mending the nets. ²⁰ And immediately Jesus called them; and they left their father Zebedee in the boat with the hired servants, and followed Jesus.

☆RSV *kingdom.* See Appendix.

EPIPHANY 4

Lesson 1 ～ Deuteronomy 18:15–20

God promises to send a prophet like Moses.

¹⁵ The SOVEREIGN [*or* LORD] your God will raise up for you a prophet like me from among you, from your own people—that prophet you shall heed—¹⁶ just as you desired of the SOVEREIGN [*or* LORD] your God at Horeb on the day of the assembly, when you said, "Let me not hear again the voice of the SOVEREIGN [*or* LORD] my God, or see this great fire anymore, lest I die." ¹⁷ And GOD [*or* the LORD] said to me, "They have rightly said all that they have spoken. ¹⁸ I will raise up for them a prophet like you from among their people; and I will put my words in the mouth of that prophet, who shall speak to them all that I command. ¹⁹ And whoever will not give heed to my words which the prophet shall speak in my name, I myself will require it of them. ²⁰ But the prophet who presumes to speak a word in my name which I have not commanded to be spoken, or who speaks in the name of other gods, that same prophet shall die."

Psalm 111

¹ Praise GOD [*or* the LORD]!
  I will give thanks to GOD [*or* the LORD] with my whole heart,
      in the company of the upright, in the congregation.
² Great are the works of GOD [*or* the LORD],
      studied by all who have pleasure in them.
³ Full of honor and majesty is God's work,
      and God's righteousness endures forever.
⁴ God has caused God's wonderful works to be remembered,
      and is gracious and merciful,
⁵ providing food for those who fear God
      and being ever mindful of the covenant.
⁶ God has shown God's people the power of God's works,
      in giving them the heritage of the nations.
⁷ The works of God's hands are faithful and just;
      all God's precepts are trustworthy,
⁸ they are established forever and ever,
      to be performed with faithfulness and uprightness.

⁹ God sent redemption to God's people,
   and has commanded the covenant forever.
   Holy and terrible is God's name!
¹⁰ The fear of GOD [[or the LORD]] is the beginning of wisdom;
   a good understanding have all those who practice it.
   God's praise endures forever!

Lesson 2 ～ 1 Corinthians 8:1–13

Paul writes to the Corinthians about their ethical responsibilities to one another.

¹ Now concerning food offered to idols: we know that "all of us possess knowledge." "Knowledge" puffs up, but love builds up. ² If any imagine that they know something, they do not yet know as they ought to know. ³ But if one loves God, one is known by God.

⁴ Hence, as to the eating of food offered to idols, we know that "an idol has no real existence," and that "there is no God but one." ⁵ For although there may be so-called gods in heaven or on earth—as indeed there are many "gods" and many "sovereigns" [[or "lords"]]— ⁶ yet for us there is one God, the Father [and Mother*], from whom are all things and for whom we exist, and one Sovereign [[or Lord]], Jesus Christ, through whom are all things and through whom we exist.

⁷ However, not all possess this knowledge. But some, through being hitherto accustomed to idols, eat food as really offered to an idol; and their conscience, being weak, is defiled. ⁸ Food will not commend us to God. We are no worse off if we do not eat, and no better off if we do. ⁹ Only take care lest this liberty of yours somehow become a stumbling block to the weak. ¹⁰ For if anyone, having a weak conscience, sees you, a person of knowledge, at table in an idol's temple, might that one not be encouraged to eat food offered to idols? ¹¹ And so by your knowledge that weak person is destroyed, the sister or brother for whom Christ died. ¹² Thus, sinning against your brothers or sisters and wounding their conscience when it is weak, you sin against Christ. ¹³ Therefore, if food is a cause of my sister's or brother's falling, I will never eat meat, lest I cause that person to fall.

---

*Addition to the text. See "Metaphor" and "God the Father and Mother" in the Appendix.

Gospel ～ Mark 1:21–28

Jesus speaks with authority to an unclean spirit.

[21] And they went into Capernaum; and immediately on the sabbath Jesus entered the synagogue and taught. [22] And they were astonished at Jesus' teaching, for he taught them as one who had authority, and not as the scribes. [23] And immediately there was in their synagogue someone with an unclean spirit [24] who cried out, "What have you to do with us, Jesus of Nazareth? Have you come to destroy us? I know who you are, the Holy One of God." [25] But Jesus rebuked the spirit, saying, "Be silent, and come out!" [26] And the unclean spirit, convulsing the person and crying with a loud voice, came out. [27] And they were all amazed, so that they questioned among themselves, saying, "What is this? A new teaching! With authority Jesus commands even the unclean spirits, and they obey." [28] And at once Jesus' fame spread everywhere throughout all the surrounding region of Galilee.

EPIPHANY 5

Lesson 1 ~ Job 7:1–7

Job speaks about the pain of human life.

¹ Have not human beings a hard service upon earth,
    and are not their days like the days of a hireling?
² Like a slave who longs for the shadow of evening,
    and like a hireling who looks for wages,
³ so I am allotted months of emptiness,
    and nights of misery are apportioned to me.
⁴ When I lie down I say, "When shall I arise?"
    But the night is long,
    and I am full of tossing till the dawn.
⁵ My flesh is clothed with worms and dirt;
    my skin hardens, then breaks out afresh.
⁶ My days are swifter than a weaver's shuttle,
    and come to their end without hope.
⁷ Remember that my life is a breath;
    my eye will never again see good.

Psalm 147:1–11

¹ Praise GOD [[*or* the LORD]]!
For it is good to sing praises to our God;
    for God is gracious, and a song of praise is seemly.
² GOD [[*or* The LORD]] builds up Jerusalem,
    and gathers the outcasts of Israel,
³ heals the brokenhearted,
    and binds up their wounds,
⁴ determines the number of the stars,
    and gives to all of them their names.
⁵ Great is our GOD [[*or* LORD]], and abundant in power,
    with understanding beyond measure.
⁶ GOD [[*or* The LORD]] lifts up the downtrodden,
    and casts the wicked to the ground.
⁷ Sing to GOD [[*or* the LORD]] with thanksgiving;
    make melody upon the lyre to our God,
⁸ who covers the heavens with clouds,
    prepares rain for the earth,
    and makes grass grow upon the hills,

[9] who gives to the beasts their food,
  and to the young ravens which cry!
[10] God does not delight in the strength of the horse,
  nor take pleasure in the might of a human being;
[11] but GOD [[or the LORD]] takes pleasure in those who fear God,
  in those who hope in God's steadfast love.

Lesson 2 ~ 1 Corinthians 9:16–23

Paul writes about his mandate to preach the gospel under all circumstances.

[16] For if I preach the gospel, that gives me no ground for boasting. For necessity is laid upon me. Woe to me if I do not preach the gospel! [17] For if I do this of my own will, I have a reward; but if not of my own will, I am entrusted with a commission. [18] What then is my reward? Just this: that in my preaching I may offer the gospel free of charge, not making full use of my right in the gospel.

[19] For though I am free from all people, I have made myself a slave to all, that I might win the more. [20] To the Jews I became as a Jew, in order to win Jews; to those under the law I became as one under the law—though not being myself under the law—that I might win those under the law. [21] To those outside the law I became as one outside the law—not being without law toward God but under the law of Christ—that I might win those outside the law. [22] To the weak I became weak, that I might win the weak. I have become all things to all people, that I might by all means save some. [23] I do it all for the sake of the gospel, that I may share in its blessings.

Gospel ～ Mark 1:29–39

Jesus is engaged in a ministry of healing.

²⁹ And immediately Jesus left the synagogue, and entered the house of Simon and Andrew, with James and John. ³⁰ Now Simon's mother-in-law lay sick with a fever, and immediately they told Jesus of her. ³¹ And Jesus came and took her by the hand and lifted her up, and the fever left her; and she served them.

³² That evening, at sundown, they brought to Jesus all who were sick or possessed with demons. ³³ And the whole city was gathered together about the door. ³⁴ And Jesus healed many who were sick with various diseases, and cast out many demons, and would not permit the demons to speak, because they knew him.

³⁵ And in the morning, a great while before day, Jesus rose and went out to a lonely place, and there Jesus prayed. ³⁶ And Simon and those who were with him pursued Jesus, ³⁷ and they found him and said, "Everyone is searching for you." ³⁸ And Jesus replied, "Let us go on to the next towns, that I may preach there also; for that is why I came out." ³⁹ And Jesus went throughout all Galilee, preaching in their synagogues and casting out demons.

EPIPHANY 6

Lesson 1 ~ 2 Kings 5:1–14

Naaman is cured of leprosy.

¹ Naaman, commander of the army of the king of Syria, was a great man with his master and in high favor, because by Naaman GOD [[*or* the LORD]] had given victory to Syria. Naaman was a mighty man of valor, but he had leprosy. ² Now the Syrians on one of their raids had carried off a young girl from the land of Israel, and she waited on Naaman's wife, ³ and said to her, "Would that my lord were with the prophet who is in Samaria! The prophet would cure Naaman of leprosy." ⁴ So Naaman went in and told his lord, "Thus and so spoke the girl from the land of Israel." ⁵ And the king of Syria said, "Go now, and I will send a letter to the king of Israel."

So Naaman went, taking ten talents of silver, six thousand shekels of gold, and ten festal garments. ⁶ And Naaman brought the letter to the king of Israel, which read, "When this letter reaches you, know that I have sent to you Naaman my servant, that you may cure him of leprosy." ⁷ And when the king of Israel read the letter, he rent his clothes and said, "Am I God, to kill and to make alive, that the king of Syria sends word to me to cure someone of leprosy? Only consider, and see how that king is seeking a quarrel with me."

⁸ But when Elisha the prophet of God heard that the king of Israel had rent his clothes, Elisha sent to the king, saying, "Why have you rent your clothes? Let Naaman come now to me, that he may know that there is a prophet in Israel." ⁹ So Naaman came with horses and chariots, and halted at the door of Elisha's house. ¹⁰ And Elisha sent a messenger to Naaman, saying, "Go and wash in the Jordan seven times, and your flesh shall be restored, and you shall be clean." ¹¹ But Naaman was angry, and went away, saying, "I thought that Elisha would surely come out to me, and stand, and call on the name of the SOVEREIGN [[*or* LORD]] his God, and wave his hand over the place, and cure the one with leprosy. ¹² Are not Abana and Pharpar, the rivers of Damascus, better than all the waters of Israel? Could I not wash in them, and be clean?" So Naaman turned and went away in a rage. ¹³ But his servants came near and said to Naaman, "My father, if the prophet had commanded you to do some great thing, would you not have done it? How much rather, then, when Elisha says to you, 'Wash, and be clean'?" ¹⁴ So Naaman went down and dipped himself seven times in the Jordan, according to the word of the prophet of God; and Naaman's flesh was restored like the flesh of a little child, and he was clean.

Psalm 32

¹ Blessed is the one whose transgression is forgiven,
    whose sin is covered.
² Blessed is the person to whom GOD [*or* the LORD] imputes no
      iniquity,
    and in whose spirit there is no deceit.
³ When I declared not my sin, my body wasted away
    through my groaning all day long.
⁴ For day and night your hand was heavy upon me;
    my strength was dried up as by the heat of summer.
⁵ I acknowledged my sin to you,
    and I did not hide my iniquity;
  I said, "I will confess my transgressions to GOD [*or* the LORD]";
    then you forgave the guilt of my sin.
⁶ Therefore let all who are godly
    offer prayer to you;
  at a time of distress, the rush of great waters
    shall not reach them.
⁷ You are a hiding place for me,
    you preserve me from trouble;
    you encompass me with deliverance.
⁸ I will instruct you and teach you
    the way you should go;
    I will counsel you with my eye upon you.
⁹ Be not like a horse or a mule, without understanding,
    which must be curbed with bit and bridle,
    else it will not keep with you.
¹⁰ Many are the pangs of the wicked;
    but steadfast love surrounds the one who trusts in GOD [*or*
    the LORD].
¹¹ Be glad in GOD [*or* the LORD], and rejoice, O righteous,
    and shout for joy, all you upright in heart!

Lesson 2 ∼ 1 Corinthians 9:24–27

Paul speaks about the importance of self-discipline.

²⁴ Do you not know that in a race all the runners compete, but only one receives the prize? So run that you may obtain it. ²⁵ Every athlete exercises self-control in all things. They do it to receive a perishable wreath, but we an imperishable. ²⁶ Well, I do not run aimlessly, I do not box as one beating the air; ²⁷ but I pommel my body and subdue it, lest after preaching to others I myself should be disqualified.

Gospel ~ Mark 1:40–45

A person with leprosy comes to Jesus for healing.

[40] A person with leprosy came beseeching Jesus, and kneeling said to him, "If you will, you can make me clean." [41] Moved with pity, Jesus reached out and touched the person, and said, "I will; be clean." [42] And immediately the leprosy went away and the person was made clean. [43] And Jesus sternly charged and sent away the one whom he had healed, [44] saying, "See that you say nothing to anyone; but go, show yourself to the priest, and offer for your cleansing what Moses commanded, for a proof to the people." [45] But the one who had been healed went out and began to talk freely about it, and to spread the news, so that Jesus could no longer openly enter a town, but was out in the country; and people came to Jesus from every quarter.

EPIPHANY 7

Lesson 1 ~ Isaiah 43:18–25

Isaiah announces God's forgiveness and redemption.

¹⁸ Remember not the former things,
    nor consider the things of old.
¹⁹ Behold, I am doing a new thing;
    now it springs forth, do you not perceive it?
  I will make a way in the wilderness
    and rivers in the desert.
²⁰ The wild beasts will honor me,
    the jackals and the ostriches;
  for I give water in the wilderness,
    rivers in the desert,
  to give drink to my chosen people,
²¹   the people whom I formed for myself
    that they might declare my praise.
²² Yet you did not call upon me, O Jacob;
    but you have been weary of me, O Israel!
²³ You have not brought me your sheep for burnt offerings,
    or honored me with your sacrifices.
  I have not burdened you with offerings,
    or wearied you with frankincense.
²⁴ You have not bought me sweet cane with money,
    or satisfied me with the fat of your sacrifices.
  But you have burdened me with your sins,
    you have wearied me with your iniquities.
²⁵ I, I am the One
    who blots out your transgressions for my own sake,
    and I will not remember your sins.

Psalm 41

¹ Blessed are those who consider the poor!
  GOD [*or* The LORD] delivers them in the day of trouble;
² GOD [*or* the LORD] protects them and keeps them alive;
  they are called blessed in the land;
  you do not give them up to the will of their enemies.
³ GOD [*or* The LORD] sustains them on their sickbed;
  in their illness you heal all their infirmities.

⁴ As for me, I said, "O GOD ⟦*or* LORD⟧, be gracious to me;
   heal me, for I have sinned against you!"
⁵ My enemies say of me in malice:
   "When will that one die, and that name perish?"
⁶ And when people come to see me, uttering empty words,
   their heart gathers mischief;
   and when they go out, they tell it abroad.
⁷ All who hate me whisper together about me;
   they imagine the worst for me.
⁸ They say, "A deadly thing has fastened upon that one,
   who has lain down never to rise again."
⁹ Even my bosom friend in whom I trusted,
   who ate of my bread, has betrayed me.
¹⁰ But you, O GOD ⟦*or* LORD⟧, be gracious to me,
   and raise me up, that I may repay them!
¹¹ By this I know that you are pleased with me,
   in that my enemy has not triumphed over me.
¹² But you have upheld me because of my integrity,
   and set me in your presence forever.
¹³ Blessed be the SOVEREIGN ⟦*or* LORD⟧, the God of Israel,
   from everlasting to everlasting!
   Amen and Amen.

Lesson 2 ∼ 2 Corinthians 1:18–22

All God's promises are affirmed in Christ.

¹⁸ As surely as God is faithful, our word to you has not been Yes and No. ¹⁹ For the Child◇ of God, Jesus Christ, whom we preached among you, Silvanus and Timothy and I, was not Yes and No; but in Christ it is always Yes. ²⁰ For all the promises of God find their Yes in Christ. That is why we utter the Amen through Jesus Christ, to the glory of God. ²¹ But it is God who establishes us with you in Christ, and has commissioned us; ²² God has put God's seal upon us and given us the Spirit of God in our hearts as a guarantee.

◇RSV *Son.* See Appendix.

68

Gospel ~ Mark 2:1–12

Mark tells the story of Jesus healing someone who was paralyzed.

[1] And when Jesus returned to Capernaum after some days, it was reported that he was at home. [2] And many were gathered together, so that there was no longer room for them, not even about the door; and Jesus was preaching the word to them. [3] And some people came, bringing to Jesus a person who was paralyzed, carried by four men. [4] And when they could not get near Jesus because of the crowd, they removed the roof above him; and when they had made an opening, they let down the pallet on which the person lay. [5] And having seen their faith, Jesus said to the one who was paralyzed, "My child, your sins are forgiven." [6] Now some of the scribes were sitting there, questioning in their hearts, [7] "Why does this man speak thus? It is blasphemy! Who can forgive sins but God alone?" [8] And immediately Jesus, perceiving in his spirit that they thus questioned within themselves, said to them, "Why do you question thus in your hearts? [9] Which is easier, to say to the one paralyzed, 'Your sins are forgiven,' or to say, 'Rise, take up your pallet and walk'? [10] But that you may know that the Human One[°] has authority on earth to forgive sins"—Jesus said to the one who was paralyzed—[11] "I say to you, rise, take up your pallet and go home." [12] And the one who had been paralyzed arose, and immediately took up the pallet and went out before them all; so that they were all amazed and glorified God, saying, "We never saw anything like this!"

[°]RSV *Son of man.* See Appendix.

EPIPHANY 8

Lesson 1 ~ Hosea 2:14–20

Through the prophet Hosea, God speaks of God's love for Israel.

¹⁴ Therefore I will allure Israel,
and bring them into the wilderness,
and speak tenderly to them.
¹⁵ And there I will give Israel vineyards,
and make the Valley of Achor a door of hope.
And there Israel shall answer as in the days of their youth,
as at the time when they came out of the land of Egypt.

¹⁶ And in that day, says the SOVEREIGN [or LORD], you will call me, "My beloved," and no longer will you call me, "My Baal." ¹⁷ For I will remove the names of the Baals from Israel's mouth, and they shall be mentioned by name no more. ¹⁸ And I will make for you a covenant on that day with the beasts of the field, the birds of the air, and the creeping things of the ground; and I will abolish the bow, the sword, and war from the land; and I will make you lie down in safety. ¹⁹ And I will join you to me forever; I will join you to me in righteousness and in justice, in steadfast love, and in mercy. ²⁰ I will join you to me in faithfulness; and you shall know the SOVEREIGN [or LORD].

Psalm 103:1–13

¹ Bless GOD [or the LORD], O my soul;
and all that is within me, bless God's holy name!
² Bless GOD [or the LORD], O my soul,
and forget not all God's benefits,
³ who forgives all your iniquity,
who heals all your diseases,
⁴ who redeems your life from the Pit,
who crowns you with steadfast love and mercy,
⁵ who satisfies you with good as long as you live
so that your youth is renewed like the eagle's.
⁶ GOD [or The LORD] works vindication
and justice for all who are oppressed.
⁷ God made known God's ways to Moses,
God's acts to the people of Israel.
⁸ GOD [or The LORD] is merciful and gracious,
slow to anger and abounding in steadfast love,

⁹ not always chiding,
   and not remaining angry forever.
¹⁰ God does not deal with us according to our sins,
   nor repay us according to our iniquities.
¹¹ For as the heavens are high above the earth,
   so great is God's steadfast love toward those who fear God;
¹² as far as the east is from the west,
   so far does God remove our transgressions from us.
¹³ As parents pity their children,
   so GOD [or the LORD] pities those who fear God.

Lesson 2 ∼ 2 Corinthians 3:1–6

Paul defends his apostolic authority.

¹ Are we beginning to commend ourselves again? Or do we need, as some do, letters of recommendation to you, or from you? ² You yourselves are our letter of recommendation, written on your hearts, to be known and read by all; ³ and you show that you are a letter from Christ delivered by us, written not with ink but with the Spirit of the living God, not on tablets of stone but on tablets of human hearts.

⁴ Such is the confidence that we have through Christ toward God. ⁵ Not that we are competent of ourselves to claim anything as coming from us; our competence is from God, ⁶ who has made us competent to be ministers of a new covenant, not in a written code but in the Spirit; for the written code kills, but the Spirit gives life.

Gospel ∼ Mark 2:18–22

Jesus responds to a question about why his disciples do not fast.

¹⁸ Now John's disciples and the Pharisees were fasting; and people came and said to Jesus, "Why do John's disciples and the disciples of the Pharisees fast, but your disciples do not fast?" ¹⁹ And Jesus said to them, "Can the wedding guests fast while the bridegroom is with them? As long as they have the bridegroom with them, they cannot fast. ²⁰ The days will come, when the bridegroom is taken away from them, and then they will fast in that day. ²¹ No one sews a piece of unshrunk cloth on an old garment; if one does, the patch tears away from it, the new from the old, and a worse tear is made. ²² And no one puts new wine into old wineskins; if one does, the wine will burst the skins, and the wine is lost, and so are the skins; but new wine is for fresh skins."

LAST SUNDAY AFTER EPIPHANY

Lesson 1 ~ 2 Kings 2:1–12a

Elijah passes his spirit to Elisha.

¹ Now when GOD [*or* the LORD] was about to take Elijah up to heaven by a whirlwind, Elijah and Elisha were on their way from Gilgal. ² And Elijah said to Elisha, "Wait here, please; for GOD [*or* the LORD] has sent me as far as Bethel." But Elisha said, "As GOD [*or* the LORD] lives, and as you yourself live, I will not leave you." So they went down to Bethel. ³ And the prophets who were in Bethel came out to Elisha, and said, "Do you know that today GOD [*or* the LORD] will take away your teacher from over you?" And Elisha said, "Yes, I know it; hold your peace."

⁴ Elijah said to him, "Elisha, wait here, please; for GOD [*or* the LORD] has sent me to Jericho." But Elisha said, "As GOD [*or* the LORD] lives, and as you yourself live, I will not leave you." So they came to Jericho. ⁵ The prophets who were at Jericho drew near to Elisha, and said to him, "Do you know that today GOD [*or* the LORD] will take away your teacher from over you?" And Elisha answered, "Yes, I know it; hold your peace."

⁶ Then Elijah said to Elisha, "Wait here, please; for GOD [*or* the LORD] has sent me to the Jordan." But Elisha said, "As GOD [*or* the LORD] lives, and as you yourself live, I will not leave you." So the two of them went on. ⁷ Fifty of the prophets also went, and stood at some distance from them, as they both were standing by the Jordan. ⁸ Then Elijah took his mantle, and rolled it up, and struck the water, and the water was parted to the one side and to the other, till the two of them could go over on dry ground.

⁹ When they had crossed, Elijah said to Elisha, "Ask what I shall do for you, before I am taken from you." And Elisha said, "Please, let me inherit a double share of your spirit." ¹⁰ And Elijah said, "You have asked a hard thing; yet, if you see me as I am being taken from you, it shall be so for you; but if you do not see me, it shall not be so." ¹¹ And as they still went on and talked, a chariot of fire and horses of fire separated the two of them. And Elijah went up by a whirlwind into heaven. ¹² And Elisha saw it and cried out, "My teacher, my teacher! the chariots of Israel and its riders!"

Psalm 50:1–6

¹ The Mighty One, God the SOVEREIGN [*or* LORD],
  speaks and summons the earth
  from the rising of the sun to its setting.
² Out of Zion, the perfection of beauty,
  God shines forth.

³ Our God comes and does not keep silence,
  before God is a devouring fire,
  round about God a mighty tempest.
⁴ God calls to the heavens above
  and to the earth, in order to judge God's people:
⁵ "Gather to me my faithful ones,
  who made a covenant with me by sacrifice!"
⁶ The heavens declare God's righteousness,
  for it is God who judges!

Lesson 2 ~ 2 Corinthians 4:3–6

Paul clarifies for the Corinthians the meaning of the gospel.

³ And even if our gospel is veiled, it is veiled only to those who are perishing. ⁴ In their case the god of this world has blinded the minds of the unbelievers, to keep them from seeing the light of the gospel of the glory of Christ, who is the likeness of God. ⁵ For what we preach is not ourselves, but Jesus Christ as Sovereign [*or* Lord], with ourselves as your servants for Jesus' sake. ⁶ For it is the God who said, "Let light shine out of darkness," who has shone in our hearts to give the light of the knowledge of the glory of God in the face of Christ.

Gospel ~ Mark 9:2–9

Peter, James, and John witness the transfiguration of Jesus.

² And after six days Jesus took with him Peter and James and John, and led them up a high mountain apart by themselves; and Jesus was transfigured before them, ³ and his garments became glistening, intensely bright, as no one on earth could bleach them. ⁴ And there appeared to them Elijah with Moses; and they were talking to Jesus. ⁵ And Peter said to Jesus, "Rabbi, it is well that we are here; let us make three booths, one for you and one for Moses and one for Elijah." ⁶ For Peter did not know what to say, for they were exceedingly afraid. ⁷ And a cloud overshadowed them, and a voice came out of the cloud, "This is my beloved Child;◇ to this one you shall listen." ⁸ And suddenly looking around they no longer saw anyone with them but Jesus only.

⁹ And as they were coming down the mountain, Jesus charged them to tell no one what they had seen, until the Human One○ should have risen from the dead.

◇RSV *Son.* See Appendix.
○RSV *Son of man.* See Appendix.

ASH WEDNESDAY

God calls the people to fasting and repentance.

¹ Blow the trumpet in Zion;
  sound the alarm on my holy mountain!
Let all the inhabitants of the land tremble,
  for the day of GOD [*or* the LORD] is coming, it is near,
² a day of shadow and gloom,
  a day of clouds and thick shadow!
Like a blanket there is spread upon the mountains
  a great and powerful people;
their like has never been from of old,
  nor will be again after them
  through the years of all generations.
¹² "Yet even now," says the SOVEREIGN [*or* LORD],
  "return to me with all your heart,
  with fasting, with weeping, and with mourning;
¹³   and rend your hearts and not your garments."
Return to the SOVEREIGN [*or* LORD], your God,
  for God is gracious and merciful,
  slow to anger, and abounding in steadfast love,
  and repents of evil.
¹⁴ Who knows whether God will not turn and repent,
  and leave a blessing behind,
a cereal offering and a drink offering
  for the SOVEREIGN [*or* LORD], your God?
¹⁵ Blow the trumpet in Zion;
  sanctify a fast;
call a solemn assembly;
¹⁶   gather the people.
Sanctify the congregation;
  assemble the elders;
gather the children,
  even nursing infants.
Let the bridegroom leave his room,
  and the bride her chamber.
¹⁷ Between the vestibule and the altar
  let the priests, the ministers of GOD [*or* the LORD], weep
and say, "Spare your people, O SOVEREIGN [*or* LORD],
  and make not your heritage a reproach,
  a byword among the nations."

Psalm 51:1–12

[1] Have mercy on me, O God, according to your steadfast love;
    according to your abundant mercy blot out my transgressions.
[2] Wash me thoroughly from my iniquity,
    and cleanse me from my sin!
[3] For I know my transgressions,
    and my sin is ever before me.
[4] Against you, you only, have I sinned,
    and done that which is evil in your sight,
  so that you are justified in your sentence
    and blameless in your judgment.
[5] I was brought forth in iniquity,
    and in sin did my mother conceive me.
[6] You desire truth in the inward being;
    therefore teach me wisdom in my secret heart.
[7] Purge me with hyssop, and I shall be clean;
    wash me, and I shall be cleaner than snow.
[8] Fill me with joy and gladness;
    let the bones which you have broken rejoice.
[9] Hide your face from my sins,
    and blot out all my iniquities.
[10] Create in me a clean heart, O God,
    and put a new and right spirit within me.
[11] Cast me not away from your presence,
    and take not your holy Spirit from me.
[12] Restore to me the joy of your salvation,
    and uphold me with a willing spirit.

Lesson 2 ∼ 2 Corinthians 5:20b–6:2 (3–10 optional)

Paul writes to the Corinthians of his ministry of reconciliation.

[20] We beseech you on behalf of Christ, be reconciled to God. [21] For our sake God made to be sin the one who knew no sin, so that in this very one we might become the righteousness of God.

[6:1] Working together with God, then, we entreat you not to accept the grace of God in vain. [2] For God says,

"At the acceptable time I have listened to you,
and helped you on the day of salvation."

Now is the acceptable time; now is the day of salvation. [3] We put no obstacle in anyone's way, so that no fault may be found with our ministry, [4] but as servants of God we commend ourselves in every way: through great endurance, in afflictions, hardships, calamities, 5 beatings, imprisonments, tumults, labors, watching, hunger; 6 by purity, knowledge, forbearance, kindness, the Holy Spirit, genuine love, 7 truthful speech, and the power of God; with the weapons of righteousness for the right hand and for the left; 8 in honor and dishonor, in ill repute and good repute. We are treated as impostors, and yet are true; 9 as unknown, and yet well known; as dying, and yet we live; as punished, and yet not killed; 10 as sorrowful, yet always rejoicing; as poor, yet making many rich; as having nothing, and yet possessing everything.

Gospel ～ Matthew 6:1–6, 16–21

Jesus tells the disciples to lay up treasure in heaven.

1 Beware of practicing your piety before others in order to be seen by them; for then you will have no reward from [*God*] your Father [*and Mother**] who is in heaven.

2 Thus, when you give alms, sound no trumpet before you, as the hypocrites do in the synagogues and in the streets, that they may be praised by others. Truly, I say to you, they have received their reward. 3 But when you give alms, do not let your left hand know what your right hand is doing, 4 so that your alms may be in secret; and God⊗ who sees in secret will reward you.

5 And when you pray, you must not be like the hypocrites; for they love to stand and pray in the synagogues and at the street corners, that they may be seen by others. Truly, I say to you, they have received their reward. 6 But when you pray, go into your room and shut the door and pray to God⊗ who is in secret; and God⊗ who sees in secret will reward you.

16 And when you fast, do not look dismal, like the hypocrites, for they disfigure their faces that their fasting may be seen by others. Truly, I say to you, they have received their reward. 17 But when you fast, anoint your head and wash your face, 18 that your fasting may not be seen by others but by God⊗ who is in secret; and God⊗ who sees in secret will reward you.

19 Do not lay up for yourselves treasures on earth, where moth and rust consume and where thieves break in and steal, 20 but lay up for yourselves treasures in heaven, where neither moth nor rust consumes and where thieves do not break in and steal. 21 For where your treasure is, there will your heart be also.

---

*Addition to the text. See "Metaphor" and "God the Father and Mother" in the Appendix.
⊗RSV *your Father*. See Appendix.

LENT 1

Lesson 1 ~ Genesis 9:8–17

After the flood, God establishes a new covenant with Noah.

[8] Then God said to Noah and to his children, [9] "Behold, I establish my covenant with you and your descendants after you, [10] and with every living creature that is with you, the birds, the cattle, and every beast of the earth with you, as many as came out of the ark. [11] I establish my covenant with you, that never again shall all flesh be cut off by the waters of a flood, and never again shall there be a flood to destroy the earth." [12] And God said, "This is the sign of the covenant which I make between me and you and every living creature that is with you, for all future generations: [13] I set my bow in the cloud, and it shall be a sign of the covenant between me and the earth. [14] When I bring clouds over the earth and the bow is seen in the clouds, [15] I will remember my covenant which is between me and you and every living creature of all flesh; and the waters shall never again become a flood to destroy all flesh. [16] When the bow is in the clouds, I will look upon it and remember the everlasting covenant between God and every living creature of all flesh that is upon the earth." [17] God said to Noah, "This is the sign of the covenant which I have established between me and all flesh that is upon the earth."

Psalm 25:1–10

[1] To you, O GOD [[*or* LORD]], I lift up my soul.
[2] O my God, in you I trust,
    let me not be put to shame;
    let not my enemies exult over me.
[3] Let none that wait for you be put to shame;
    let them be ashamed who are wantonly treacherous.
[4] Make me to know your ways, O GOD [[*or* LORD]];
    teach me your paths.
[5] Lead me in your truth, and teach me,
    for you are the God of my salvation;
    for you I wait all the day long.
[6] Be mindful of your mercy, O GOD [[*or* LORD]], and of your steadfast love,
    for they have been from of old.
[7] Remember not the sins of my youth, or my transgressions;
    according to your steadfast love remember me,
    for your goodness' sake, O GOD [[*or* LORD]]!

⁸ Good and upright is GOD [[*or* the LORD]],
    who therefore instructs sinners in the way.
⁹ God leads the humble in what is right,
    and teaches the humble God's way.
¹⁰ All the paths of GOD [[*or* the LORD]] are steadfast love and
        faithfulness,
    for those who keep God's covenant and testimonies.

Lesson 2 ~ 1 Peter 3:18–22

The author writes of the saving work of baptism through Jesus' resurrection.

¹⁸ For Christ also died for sins once for all, the righteous for the unright-eous, in order to bring us to God, being put to death in the flesh but made alive in the spirit, ¹⁹ in which Christ went and preached to the spirits in prison. ²⁰ They formerly did not obey, when God's patience waited in the days of Noah, during the building of the ark, in which a few, that is, eight persons, were saved through water. ²¹ Baptism, which corresponds to this, now saves you, not as a removal of dirt from the body but as an appeal to God for a clear conscience, through the resurrection of Jesus Christ, ²² who has gone into heaven and is at the right hand of God, to rule over angels, authorities, and powers.

Gospel ~ Mark 1:9–15

Mark tells about Jesus' baptism and temptation, and about the beginning of Jesus' ministry.

⁹ In those days Jesus came from Nazareth of Galilee and was baptized by John in the Jordan. ¹⁰ And having come up out of the water, immediately Jesus saw the heavens opened and the Spirit descending upon him like a dove; ¹¹ and a voice came from heaven, "You are my beloved Child;◊ with you I am well pleased."

¹² The Spirit immediately drove Jesus out into the wilderness. ¹³ And Jesus was in the wilderness forty days, tempted by Satan; and he was with the wild beasts; and the angels ministered to him.

¹⁴ Now after John was arrested, Jesus came into Galilee, preaching the gospel of God, ¹⁵ and saying, "The time is fulfilled, and the realm☆ of God is at hand; repent, and believe in the gospel."

◊RSV *Son.* See Appendix.
☆RSV *kingdom.* See Appendix.

LENT 2

Lesson 1 ~ Genesis 17:1–10, 15–19

God makes a covenant with Abraham, and bestows blessings upon both Abraham and Sarah.

[1] When Abram was ninety-nine years old the SOVEREIGN [[or LORD]] appeared to Abram, and said, "I am God Almighty; walk before me, and be blameless. [2] And I will make my covenant between me and you, and will multiply you exceedingly." [3] Then Abram fell on his face; and God said, [4] "My covenant is with you, and you shall be the ancestor of a multitude of nations. [5] No longer shall your name be Abram, but your name shall be Abraham; for I have made you the ancestor of a multitude of nations. [6] I will make you exceedingly fruitful; and I will make nations of you, and rulers[] shall come forth from you. [7] And I will establish my covenant between me and you and your descendants after you throughout their generations for an everlasting covenant, to be God to you and to your descendants after you. [8] And I will give to you, and to your descendants after you, the land of your sojournings, all the land of Canaan, for an everlasting possession; and I will be their God."

[9] And God said to Abraham, "As for you, you shall keep my covenant, you and your descendants after you throughout their generations. [10] This is my covenant, which you shall keep, between me and you and your descendants after you: Every male among you shall be circumcised."

[15] And God said to Abraham, "As for Sarai your wife, you shall not call her name Sarai, but Sarah shall be her name. [16] I will bless her, and moreover I will give you a child by her; I will bless her, and she shall be a mother of nations; rulers[] of peoples shall come from her." [17] Then Abraham fell on his face and laughed, and said to himself, "Shall a child be born to a man who is a hundred years old? Shall Sarah, who is ninety years old, bear a child?" [18] And Abraham said to God, "O that Ishmael might live in your sight!" [19] God said, "No, but Sarah your wife shall bear you a son, and you shall call his name Isaac. I will establish my covenant with Isaac as an everlasting covenant for his descendants."

[]RSV *kings.* See Appendix.

¹ O give thanks to GOD [*or* the LORD], call on God's name,
    make known God's deeds among the nations!
² Sing to God, sing praises to God,
    tell of all God's wonderful works!
³ Glory in God's holy name;
    let the hearts of those who seek GOD [*or* the LORD] rejoice!
⁴ Seek GOD [*or* the LORD] and God's strength,
    seek God's presence continually!
⁵ Remember the wonderful works that God has done,
    the miracles, and the judgments God uttered,
⁶ O offspring of Abraham [*and Sarah,**] God's servants,
    children of Jacob, [*Rachel, and Leah,**] God's chosen ones!
⁷ This is the SOVEREIGN [*or* LORD] our God,
    whose judgments are in all the earth.
⁸ God is mindful of the covenant forever,
    of the word commanded for a thousand generations,
⁹ the covenant which God made with Abraham,
    God's sworn promise to Isaac,
¹⁰ confirmed to Jacob as a statute,
    to Israel as an everlasting covenant,
¹¹ saying, "To you I will give the land of Canaan
    as your portion for an inheritance."

Lesson 2 ~ Romans 4:16–25

Paul writes that our justification, like that of Abraham and Sarah, is by faith, not by obedience to the law.

¹⁶ That is why it depends on faith, in order that the promise may rest on grace and be guaranteed to all their descendants—not only to the adherents of the law but also to those who share the faith of Abraham, who [*with Sarah**] is the ancestor of us all; ¹⁷ as it is written, "I have made you the ancestor of many nations"—in the presence of the God in whom Abraham believed, who gives life to the dead and calls into existence the things that do not exist. ¹⁸ In hope Abraham believed against hope, in order to become the ancestor of many nations; as he had been told, "So shall your descendants be." ¹⁹ Abraham, being about a hundred years old, did not weaken in faith when considering his own body to be as good as dead, or when considering the barrenness of Sarah's womb. ²⁰ No distrust made Abraham waver con-

*Addition to the text. See "Addition of Women's Names to the Text" in the Appendix.

cerning the promise of God, but he grew strong in faith, giving glory to God, [21] fully convinced that God was able to do what God had promised. [22] That is why Abraham's faith was "reckoned to him as righteousness." [23] But the words, "it was reckoned to him," were written not for Abraham's sake alone, [24] but for ours also. It will be reckoned to us who believe in the one who raised from the dead Jesus our Sovereign [[or Lord]], [25] who was put to death for our trespasses and raised for our justification.

Gospel ～ Mark 8:31–38

Jesus speaks about the passion and teaches about discipleship.

[31] And Jesus began to teach them that the Human One° must suffer many things, and be rejected by the elders and the chief priests and the scribes, and be killed, and after three days rise again. [32] And he said this plainly. And Peter took Jesus, and began to rebuke him. [33] But turning and seeing his disciples, Jesus rebuked Peter, and said, "Get behind me, Satan! For you are not siding with God, but with humankind."

[34] And Jesus summoned the multitude with the disciples, and said to them, "If any would come after me, let them deny themselves and take up their cross and follow me. [35] For those who would save their life will lose it; and those who lose their life for my sake and the gospel's will save it. [36] For what advantage is it, to gain the whole world and forfeit one's life? [37] For what shall one give in return for one's life? [38] For any who are ashamed of me and of my words in this adulterous and sinful generation, of them will the Human One° also be ashamed, when the Human One° comes in the glory of God⊗ with the holy angels."

°RSV *Son of man.* See Appendix.
⊗RSV *his Father.* See Appendix.

Gospel (alternate) ~ Mark 9:1-9

Peter, James, and John witness the transfiguration of Jesus.

[1] And Jesus said to them, "Truly, I say to you, there are some standing here who will not taste death before they see that the realm☆ of God has come with power."

[2] And after six days Jesus took Peter and James and John, and led them up a high mountain apart by themselves; and Jesus was transfigured before them, [3] and his garments became glistening, intensely bright, as no one on earth could bleach them. [4] And there appeared to them Elijah with Moses; and they were talking to Jesus. [5] And Peter said to Jesus, "Rabbi, it is well that we are here; let us make three booths, one for you and one for Moses and one for Elijah." [6] For Peter did not know what to say, for they were exceedingly afraid. [7] And a cloud overshadowed them, and a voice came out of the cloud, "This is my beloved Child;◇ to this one you shall listen." [8] And suddenly looking around they no longer saw anyone with them but Jesus only.

[9] And as they were coming down the mountain, Jesus charged them to tell no one what they had seen, until the Human One○ should have risen from the dead.

☆RSV *kingdom*. See Appendix.
◇RSV *Son*. See Appendix.
○RSV *Son of man*. See Appendix.

LENT 3

God gives the Ten Commandments to Moses.

¹ And God spoke all these words, saying,

² "I am the SOVEREIGN [[or LORD]] your God, who brought you out of the land of Egypt, out of the house of bondage.

³ "You shall have no other gods before me.

⁴ "You shall not make for yourself a graven image, or any likeness of anything that is in heaven above, or that is in the earth beneath, or that is in the water under the earth; ⁵ you shall not bow down to them or serve them; for I the SOVEREIGN [[or LORD]] your God am a jealous God, visiting the iniquity of the parents upon the children to the third and the fourth generation of those who hate me, ⁶ but showing steadfast love to thousands of those who love me and keep my commandments.

⁷ "You shall not take the name of the SOVEREIGN [[or LORD]] your God in vain; for GOD [[or the LORD]] will not hold anyone guiltless who takes God's name in vain.

⁸ "Remember the sabbath day, to keep it holy. ⁹ Six days you shall labor, and do all your work; ¹⁰ but the seventh day is a sabbath to the SOVEREIGN [[or LORD]] your God; in it you shall not do any work, you, or your son, or your daughter, or your manservant, or your womanservant, or your cattle, or the resident alien who is within your gates; ¹¹ for in six days GOD [[or the LORD]] made heaven and earth, the sea, and all that is in them, and rested the seventh day; therefore GOD [[or the LORD]] blessed the sabbath day and hallowed it.

¹² "Honor your father and your mother, that your days may be long in the land which the SOVEREIGN [[or LORD]] your God gives you.

¹³ "You shall not kill.

¹⁴ "You shall not commit adultery.

¹⁵ "You shall not steal.

¹⁶ "You shall not bear false witness against your neighbor.

¹⁷ "You shall not covet your neighbor's house; you shall not covet your neighbor's wife, [or *husband,* *] or manservant, or womanservant, or ox, or donkey, or anything that is your neighbor's."

---

*Addition to the text.

Psalm 19:7–14

⁷ The law of GOD [[*or* the LORD]] is perfect,
     reviving the soul;
   the testimony of GOD [[*or* the LORD]] is sure,
     making wise the simple;
⁸ the precepts of GOD [[*or* the LORD]] are right,
     rejoicing the heart;
   the commandment of GOD [[*or* the LORD]] is pure,
     enlightening the eyes;
⁹ the fear of GOD [[*or* the LORD]] is clean,
     enduring forever;
   the ordinances of GOD [[*or* the LORD]] are true,
     and righteous altogether.
¹⁰ More to be desired are they than gold,
     even much fine gold;
   sweeter also than honey
     and drippings of the honeycomb.
¹¹ Moreover by them is your servant warned;
     in keeping them there is great reward.
¹² But who can discern one's errors?
     Clear me from hidden faults.
¹³ Keep back your servant also from presumptuous sins;
     let them not have dominion over me!
   Then I shall be blameless,
     and innocent of great transgression.
¹⁴ Let the words of my mouth and the meditation of my heart
     be acceptable in your sight,
   O GOD [[*or* LORD]], my rock and my redeemer.

Lesson 2 ～ 1 Corinthians 1:22–25

Paul writes that the wisdom of God is wiser than human wisdom.

²² For Jews demand signs and Greeks seek wisdom, ²³ but we preach Christ crucified, a stumbling block to Jews and folly to Gentiles, ²⁴ but to those who are called, both Jews and Greeks, Christ the power of God and the wisdom of God. ²⁵ For the foolishness of God is wiser than human wisdom, and the weakness of God is stronger than human strength.

Jesus cleanses the temple.

[13] The Passover was at hand, and Jesus went up to Jerusalem. [14] In the temple Jesus found those who were selling oxen and sheep and pigeons, and the money-changers at their business. [15] And making a whip of cords, Jesus drove them all, with the sheep and oxen, out of the temple, pouring out the coins of the money-changers and overturning their tables. [16] And Jesus told those who sold the pigeons, "Take these things away; you shall not make God's⊗ house a house of trade." [17] The disciples remembered that it was written, "Zeal for your house will consume me." [18] The religious authorities▽ then said to Jesus, "What sign have you to show us for doing this?" [19] Jesus answered them, "Destroy this temple, and in three days I will raise it up." [20] Then the religious authorities▽ said, "It has taken forty-six years to build this temple, and will you raise it up in three days?" [21] But Jesus spoke of the temple of his body. [22] When therefore Jesus was raised from the dead, the disciples remembered that Jesus had said this; and they believed the scripture and the word which Jesus had spoken.

⊗RSV *my Father's.* See Appendix.
▽RSV v. 18 *The Jews;* v. 20 *the Jews.* See Appendix.

LENT 4

Lesson 1 (alternate) ~ Judges 4:4–9[+]

Deborah, a prophet and judge of Israel, fearlessly leads her people into battle.

⁴ Now Deborah, a prophet, the wife of Lappidoth, was judging Israel at that time. ⁵ She used to sit under the palm of Deborah between Ramah and Bethel in the hill country of Ephraim; and the people of Israel came up to her for judgment. ⁶ She sent and summoned Barak the son of Abinoam from Kedesh in Naphtali, and said to him, "The SOVEREIGN [*or* LORD], the God of Israel, commands you, 'Go, gather your soldiers at Mount Tabor, taking ten thousand from the tribe of Naphtali and the tribe of Zebulun. ⁷ And I will draw out Sisera, the general of Jabin's army, to meet you by the river Kishon with chariots and troops; and I will give Sisera into your hand.' " ⁸ Barak said to Deborah, "If you will go with me, I will go; but if you will not go with me, I will not go." ⁹ And she said, "I will surely go with you; nevertheless, the road on which you are going will not lead to your glory, for GOD [*or* the LORD] will sell Sisera into the hand of a woman." Then Deborah arose, and went with Barak to Kedesh.

Lesson 1 ~ 2 Chronicles 36:14–23

God judges the transgressions of the nation Judah.

¹⁴ All the leading priests and the people likewise were exceedingly unfaithful, following all the abominations of the nations; and they polluted the house of GOD [*or* the LORD] which God had hallowed in Jerusalem. ¹⁵ The SOVEREIGN [*or* LORD], the God of their ancestors, sent persistently to them by messengers, because God had compassion on the people and on God's dwelling place; ¹⁶ but they kept mocking the messengers of God, despising God's words, and scoffing at God's prophets, till the wrath of the SOVEREIGN [*or* LORD] rose against God's people, till there was no remedy. ¹⁷ Therefore God brought up against them the king of the Chaldeans, who slew their young men with the sword in the house of their sanctuary, and had no compassion on young man or young woman, old people or aged; God gave them all into the king's hand. ¹⁸ And all the vessels of the house of God, great and small, and the treasures of the house of GOD [*or* the LORD], and the treasures of the king and of his princes, all these the king of the Chaldeans brought to Babylon. ¹⁹ And they burned the house of God, and broke

---

[+]Lection added. See Appendix, p. 255.

86

down the wall of Jerusalem, and burned all its palaces with fire, and destroyed all its precious vessels. 20 He took into exile in Babylon those who had escaped from the sword, and they became servants to the king and to his offspring until the establishment of the kingdom of Persia, 21 to fulfill the word of GOD [or the LORD] by the mouth of Jeremiah, until the land had enjoyed its sabbaths. All the days that it lay desolate it kept sabbath, to fulfill seventy years.

22 Now in the first year of Cyrus, king of Persia, that the word of GOD [or the LORD] by the mouth of Jeremiah might be accomplished, GOD [or the LORD] stirred up the spirit of Cyrus king of Persia so that Cyrus made a proclamation throughout all the kingdom and also put it in writing: 23 "Thus says Cyrus king of Persia, 'The SOVEREIGN [or LORD], the God of heaven, has given me all the kingdoms of the earth and has charged me to build for God a house at Jerusalem, which is in Judah. All who are among you of all God's people, may the SOVEREIGN [or LORD] their God be with them. Let them go up.' "

Psalm 137:1-6

1 By the waters of Babylon,
     there we sat down and wept,
     when we remembered Zion.
2 On the willows there
     we hung up our lyres.
3 For there our captors
     required of us songs,
   and our tormentors, mirth, saying,
     "Sing us one of the songs of Zion!"
4 How shall we sing GOD's [or the LORD's] song
     in a foreign land?
5 If I forget you, O Jerusalem,
     let my right hand wither!
6 Let my tongue cleave to the roof of my mouth,
     if I do not remember you,
   if I do not set Jerusalem
     above my highest joy!

Lesson 2 ～ Ephesians 2:4–10

Salvation in Christ is declared to be the gift of God.

⁴ But God, who is rich in mercy, out of the great love with which God loved us, ⁵ even when we were dead through our trespasses, made us alive together with Christ (by grace you have been saved), ⁶ and raised us up with Christ, and made us sit with Christ in the heavenly places in Christ Jesus, ⁷ that in the coming ages God might show the immeasurable riches of God's grace in kindness toward us in Christ Jesus. ⁸ For by grace you have been saved through faith; and this is not your own doing, it is the gift of God—⁹ not because of works, lest anyone should boast. ¹⁰ For we are God's handiwork, created in Christ Jesus for good works, which God prepared beforehand, that we should walk in them.

Gospel ～ John 3:14–21

Acceptance or rejection of God's love in Jesus Christ brings its own consequence.

¹⁴ "And as Moses lifted up the serpent in the wilderness, so must the Human One○ be lifted up, ¹⁵ that whoever believes in that one may have eternal life."
¹⁶ For God so loved the world that God gave God's only Child,◇ that whoever believes in that Child should not perish but have eternal life. ¹⁷ For God sent that Child◇ into the world, not to condemn the world, but that through that Child the world might be saved. ¹⁸ Whoever believes in the Child [*of God**] is not condemned; whoever does not believe is condemned already, for not having believed in the name of the only Child◇ of God. ¹⁹ And this is the judgment, that the light has come into the world, and people loved the night rather than light, because their deeds were evil. ²⁰ For all who do evil hate the light, and do not come to the light, lest their deeds should be exposed. ²¹ But all who do what is true come to the light, that it may be clearly seen that their deeds have been wrought in God.

○RSV *Son of man.* See Appendix.
◇RSV, vs. 16, 18 *Son;* v. 17 *the Son.* See Appendix.
*Addition to the text.

LENT 5

Lesson 1 ∼ Jeremiah 31:31–34

God promises a new covenant with the houses of Israel and Judah.

³¹ The days are coming, says the SOVEREIGN [*or* LORD], when I will make a new covenant with the house of Israel and the house of Judah, ³² not like the covenant which I made with their ancestors when I took them by the hand to bring them out of the land of Egypt, my covenant which they broke, though I was married to them, says the SOVEREIGN [*or* LORD]. ³³ But this is the covenant which I will make with the house of Israel after those days, says the SOVEREIGN [*or* LORD]: I will put my law within them, and I will write it upon their hearts; and I will be their God, and they shall be my people. ³⁴ And no longer shall each one teach a neighbor and each a brother or sister, saying, "Know GOD [*or* the LORD]," for they shall all know me, from the least of them to the greatest, says the SOVEREIGN [*or* LORD]; for I will forgive their iniquity, and I will remember their sin no more.

Psalm 51:10–17

¹⁰ Create in me a clean heart, O God,
    and put a new and right spirit within me.
¹¹ Cast me not away from your presence,
    and take not your holy Spirit from me.
¹² Restore to me the joy of your salvation,
    and uphold me with a willing spirit.
¹³ Then I will teach transgressors your ways,
    and sinners will return to you.
¹⁴ Deliver me from bloodguiltiness, O God,
    God of my salvation,
    and my tongue will sing aloud of your deliverance.
¹⁵ O God [*or* Lord], open my lips,
    and my mouth shall show forth your praise.
¹⁶ For you have no delight in sacrifice;
    were I to give a burnt offering, you would not be pleased.
¹⁷ The sacrifice acceptable to God is a broken spirit;
    a broken and contrite heart, O God, you will not despise.

Lesson 2 ~ Hebrews 5:7–10

Salvation is given through Jesus Christ, the suffering high priest.

[7] While in the flesh, Jesus offered up prayers and supplications, with loud cries and tears, to the one who was able to save him from death, and was heard for his godly fear. [8] Although the Child◇ [*of God**], Jesus learned obedience through suffering, [9] and being made perfect, became the source of eternal salvation to all who obey Jesus Christ, [10] having been designated by God a high priest after the order of Melchizedek.

Gospel ~ John 12:20–33

John speaks of the glorification of the Human One.

[20] Now among those who went up to worship at the feast were some Greeks. [21] So these came to Philip, who was from Bethsaida in Galilee, and said, "Sir, we wish to see Jesus." [22] Philip went and told Andrew; Andrew went with Philip and they told Jesus. [23] And Jesus answered them, "The hour has come for the Human One○ to be glorified. [24] Truly, truly, I say to you, unless a grain of wheat falls into the earth and dies, it remains alone; but if it dies, it bears much fruit. [25] Whoever loves their life loses it, and whoever hates their life in this world will keep it for eternal life. [26] Anyone who serves me must follow me; and where I am, there shall my servant be also; anyone who serves me will be honored by [*God*] the Father [*and Mother**]."

[27] "Now is my soul troubled. And what shall I say? 'God,⊛ save me from this hour'? No, for this purpose I have come to this hour. [28] God,⊛ glorify your name." Then a voice came from heaven, "I have glorified it, and I will glorify it again." [29] The crowd standing by heard it and said that it had thundered. Others said, "An angel has spoken to him." [30] Jesus answered, "This voice has come for your sake, not for mine. [31] Now is the judgment of this world, now shall the ruler of this world be cast out; [32] and I, when I am lifted up from the earth, will draw all people to myself." [33] Jesus said this to show by what death he was to die.

◇RSV *a Son.* See Appendix.
*Addition to the text.
○RSV *Son of man.* See Appendix.
**Addition to the text. See "Metaphor" and "God the Father and Mother" in the Appendix.
⊛RSV *Father.* See Appendix.

LENT 6, PASSION SUNDAY

Lesson 1 ～ Isaiah 50:4–9a

The prophet Isaiah tells of the suffering of the one who obeys God.

⁴ The Sovereign [*or* Lord] GOD has given me
   the tongue of those who are taught,
 that I may know how to sustain with a word
   one who is weary.
 Morning by morning God wakens,
   God wakens my ear
 to hear as those who are taught.
⁵ The Sovereign [*or* Lord] GOD has opened my ear,
   and I was not rebellious,
   I turned not backward.
⁶ I gave my back to the smiters,
   and my cheeks to those who pulled out my beard;
 I hid not my face
   from shame and spitting.
⁷ For the Sovereign [*or* Lord] GOD helps me;
   therefore I have not been confounded;
 therefore I have set my face like a flint,
   and I know that I shall not be put to shame;
⁸   the one who vindicates me is near.
 Who will contend with me?
   Let us stand together.
 Who are my adversaries?
   Let them come near to me.
⁹ The Sovereign [*or* Lord] GOD helps me;
   who will declare me guilty?

Psalm 31:9–16

⁹ Be gracious to me, O GOD [*or* LORD], for I am in distress;
   my eye is wasted from grief,
   my soul and my body also.
¹⁰ For my life is spent with sorrow,
   and my years with sighing;
   my strength fails because of my misery,
   and my bones waste away.

¹¹ I am the scorn of all my adversaries,
    a horror to my neighbors,
  an object of dread to my acquaintances;
    those who see me in the street flee from me.
¹² I have passed out of mind like one who is dead;
    I have become like a broken vessel.
¹³ For I hear the whispering of many—
    terror on every side!—
  as they scheme together against me,
    as they plot to take my life.
¹⁴ But I trust in you, O GOD [[*or* LORD]],
    I say, "You are my God."
¹⁵ My times are in your hand;
    deliver me from the hand of my enemies and persecutors!
¹⁶ Let your face shine on your servant;
    save me in your steadfast love!

Lesson 2 ～ Philippians 2:5–11

Paul speaks about the Sovereign Jesus Christ.

⁵ Have this mind among yourselves, which is yours in Christ Jesus, ⁶ who, though being in the form of God, did not count equality with God a thing to be grasped, ⁷ but emptied Christ's self, taking the form of a servant, being born in the likeness of human beings. ⁸ And being found in human form, Christ humbled Christ's self and became obedient unto death, even death on a cross. ⁹ Therefore God has highly exalted Jesus and bestowed on Jesus the name which is above every name, ¹⁰ that at the name of Jesus every knee should bow, in heaven and on earth and under the earth, ¹¹ and every tongue confess that Jesus Christ is Sovereign [[*or* Lord]], to the glory of God the Father [*and Mother**].

Gospel ～ Mark 14–15 (or 15:1–39)

Mark gives an account of the final events of Jesus' earthly life.

¹ It was now two days before the Passover and the feast of Unleavened Bread. And the chief priests and the scribes were seeking how to arrest Jesus by stealth, and kill him; ² for they said, "Not during the feast, lest there be a tumult of the people."

---

*Addition to the text. See "Metaphor" and "God the Father and Mother" in the Appendix.

³ And while Jesus was at Bethany sitting at table in the house of Simon—a man who had leprosy—a woman came with an alabaster flask of ointment of pure nard, very costly, and she broke the flask and poured it over Jesus' head. ⁴ But there were some who said to themselves indignantly, "Why was the ointment thus wasted? ⁵ For this ointment might have been sold for more than three hundred denarii, and given to the poor." And they reproached her. ⁶ But Jesus said, "Let her alone; why do you trouble her? She has done a beautiful thing to me. ⁷ For you always have the poor with you, and whenever you will, you can do good to them; but you will not always have me. ⁸ She has done what she could; she has anointed my body beforehand for burying. ⁹ And truly, I say to you, wherever the gospel is preached in the whole world, what she has done will be told in memory of her."

¹⁰ Then Judas Iscariot, who was one of the twelve, went to the chief priests in order to betray Jesus to them. ¹¹ And when they heard it they were glad, and promised to give Judas money. And Judas sought an opportunity to betray Jesus.

¹² And on the first day of Unleavened Bread, when they sacrificed the passover lamb, the disciples said to Jesus, "Where will you have us go and prepare for you to eat the passover?" ¹³ And Jesus sent two of the disciples, and said to them, "Go into the city, and a man carrying a jar of water will meet you; follow him, ¹⁴ and wherever he enters, say to the householder, 'The Teacher says, Where is my guest room, where I am to eat the passover with my disciples?' ¹⁵ And the householder will show you a large upper room furnished and ready; there prepare for us." ¹⁶ And the disciples set out and went to the city, and found it as Jesus had told them; and they prepared the passover.

¹⁷ And when it was evening Jesus came with the twelve. ¹⁸ And as they were at table eating, Jesus said, "Truly, I say to you, one of you will betray me, the one who is eating with me." ¹⁹ They began to be sorrowful, and to say to Jesus one after another, "Is it I?" ²⁰ Jesus said to them, "It is one of the twelve, the one who is dipping bread into the dish with me. ²¹ For the Human One° goes as it is written, but woe to that person by whom the Human One° is betrayed! It would have been better for that person not to have been born."

²² And as they were eating, Jesus took bread, and blessed, and broke it, and gave it to them, and said, "Take; this is my body." ²³ And Jesus took a cup, and after giving thanks, gave it to them, and they all drank of it. ²⁴ And Jesus said to them, "This is my blood of the covenant, which is poured out for many. ²⁵ Truly, I say to you, I shall not drink again of the fruit of the vine until that day when I drink it new in the realm☆ of God."

²⁶ And when they had sung a hymn, they went out to the Mount of Olives.

°RSV *Son of man.* See Appendix.
☆RSV *kingdom.* See Appendix.

⁲⁷ And Jesus said to them, "You will all fall away; for it is written, 'I will strike the shepherd, and the sheep will be scattered.' ²⁸ But after I am raised up, I will go before you to Galilee." ²⁹ Peter said to Jesus, "Even though they all fall away, I will not." ³⁰ And Jesus said to Peter, "Truly, I say to you, this very night, before the cock crows twice, you will deny me three times." ³¹ But Peter said vehemently, "If I must die with you, I will not deny you." And they all said the same.

³² And they went to a place which was called Gethsemane; and Jesus said to the disciples, "Sit here, while I pray." ³³ And taking Peter and James and John, Jesus began to be greatly distressed and troubled. ³⁴ And he said to them, "My soul is very sorrowful, even to death; remain here, and watch." ³⁵ And going a little farther, Jesus fell on the ground and prayed that, if it were possible, the hour might pass from him. ³⁶ And Jesus said, "[*God, my Mother and**] Father, all things are possible to you; remove this cup from me; yet not what I will, but what you will." ³⁷ And Jesus came and found them sleeping, and said to Peter, "Simon, are you asleep? Could you not watch one hour? ³⁸ Watch and pray that you may not enter into temptation; the spirit indeed is willing, but the flesh is weak." ³⁹ And again Jesus went away and prayed, saying the same words. ⁴⁰ And again he came and found them sleeping, for their eyes were very heavy; and they did not know what to answer. ⁴¹ And Jesus came the third time, and said to them, "Are you still sleeping and taking your rest? It is enough; the hour has come; the Human One° is betrayed into the hands of sinners. ⁴² Rise, let us be going; see, my betrayer is at hand."

⁴³ And immediately, while Jesus was still speaking, Judas came, one of the twelve, and with him a crowd with swords and clubs, from the chief priests and the scribes and the elders. ⁴⁴ Now the betrayer had given them a sign, saying, "The one I shall kiss is the man; seize him and lead him away under guard." ⁴⁵ And when Judas came, he went up to Jesus at once, and said, "Rabbi!" And Judas kissed Jesus. ⁴⁶ And they laid hands on Jesus and seized him. ⁴⁷ But one of those who stood by drew a sword, and struck the slave of the high priest and cut off his ear. ⁴⁸ And Jesus said to them, "Have you come out as against a robber, with swords and clubs to capture me? ⁴⁹ Day after day I was with you in the temple teaching, and you did not seize me. But let the scriptures be fulfilled." ⁵⁰ And they all forsook Jesus, and fled.

⁵¹ And a young man followed Jesus, with nothing but a linen cloth about his body; and they seized him, ⁵² but he left the linen cloth and ran away naked.

⁵³ And they led Jesus to the high priest; and all the chief priests and the elders and the scribes were assembled. ⁵⁴ And Peter had followed Jesus at

---

*Addition to the text. RSV *"Abba."* See "Metaphor" and "God the Father and Mother" in the Appendix.
°RSV *Son of man.* See Appendix.

a distance, right into the courtyard of the high priest, and was sitting with the guards, warming himself at the fire. ⁵⁵ Now the chief priests and the whole council sought testimony against Jesus to put him to death; but they found none. ⁵⁶ For many bore false witness against Jesus, and their witness did not agree. ⁵⁷ And some stood up and bore false witness, saying, ⁵⁸ "We heard Jesus say, 'I will destroy this temple that is made with hands, and in three days I will build another, not made with hands.'" ⁵⁹ Yet not even so did their testimony agree. ⁶⁰ And the high priest stood up in the midst, and asked Jesus, "Have you no answer to make? What is it that these witnesses testify against you?" ⁶¹ But Jesus was silent and made no answer. Again the high priest asked Jesus, "Are you the Christ, the Child◇ of the Blessed?" ⁶² And Jesus said, "I am; and you will see the Human One○ seated at the right hand of Power, and coming with the clouds of heaven." ⁶³ And the high priest tore the priestly garments, and said, "Why do we still need witnesses? ⁶⁴ You have heard his blasphemy. What is your decision?" And they all condemned Jesus as deserving death. ⁶⁵ And some began to spit on Jesus, and to cover his face, and to strike him, saying, "Prophesy!" And the guards received Jesus with blows.

⁶⁶ And as Peter was below in the courtyard, one of the maids of the high priest came; ⁶⁷ and seeing Peter warming himself, she looked at him, and said, "You also were with the Nazarene, Jesus." ⁶⁸ But Peter denied it, saying, "I neither know nor understand what you mean." And he went out into the gateway. ⁶⁹ And the maid saw him, and began again to say to the bystanders, "This is one of them." ⁷⁰ But again Peter denied it. And after a little while again the bystanders said to Peter, "Certainly you are one of them; for you are a Galilean." ⁷¹ But Peter began to invoke a curse on himself and to swear, "I do not know this one of whom you speak." ⁷² And immediately the cock crowed a second time. And Peter remembered how Jesus had said, "Before the cock crows twice, you will deny me three times." And Peter broke down and wept.

¹⁵:¹ And as soon as it was morning the chief priests, with the elders and scribes, and the whole council held a consultation; and they bound Jesus and led him away and delivered him to Pilate. ² And Pilate asked Jesus, "Are you the King of the Jews?" And Jesus answered, "You have said so." ³ And the chief priests accused Jesus of many things. ⁴ And Pilate again asked Jesus, "Have you no answer to make? See how many charges they bring against you." ⁵ But Jesus made no further answer, so that Pilate wondered.

⁶ Now at the feast Pilate used to release for them one prisoner for whom they asked. ⁷ And among the rebels in prison, who had committed murder in the insurrection, there was a man called Barabbas. ⁸ And the crowd came up and began to ask Pilate to do as he was wont to do for them. ⁹ And Pilate

---

◇RSV Son. See Appendix.
○RSV Son of man. See Appendix.

answered them, "Do you want me to release for you the King of the Jews?" [10] For Pilate perceived that it was out of envy that the chief priests had delivered up Jesus. [11] But the chief priests stirred up the crowd to have Pilate release for them Barabbas instead. [12] And Pilate again said to them, "Then what shall I do with the one whom you call the King of the Jews?" [13] And they cried out again, "Crucify him." [14] And Pilate said to them, "Why, what evil has he done?" But they shouted all the more, "Crucify him." [15] So Pilate, wishing to satisfy the crowd, released for them Barabbas; and having scourged Jesus, Pilate delivered him to be crucified.

[16] And the soldiers led Jesus away inside the palace (that is, the praetorium); and they called together the whole battalion. [17] And they clothed Jesus in a purple cloak, and plaiting a crown of thorns they put it on him. [18] And they began to salute Jesus, "Hail, King of the Jews!" [19] And they struck Jesus' head with a reed, and spat upon him, and they knelt down in homage to him. [20] And when they had mocked Jesus, they stripped him of the purple cloak, and put his own clothes on him. And they led Jesus out to be crucified.

[21] And they compelled a passer-by, Simon of Cyrene, who was coming in from the country, the father of Alexander and Rufus, to carry Jesus' cross. [22] And they brought Jesus to the place called Golgotha (which means the place of a skull). [23] And they offered Jesus wine mingled with myrrh; but he did not take it. [24] And they crucified Jesus, and divided his garments among them, casting lots for them, to decide what each should take. [25] And it was the third hour, when they crucified Jesus. [26] And the inscription of the charge against him read, "The King of the Jews." [27] And with Jesus they crucified two robbers, one on the right and one on the left. [29] And those who passed by derided Jesus, wagging their heads, and saying, "Aha! You who would destroy the temple and build it in three days, [30] save yourself, and come down from the cross!" [31] So also the chief priests, together with the scribes, mocked Jesus, saying to one another, "He saved others, but cannot save himself. [32] Let the Christ, the King of Israel, come down now from the cross, that we may see and believe." Those who were crucified with Jesus also reviled him.

[33] And when the sixth hour had come, there was darkness over the whole land until the ninth hour. [34] And at the ninth hour Jesus cried with a loud voice, "Eloi, Eloi, lama sabachthani?" which means, "My God, my God, why have your forsaken me?" [35] And some of the bystanders hearing it said, "Behold, Jesus is calling Elijah." [36] And one ran and, filling a sponge full of vinegar, put it on a reed and gave it to Jesus to drink, saying, "Wait, let us see whether Elijah will come to take Jesus down." [37] And Jesus uttered a loud cry, and died. [38] And the curtain of the temple was torn in two, from top to bottom. [39] And when the centurion, who stood facing Jesus, saw that Jesus died in this way, he said, "Truly this was the Child◇ of God!"

◇RSV *Son.* See Appendix.

⁴⁰ There were also women looking on from afar, among whom were Mary Magdalene, and Mary the mother of James the younger and of Joses, and Salome, ⁴¹ who, when Jesus was in Galilee, followed him, and ministered to him; and also many other women who came up with Jesus to Jerusalem.

⁴² And when the evening had come, since it was the day of Preparation, that is, the day before the sabbath, ⁴³ Joseph of Arimathea, a respected member of the council, who was also looking for the realm✩ of God, took courage and went to Pilate, and asked for the body of Jesus. ⁴⁴ And Pilate wondered if Jesus were already dead; and summoning the centurion, Pilate asked him whether Jesus was already dead. ⁴⁵ And on learning from the centurion that Jesus was dead, Pilate granted the body to Joseph. ⁴⁶ And Joseph bought a linen shroud, and taking him down, wrapped him in the linen shroud, and laid him in a tomb which had been hewn out of the rock; and Joseph rolled a stone against the door of the tomb. ⁴⁷ Mary Magdalene and Mary the mother of Joses saw where Jesus was laid.

✩RSV *kingdom*. See Appendix.

LENT 6, PALM SUNDAY

Lesson 1 ~ Isaiah 50:4–9a

The prophet Isaiah tells of the suffering of the one who obeys God.

⁴ The Sovereign [*or* Lord] GOD has given me
   the tongue of those who are taught,
 that I may know how to sustain with a word
   one who is weary.
 Morning by morning God wakens,
   God wakens my ear
   to hear as those who are taught.
⁵ The Sovereign [*or* Lord] GOD has opened my ear,
   and I was not rebellious,
   I turned not backward.
⁶ I gave my back to the smiters,
   and my cheeks to those who pulled out my beard;
 I hid not my face
   from shame and spitting.
⁷ For the Sovereign [*or* Lord] GOD helps me;
   therefore I have not been confounded;
 therefore I have set my face like a flint,
   and I know that I shall not be put to shame;
⁸   the one who vindicates me is near.
 Who will contend with me?
   Let us stand together.
 Who are my adversaries?
   Let them come near to me.
⁹ The Sovereign [*or* Lord] GOD helps me;
   who will declare me guilty?

Psalm 118:19–29

¹⁹ Open to me the gates of righteousness,
    that I may enter through them
    and give thanks to GOD [*or* the LORD].
²⁰ This is the gate of GOD [*or* the LORD];
    the righteous shall enter through it.
²¹ I thank you that you have answered me
    and have become my salvation.
²² The stone which the builders rejected
    has become the head of the corner.

²³ This is GOD'S [*or* the LORD'S] doing;
    it is marvelous in our eyes.
²⁴ This is the day which GOD [*or* the LORD] has made;
    let us rejoice and be glad in it.
²⁵ Save us, we beseech you, O GOD [*or* LORD]!
    O GOD [*or* LORD], we beseech you, give us success!
²⁶ Blessed be the one who enters in the name of GOD [*or* the LORD]!
    We bless you from the house of GOD [*or* the LORD].
²⁷ The SOVEREIGN [*or* LORD] is God,
    who has caused light to shine upon us.
  Bind the festal procession with branches,
    up to the horns of the altar!
²⁸ You are my God, and I will give thanks to you;
    you are my God, I will extol you.
²⁹ O give thanks to GOD [*or* the LORD], for God is good;
    for God's steadfast love endures forever!

Lesson 2 ~ Philippians 2:5–11

Paul speaks about the Sovereign Jesus Christ.

⁵ Have this mind among yourselves, which is yours in Christ Jesus, ⁶ who, though being in the form of God, did not count equality with God a thing to be grasped, ⁷ but emptied Christ's self, taking the form of a servant, being born in the likeness of human beings. ⁸ And being found in human form, Christ humbled Christ's self and became obedient unto death, even death on a cross. ⁹ Therefore God has highly exalted Jesus and bestowed on Jesus the name which is above every name, ¹⁰ that at the name of Jesus every knee should bow, in heaven and on earth and under the earth, ¹¹ and every tongue confess that Jesus Christ is Sovereign [*or* Lord], to the glory of God the Father [*and Mother**].

---

*Addition to the text. See "Metaphor" and "God the Father and Mother" in the Appendix.

Gospel ~ Mark 11:1–11

Jesus enters Jerusalem amid shouts of the people.

¹ And when they drew near to Jerusalem, to Bethphage and Bethany, at the Mount of Olives, Jesus sent two of the disciples, ² and said to them, "Go into the village opposite you, and immediately as you enter it you will find a colt tied, on which no one has ever sat; untie it and bring it. ³ If anyone says to you, 'Why are you doing this?' say, 'The Sovereign [[*or* Lord]] has need of it and will send it back here immediately.' " ⁴ And they went away, and found a colt tied at the door out in the open street; and they untied it. ⁵ And those who stood there said to them, "What are you doing, untying the colt?" ⁶ And the disciples told them what Jesus had said; and they let the disciples go. ⁷ And the disciples brought the colt to Jesus, and threw their garments on it; and Jesus sat upon it. ⁸ And many spread their garments on the road, and others spread leafy branches which they had cut from the fields. ⁹ And those who went before and those who followed cried out, "Hosanna! Blessed is the one who comes in the name of the Sovereign [[*or* Lord]]! ¹⁰ Blessed is the realm☆ of our ancestor David! Hosanna in the highest!"

¹¹ And Jesus entered Jerusalem, and went into the temple; and having looked round at everything, since it was already late, he went out to Bethany with the twelve.

☆RSV *kingdom.* See Appendix.

MONDAY OF HOLY WEEK

Lesson 1 ~ Isaiah 42:1–9

God speaks through the prophet Isaiah about God's servant.

¹ Here is my servant, whom I uphold,
 my chosen, in whom my soul delights;
 I have put my Spirit upon my servant,
 who will bring forth justice to the nations.
² My servant will not cry or speak out,
 nor be heard in the street;
³ my servant will not break a bruised reed,
 nor quench a dimly burning wick,
 but will faithfully bring forth justice.
⁴ My servant will not fail or be discouraged
 till justice has been established in the earth;
 and the coastlands wait for the servant's law.
⁵ Thus says God, the SOVEREIGN [[or LORD]],
 who created the heavens and stretched them out,
 who spread forth the earth and what comes from it,
 who gives breath to the people upon it
 and spirit to those who walk in it:
⁶ "I am the SOVEREIGN [[or LORD]], I have called you in righteousness,
 I have taken you by the hand and kept you;
 I have given you as a covenant to the people,
 a light to the nations,
⁷ to open the eyes that are blind,
 to bring out the prisoners from the dungeon,
 from the prison those who sit with no light.
⁸ I am the SOVEREIGN [[or LORD]], that is my name;
 my glory I give to no other,
 nor my praise to graven images.
⁹ Now the former things have come to pass,
 and new things I declare;
 before they spring forth
 I tell you of them."

Psalm 36:5–10

⁵ Your steadfast love, O GOD [[*or* LORD]], extends to the heavens,
   your faithfulness to the clouds.
⁶ Your righteousness is like the mountains of God,
   your judgments are like the great deep;
   all living things you save, O GOD [[*or* LORD]].
⁷ How precious is your steadfast love, O God!
   All people may take refuge in the shadow of your wings.
⁸ They feast on the abundance of your house,
   and you give them drink from the river of your delights.
⁹ For with you is the fountain of life;
   in your light do we see light.
¹⁰ O continue your steadfast love to those who know you,
   and your salvation to the upright of heart!

Lesson 2 ∼ Hebrews 9:11–15

Christ is the mediator of a new covenant.

¹¹ But when Christ appeared as a high priest of the good things that have come, then through the greater and more perfect tent (not made with hands, that is, not of this creation) ¹² Christ entered once for all into the Holy Place, taking not the blood of goats and calves but Christ's own blood, thus securing an eternal redemption. ¹³ For if the sprinkling of defiled persons with the blood of goats and bulls and with the ashes of a heifer sanctifies for the purification of the flesh, ¹⁴ how much more shall the blood of Christ—who through the eternal Spirit offered Christ's self as an unblemished sacrifice to God—purify your conscience from dead works to serve the living God.

¹⁵ Therefore Christ is the mediator of a new covenant, so that those who are called may receive the promised eternal inheritance, since a death has occurred which redeems them from the transgressions under the first covenant.

Gospel ~ John 12:1–11

Mary of Bethany anoints the feet of Jesus.

¹ Six days before the Passover, Jesus came to Bethany, where Lazarus was, whom Jesus had raised from the dead. ² There they made Jesus a supper; Martha served, and Lazarus was one of those at the table. ³ Mary took a pound of costly ointment of pure nard and anointed the feet of Jesus and wiped them with her hair; and the house was filled with the fragrance of the ointment. ⁴ But Judas Iscariot, one of the disciples (the one who was to betray Jesus), said, ⁵ "Why was this ointment not sold for three hundred denarii and given to the poor?" ⁶ This Judas said, not that he cared for the poor but because he was a thief, and having the money box, he used to take what was put into it. ⁷ Jesus said, "Let her alone, let her keep it for the day of my burial. ⁸ The poor you always have with you, but you do not always have me."

⁹ When the great crowd of the Jews learned that Jesus was there, they came, not only on account of Jesus but also to see Lazarus, whom Jesus had raised from the dead. ¹⁰ So the chief priests planned to put Lazarus also to death, ¹¹ because on account of him many of the Jews were going away and believing in Jesus.

TUESDAY OF HOLY WEEK

Lesson 1 ~ Isaiah 49:1-7

The prophet Isaiah speaks of the servant of God.

¹ Listen to me, O coastlands,
    and hearken, you nations from afar.
GOD [*or* The LORD] called me from the womb,
    and from the body of my mother God named my name.
² God made my mouth like a sharp sword,
    in the shadow of God's hand I was hidden;
God made me a polished arrow,
    in the quiver I was hidden away.
³ And God said to me, "You are my servant,
    Israel, in whom I will be glorified."
⁴ But I said, "I have labored in vain,
    I have spent my strength for nothing and vanity;
yet surely my right is with the SOVEREIGN [*or* LORD],
    and my recompense with my God."
⁵ And now GOD [*or* the LORD] says,
    who formed me from the womb to be God's servant,
to bring Jacob back to God,
    and that Israel might be gathered to God,
for I am honored in the eyes of the SOVEREIGN [*or* LORD],
    and my God has become my strength—
⁶ God says:
"It is too light a thing that you should be my servant
    to raise up the tribes of Jacob
    and to restore the preserved of Israel;
I will give you as a light to the nations,
    that my salvation may reach to the end of the earth."
⁷ Thus says the SOVEREIGN [*or* LORD],
    the Redeemer of Israel and Israel's Holy One,
to one deeply despised, abhorred by the nations,
    the servant of rulers:
"Monarchs[a] shall see and arise;
    rulers, and they shall prostrate themselves;
because of the SOVEREIGN [*or* LORD], who is faithful,
    the Holy One of Israel, who has chosen you."

---

[a]RSV *Kings.* See Appendix.

Psalm 71:1–12

¹ In you, O GOD [[*or* LORD]], do I take refuge;
    let me never be put to shame!
² In your righteousness deliver me and rescue me;
    incline your ear to me, and save me!
³ Be to me a rock of refuge,
    a strong fortress, to save me,
    for you are my rock and my fortress.
⁴ Rescue me, O my God, from the hand of the wicked,
    from the grasp of the unjust and the cruel.
⁵ For you, O God [[*or* Lord]], are my hope,
    my trust, O GOD [[*or* LORD]], from my youth.
⁶ Upon you I have leaned from my birth;
    you are the one who took me from my mother's womb.
  My praise is continually of you.
⁷ I have been as a portent to many;
    but you are my strong refuge.
⁸ My mouth is filled with your praise,
    and with your glory all the day.
⁹ Do not cast me off in the time of old age;
    forsake me not when my strength is spent.
¹⁰ For my enemies speak concerning me,
    those who watch for my life consult together,
¹¹ and say, "God has forsaken the one who trusted;
    pursue and seize the forsaken one,
    for there is no one to give deliverance."
¹² O God, be not far from me;
    O my God, make haste to help me!

Lesson 2 ~ 1 Corinthians 1:18–31

Paul writes to the Christians at Corinth about the wisdom of God.

¹⁸ For the word of the cross is folly to those who are perishing, but to us who are being saved it is the power of God. ¹⁹ For it is written,

"I will destroy the wisdom of the wise,
and the cleverness of the clever I will thwart."

²⁰ Where is the wise one? Where is the scribe? Where is the debater of this age? Has not God made foolish the wisdom of the world? ²¹ For since, in the wisdom of God, the world did not know God through wisdom, it pleased God through the folly of what we preach to save those who believe. ²² For Jews demand signs and Greeks seek wisdom, ²³ but we preach Christ crucified, a stumbling block to Jews and folly to Gentiles, ²⁴ but to those who are called, both Jews and Greeks, Christ the power of God and the wisdom of God. ²⁵ For the foolishness of God is wiser than human wisdom, and the weakness of God is stronger than human strength.

²⁶ For consider your call, my friends; not many of you were wise according to worldly standards, not many were powerful, not many were of noble birth; ²⁷ but God chose what is foolish in the world to shame the wise, God chose what is weak in the world to shame the strong, ²⁸ God chose what is low and despised in the world, even things that are not, to bring to nothing things that are, ²⁹ so that no human being might boast in the presence of God. ³⁰ God is the source of your life in Christ Jesus, whom God made our wisdom, our righteousness and sanctification and redemption; ³¹ therefore, as it is written, "Let the one who boasts, boast of the Sovereign [[*or* Lord]]."

Gospel ~ John 12:20–36

Jesus speaks of the glorification of the Human One.

[20] Now among those who went up to worship at the feast were some Greeks. [21] So these came to Philip, who was from Bethsaida in Galilee, and said, "Sir, we wish to see Jesus." [22] Philip went and told Andrew; Andrew went with Philip and they told Jesus. [23] And Jesus answered them, "The hour has come for the Human One° to be glorified. [24] Truly, truly, I say to you, unless a grain of wheat falls into the earth and dies, it remains alone; but if it dies, it bears much fruit. [25] Whoever loves their life loses it, and whoever hates their life in this world will keep it for eternal life. [26] Anyone who serves me must follow me; and where I am, there shall my servant be also; anyone who serves me will be honored by [*God*] the Father [*and Mother**].

[27] "Now is my soul troubled. And what shall I say? 'God,⊗ save me from this hour'? No, for this purpose I have come to this hour. [28] God,⊗ glorify your name." Then a voice came from heaven, "I have glorified it, and I will glorify it again." [29] The crowd standing by heard it and said that it had thundered. Others said, "An angel has spoken to him." [30] Jesus answered, "This voice has come for your sake, not for mine. [31] Now is the judgment of this world, now shall the ruler of this world be cast out; [32] and I, when I am lifted up from the earth, will draw all people to myself." [33] Jesus said this to show by what death he was to die. [34] The crowd answered, "We have heard from the law that the Christ remains forever. How can you say that the Human One° must be lifted up? Who is this Human One°?" [35] Jesus said to them, "The light is with you for a little longer. Walk while you have the light, lest the night overtake you; those who walk in the night do not know where they are going. [36] While you have the light, believe in the light, that you may become children of light."

Having said this, Jesus departed and hid from them.

°RSV *Son of man.* See Appendix.
*Addition to the text. See "Metaphor" and "God the Father and Mother" in the Appendix.
⊗RSV *Father.* See Appendix.

WEDNESDAY OF HOLY WEEK

Lesson 1 ~ Isaiah 50:4–9a

The prophet Isaiah tells of the suffering of the one who obeys God.

⁴ The Sovereign [*or* Lord] GOD has given me
    the tongue of those who are taught,
that I may know how to sustain with a word
    one who is weary.
Morning by morning God wakens,
    God wakens my ear
    to hear as those who are taught.
⁵ The Sovereign [*or* Lord] GOD has opened my ear,
    and I was not rebellious,
    I turned not backward.
⁶ I gave my back to the smiters,
    and my cheeks to those who pulled out my beard;
    I hid not my face
    from shame and spitting.
⁷ For the Sovereign [*or* Lord] GOD helps me;
    therefore I have not been confounded;
therefore I have set my face like a flint,
    and I know that I shall not be put to shame;
⁸   the one who vindicates me is near.
Who will contend with me?
    Let us stand together.
Who are my adversaries?
    Let them come near to me.
⁹ The Sovereign [*or* Lord] GOD helps me;
    who will declare me guilty?

Psalm 70

¹ Be pleased, O God, to deliver me!
    O GOD [*or* LORD], make haste to help me!
² Let them be put to shame and confusion
    who seek my life!
Let them be turned back and brought to dishonor
    who desire my hurt!
³ Let them be appalled because of their shame
    who say, "Aha, Aha!"

⁴ May all who seek you
    rejoice and be glad in you!
May those who love your salvation
    say evermore, "God is great!"
⁵ But I am poor and needy;
    hasten to me, O God!
You are my help and my deliverer;
    O GOD [[*or* LORD]], do not tarry!

Lesson 2 ~ Hebrews 12:1–3

Jesus is the pioneer and perfecter of our faith.

¹ Therefore, since we are surrounded by so great a cloud of witnesses, let us also lay aside every weight, and sin which clings so closely, and let us run with perseverance the race that is set before us, ² looking to Jesus the pioneer and perfecter of our faith, who for the joy that was set before him endured the cross, despising the shame, and is seated at the right hand of the throne of God.

³ Consider the one who endured from sinners such hostility against himself, so that you may not grow weary or fainthearted.

Gospel ~ John 13:21–30

Judas is identified as the one who will betray Jesus.

²¹ Having spoken thus, Jesus was troubled in spirit, and testified, "Truly, truly, I say to you, one of you will betray me." ²² The disciples looked at one another, uncertain of whom he spoke. ²³ One of the disciples, whom Jesus loved, was lying close to his breast; ²⁴ so Simon Peter beckoned to that disciple and said, "Tell us who it is of whom he speaks." ²⁵ So lying thus, close to the breast of Jesus, the one whom Jesus loved said to him, "Sovereign [[*or* Lord]], who is it?" ²⁶ Jesus answered, "It is the one to whom I shall give this morsel when I have dipped it." Having dipped the morsel, he gave it to Judas, the son of Simon Iscariot. ²⁷ Then after the morsel, Satan entered into Judas. Jesus said to him, "What you are going to do, do quickly." ²⁸ Now no one at the table knew why Jesus said this to Judas. ²⁹ Some thought that, because Judas had the money box, Jesus was telling him, "Buy what we need for the feast," or that Judas should give something to the poor. ³⁰ So, after receiving the morsel, Judas immediately went out; and it was night.

MAUNDY THURSDAY

(For those who want the foot washing emphasis every year, the Year A readings are used each year.)

Lesson 1 ~ Exodus 24:3–8

The covenant is ratified by Moses and the people.

³ Moses came and told the people all the words of GOD [*or* the LORD] and all the ordinances; and all the people answered with one voice, and said, "All the words which GOD [*or* the LORD] has spoken we will do." ⁴ And Moses wrote all the words of GOD [*or* the LORD]. And Moses rose early in the morning, and built an altar at the foot of the mountain, and twelve pillars, according to the twelve tribes of Israel. ⁵ And Moses sent some young people of Israel to offer burnt offerings and to sacrifice peace offerings of oxen to GOD [*or* the LORD]. ⁶ And Moses took half of the blood and put it in basins, and half of the blood he threw against the altar. ⁷ Then Moses took the book of the covenant, and read it in the hearing of the people; and they said, "All that GOD [*or* the LORD] has spoken we will do, and we will be obedient." ⁸ And Moses took the blood and threw it upon the people, and said, "Behold the blood of the covenant which GOD [*or* the LORD] has made with you in accordance with all these words."

Psalm 116:12–19

(Psalm 116:12–19 is used at the Eucharist on Maundy [Holy] Thursday. Psalm 89:20–21, 24, 26, on page 168, is used at the Chrism service.)

¹² What shall I render to GOD [*or* the LORD]
    for all God's bounty to me?
¹³ I will lift up the cup of salvation
    and call on the name of GOD [*or* the LORD],
¹⁴ I will pay my vows to GOD [*or* the LORD]
    in the presence of all God's people.
¹⁵ Precious in the sight of GOD [*or* the LORD]
    is the death of the saints.
¹⁶ O GOD [*or* LORD], I am your servant;
    I am your servant, the child of your womanservant.
    You have loosed my bonds.
¹⁷ I will offer to you the sacrifice of thanksgiving
    and call on the name of GOD [*or* the LORD].
¹⁸ I will pay my vows to GOD [*or* the LORD]
    in the presence of all God's people,
¹⁹ in the courts of the house of GOD [*or* the LORD],
    in your midst, O Jerusalem.
  Praise GOD [*or* the LORD]!

Lesson 2 ～ 1 Corinthians 10:16–17

Partaking of the bread and the cup is an act of unity in Jesus Christ.

[16] The cup of blessing which we bless, is it not a participation in the blood of Christ? The bread which we break, is it not a participation in the body of Christ? [17] Because there is one bread, we who are many are one body, for we all partake of the one bread.

Gospel ～ Mark 14:12–26

Mark tells about Jesus' last supper with the disciples.

[12] And on the first day of Unleavened Bread, when they sacrificed the passover lamb, the disciples said to Jesus, "Where will you have us go and prepare for you to eat the passover?" [13] And Jesus sent two of the disciples, and said to them, "Go into the city, and a man carrying a jar of water will meet you; follow him, [14] and wherever he enters, say to the householder, 'The Teacher says, Where is my guest room, where I am to eat the passover with my disciples?' [15] And the householder will show you a large upper room furnished and ready; there prepare for us." [16] And the disciples set out and went to the city, and found it as Jesus had told them; and they prepared the passover.

[17] And when it was evening Jesus came with the twelve. [18] And as they were at table eating, Jesus said, "Truly, I say to you, one of you will betray me, the one who is eating with me." [19] They began to be sorrowful, and to say to Jesus one after another, "Is it I?" [20] Jesus said to them, "It is one of the twelve, the one who is dipping bread into the dish with me. [21] For the Human One○ goes as it is written, but woe to that person by whom the Human One○ is betrayed! It would have been better for that person not to have been born."

[22] And as they were eating, Jesus took bread, and blessed, and broke it, and gave it to them, and said, "Take; this is my body." [23] And Jesus took a cup, and after giving thanks, gave it to them, and they all drank of it. [24] And Jesus said to them, "This is my blood of the covenant, which is poured out for many. [25] Truly, I say to you, I shall not drink again of the fruit of the vine until that day when I drink it new in the realm☆ of God."

[26] And when they had sung a hymn, they went out to the Mount of Olives.

○RSV *Son of man.* See Appendix.
☆RSV *kingdom.* See Appendix.

GOOD FRIDAY

Lesson 1 ～ Isaiah 52:13–53:12

Isaiah writes of the Suffering Servant.

¹³ My servant shall prosper,
 shall be exalted and lifted up,
 and shall be very high.
¹⁴ As many were astonished at the one
 whose appearance was so marred, beyond human semblance,
 and whose form beyond that of human beings,
¹⁵ so many nations will be startled;
 rulers[□] shall shut their mouths because of my servant;
for that which has not been told them they shall see,
 and that which they have not heard they shall understand.
^{53:1} Who has believed what we have heard?
 And to whom has the arm of GOD [*or* the LORD] been revealed?
² For the servant grew up before God like a young plant,
 and like a root out of dry ground,
with no form or comeliness that we should admire,
 and no beauty that we should desire.
³ The servant was despised and rejected by everyone,
 was full of sorrows, and acquainted with grief,
and as one from whom people hide their faces,
 was despised and not esteemed by us.
⁴ Surely this one has borne our griefs
 and carried our sorrows;
yet we esteemed the servant stricken,
 smitten by God, and afflicted.
⁵ But this servant was wounded for our transgressions,
 was bruised for our iniquities,
bore the chastisement that made us whole
 and the stripes by which we are healed.
⁶ All we like sheep have gone astray;
 we have turned everyone to our own way;
and GOD [*or* the LORD] has laid on this one
 the iniquity of us all.

[□]RSV *kings.* See Appendix.

⁷ The servant was oppressed, and was afflicted,
   yet did not say a word;
  like a lamb that is led to the slaughter,
    and like a ewe that before her shearers is dumb,
    the servant did not say a word.
⁸ By oppression and judgment the servant was taken away;
    and as for that one's generation, who considered
  that the servant was cut off out of the land of the living,
    stricken for the transgression of my people?
⁹ Although the servant had done no violence
    and had spoken no deceit,
  the servant was buried with the wicked,
    and with the rich in death.
¹⁰ Yet it was the will of GOD [or the LORD] to bruise
    and put to grief this one,
  who, after choosing to become an offering for sin,
    shall see offspring, and enjoy long life;
  the will of GOD [or the LORD] shall prosper in the servant's hand;
¹¹   my servant shall see the fruit of the soul's travail and be satisfied;
  by knowledge shall the righteous one, my servant,
    make many to be accounted righteous,
    and shall bear their iniquities.
¹² Therefore I will divide for this one a portion with the great,
    and my servant shall divide the spoil with the strong,
  because my servant poured out life and died,
    and was numbered with the transgressors,
  yet bore the sin of many,
    and made intercession for the transgressors.

Psalm 22:1–18

¹ My God, my God, why have you forsaken me?
  Why are you so far from helping me, from the words of my
    groaning?
² O my God, I cry by day, but you do not answer;
  and by night, but find no rest.
³ Yet you are holy,
  enthroned on the praises of Israel.
⁴ In you our ancestors trusted;
  they trusted, and you delivered them.
⁵ To you they cried, and were saved;
  in you they trusted, and were not disappointed.
⁶ But I am a worm, not human at all;
  scorned by everyone, and despised by the people.

⁷ All who seek me mock at me,
they make mouths at me, they wag their heads and say,
⁸ "You trusted in GOD [[or the LORD]]; let God deliver you,
let God rescue you, for God delights in you!"
⁹ Yet you, O God, are the one who took me from the womb;
you kept me safe upon my mother's breasts.
¹⁰ Upon you I was cast from my birth,
and since my mother bore me you have been my God.
¹¹ Be not far from me,
for trouble is near
and there is none to help.
¹² Many bulls encompass me,
strong bulls of Bashan surround me;
¹³ they open wide their mouths at me,
like a ravening and roaring lion.
¹⁴ I am poured out like water,
and all my bones are out of joint;
my heart is like wax,
it is melted within my breast;
¹⁵ my strength is dried up like a potsherd,
and my tongue cleaves to my jaws;
you lay me in the dust of death.
¹⁶ Even dogs are round about me;
a company of evildoers encircle me;
they have pierced my hands and feet—
¹⁷ I can count all my bones—
they stare and gloat over me;
¹⁸ they divide my garments among them,
and for my raiment they cast lots.

Lesson 2 ~ Hebrews 4:14–16; 5:7–9

Jesus the high priest learns obedience through suffering.

¹⁴ Since then we have a great high priest who has passed through the heavens, Jesus, the Child◇ of God, let us hold fast our confession. ¹⁵ For we have not a high priest who is unable to sympathize with our weaknesses, but one who in every respect has been tempted as we are, yet without sin. ¹⁶ Let us then with confidence draw near to the throne of grace, that we may receive mercy and find grace to help in time of need.

◇RSV *Son.* See Appendix.

5:7 While in the flesh, Jesus offered up prayers and supplications, with loud cries and tears, to the one who was able to save him from death, and was heard for his godly fear. 8 Although a Child◇ [of God*], Jesus learned obedience through suffering, 9 and being made perfect, became the source of eternal salvation to all who obey Jesus.

Gospel ~ John 18–19 (or 19:17–30)

John tells of the arrest and crucifixion of Jesus.

1 After praying for the disciples, Jesus went forth with them across the Kidron valley, where there was a garden which they entered. 2 Now Judas, who betrayed him, also knew the place; for Jesus often met there with the disciples. 3 So Judas, procuring a band of soldiers and some officers from the chief priests and the Pharisees, went there with lanterns and torches and weapons. 4 Then Jesus, knowing all that was to befall him, came forward and said to them, "Whom do you seek?" 5 They answered, "Jesus of Nazareth." Jesus said to them, "I am the one." Judas, the betrayer, was standing with them. 6 When Jesus said to them, "I am the one," they drew back and fell to the ground. 7 Again Jesus asked them, "Whom do you seek?" And they said, "Jesus of Nazareth." 8 He answered, "I told you that I am the one; so, if you seek me, let these others go." 9 This was to fulfill the word which he had spoken, "Of those whom you gave me I lost not one." 10 Then Simon Peter, having a sword, drew it and struck the high priest's slave and cut off his right ear. The slave's name was Malchus. 11 Jesus said to Peter, "Put your sword into its sheath; shall I not drink the cup which [God] the Father [and Mother**] has given me?"

12 So the band of soldiers and their captain and the officers of the religious authorities▽ seized and bound Jesus. 13 First they led him to Annas, who was the father-in-law of Caiaphas, the high priest that year. 14 It was Caiaphas who had given counsel to the religious authorities▽ that it was expedient that one person should die for the people.

15 Simon Peter followed Jesus, and so did another disciple, who was known to the high priest, and who entered the court of the high priest along with Jesus, 16 while Peter stood outside at the door. So the other disciple, who was known to the high priest, went out and spoke to the maid who kept the door, and brought Peter in. 17 The maid who kept the door said to Peter, "Are not you also one of this man's disciples?" Peter said, "I am not." 18 Now the servants and officers had made a charcoal fire, because it was cold, and they

---

◇RSV *Although he was a Son.* See Appendix.
*Addition to the text.
**Addition to the text. See "Metaphor" and "God the Father and Mother" in the Appendix.
▽RSV *the Jews.* See Appendix.

were standing and warming themselves; Peter also was with them, standing and warming himself.

19 The high priest then questioned Jesus about his disciples and teaching. 20 Jesus answered the high priest, "I have spoken openly to the world; I have always taught in synagogues and in the temple, where all Jews come together; I have said nothing secretly. 21 Why do you ask me? Ask those who have heard me, what I said to them; they know what I said." 22 When Jesus had said this, one of the officers standing by struck him with his hand, saying, "Is that how you answer the high priest?" 23 Jesus answered the officer, "If I have spoken wrongly, bear witness to the wrong; but if I have spoken rightly, why do you strike me?" 24 Annas then sent Jesus bound to Caiaphas the high priest.

25 Now Simon Peter was standing and warming himself. They said to him, "Are not you also one of his disciples?" He denied it and said, "I am not." 26 One of the servants of the high priest, a relative of the slave whose ear Peter had cut off, asked, "Did I not see you in the garden with him?" 27 Peter again denied it; and at once the cock crowed.

28 Then they led Jesus from the house of Caiaphas to the praetorium. It was early. They themselves did not enter the praetorium, so that they might not be defiled, but might eat the passover. 29 So Pilate went out to them and said, "What accusation do you bring against this person?" 30 They answered Pilate, "If this one were not an evildoer, we would not have handed him over." 31 Pilate said to them, "Take him yourselves and make judgment by your own law." The religious authorities▽ said to Pilate, "It is not lawful for us to put anyone to death." 32 This was to fulfill the word which Jesus had spoken to show by what death he was to die.

33 Pilate entered the praetorium again and called Jesus, and said, "Are you the King of the Jews?" 34 Jesus answered, "Do you say this of your own accord, or did others say it to you about me?" 35 Pilate answered, "Am I one of you?① Your own nation and the chief priests have handed you over to me; what have you done?" 36 Jesus answered, "My dominion☆ is not of this world; if my dominion☆ were of this world, my servants would fight, that I might not be handed over to the religious authorities;▽ but my dominion☆ is not from the world." 37 Pilate said to Jesus, "So you are a king?" Jesus answered, "You say that I am a king. For this I was born, and for this I have come into the world, to bear witness to the truth. Everyone who is of the truth hears my voice." 38 Pilate said to Jesus, "What is truth?"

And having said this, Pilate went out to the religious authorities▽ again, and told them, "I find no crime in this person. 39 But you have a custom that I should release someone for you at the Passover; will you have me release

---

▽RSV v. 31 *The Jews;* v. 38 *the Jews.* See Appendix.
①RSV *"Am I a Jew?"*
☆RSV *kingship.* See Appendix.

for you the King of the Jews?" [40] They cried out again, "Not Jesus, but Barabbas!" Now Barabbas was a robber.

[19:1] Then Pilate had Jesus scourged. [2] And the soldiers plaited a crown of thorns, and put it on Jesus' head, and arrayed him in a purple robe; [3] they came up, saying, "Hail, King of the Jews!" and struck him with their hands. [4] Pilate went out again, and said to them, "See, I am bringing him out to you, that you may know that I find no crime in him." [5] So Jesus came out, wearing the crown of thorns and the purple robe. Pilate said to them, "Here he is!" [6] When the chief priests and the officers saw Jesus, they cried out, "Crucify, crucify!" Pilate said to them, "Take him yourselves and crucify him, for I find no crime in him." [7] The religious authorities[▽] answered Pilate, "We have a law, and by that law Jesus ought to die, because he has made himself the Child[◇] of God." [8] Hearing these words, Pilate was the more afraid. [9] Pilate entered the praetorium again and said to Jesus, "Where are you from?" But Jesus gave no answer. [10] Pilate therefore said to him, "You will not speak to me? Do you not know that I have power to release you, and power to crucify you?" [11] Jesus replied, "You would have no power over me unless it had been given you from above; therefore the one who delivered me to you has the greater sin."

[12] Upon this Pilate sought to release Jesus, but the religious authorities[▽] cried out, "If you release this person, you are not Caesar's friend; everyone who claims to be a king opposes Caesar." [13] Hearing these words, Pilate brought Jesus out and sat down on the judgment seat at a place called The Pavement, and in Hebrew, Gabbatha. [14] Now it was the day of Preparation of the Passover; it was about the sixth hour. Pilate said to the Jews, "Behold your King!" [15] They cried out, "Away, away with him, crucify him!" Pilate said to them, "Shall I crucify your King?" The chief priests answered, "We have no king but Caesar." [16] Then Pilate handed him over to them to be crucified.

[17] So they took Jesus, who went out bearing his own cross, to the place called the place of a skull, which is called in Hebrew Golgotha. [18] There they crucified him, along with two others, one on either side, and Jesus between them. [19] Pilate also wrote a title and put it on the cross; it read, "Jesus of Nazareth, the King of the Jews." [20] Many of the Jews read this title, for the place where Jesus was crucified was near the city; and it was written in Hebrew, in Latin, and in Greek. [21] The chief priests of the Jews then said to Pilate, "Do not write, 'The King of the Jews,' but, 'This one said, I am King of the Jews.' " [22] Pilate answered, "What I have written I have written."

[23] When the soldiers had crucified Jesus they took his garments and made four parts, one for each soldier; also his tunic. But the tunic was without seam, woven from top to bottom; [24] so they said to one another, "Let us not

---

[▽]RSV 19:7 *The Jews;* v. 12 *the Jews.* See Appendix.
[◇]RSV *Son.* See Appendix.

tear it, but cast lots for it to see whose it shall be." This was to fulfill the scripture,

"They parted my garments among them,
and for my clothing they cast lots."

25 So the soldiers did this. But standing by the cross of Jesus were his mother, and his mother's sister, Mary the wife of Clopas, and Mary Magdalene. 26 When Jesus saw his mother, and the disciple whom he loved standing near, he said to his mother, "Woman, behold, your child!" 27 Then Jesus said to the disciple, "Behold, your mother!" And from that hour the disciple took her home.

28 After this, Jesus, knowing that all was now finished, said (to fulfill the scripture), "I thirst." 29 A bowl full of vinegar stood there; so they put a sponge full of the vinegar on hyssop and held it to his mouth. 30 After receiving the vinegar, Jesus said, "It is finished," and bowed his head and gave up the spirit.

31 Since it was the day of Preparation, in order to prevent the bodies from remaining on the cross on the sabbath (for that sabbath was a high day), the religious authorities∇ asked Pilate that their legs might be broken, and that they might be taken away. 32 So the soldiers came and broke the legs of the first, and of the other who had been crucified with Jesus; 33 but when they came to Jesus and saw that he was already dead, they did not break his legs. 34 But one of the soldiers pierced Jesus' side with a spear, and at once there came out blood and water. 35 The one who saw it has borne witness—this testimony is true, and the witness knows that it is the truth—that you also may believe. 36 For these things took place that the scripture might be fulfilled, "Not a bone of him shall be broken." 37 And again another scripture says, "They shall look on the one whom they have pierced."

38 After this Joseph of Arimathea, who was a disciple of Jesus, but secretly, for fear of the religious authorities,∇ asked Pilate for permission to take away the body of Jesus, and Pilate granted it. So Joseph came and took away Jesus' body. 39 Nicodemus also, who had at first come to Jesus by night, came bringing a mixture of myrrh and aloes, about a hundred pounds' weight. 40 They took the body of Jesus, and bound it in linen cloths with the spices, as is the burial custom of the Jews. 41 Now in the place where Jesus was crucified there was a garden, and in the garden a new tomb where no one had ever been laid. 42 So because of the Jewish day of Preparation, as the tomb was close at hand, they laid Jesus there.

∇RSV the Jews. See Appendix.

EASTER

(If the first lesson is read from the Old Testament, the lection from Acts should be read as Lesson 2.)

Lesson 1 ～ Acts 10:34-43

Peter preaches about Jesus' life, death, and resurrection.

[34] Peter proclaimed, "Truly I perceive that God shows no partiality, [35] but in every nation anyone who fears God and does what is right is acceptable to God. [36] You know the word which God sent to Israel, preaching good news of peace by Jesus Christ (Christ is Sovereign [[*or* Lord]] of all), [37] the word which was proclaimed throughout all Judea, beginning from Galilee after the baptism which John preached: [38] how God anointed Jesus of Nazareth with the Holy Spirit and with power; how Jesus went about doing good and healing all that were oppressed by the devil, for God was with him. [39] And we are witnesses to all that Jesus did both in Judea and in Jerusalem. They put Jesus to death by hanging him on a tree; [40] but God raised Jesus on the third day and made Jesus manifest; [41] not to all the people but to us who were chosen by God as witnesses, who ate and drank with Jesus after the resurrection from the dead. [42] And Jesus commanded us to preach to the people, and to testify that Jesus is the one ordained by God to be judge of the living and the dead. [43] To this one all the prophets bear witness that everyone who believes in Jesus Christ receives forgiveness of sins through Jesus' name."

Lesson 1 (alternate) ～ Isaiah 25:6-9

Isaiah speaks of God's victory over death.

[6] On this mountain the GOD [[*or* LORD]] of hosts will make for all peoples a feast of fat things, a feast of wine on the lees, of fat things full of marrow, of wine on the lees well refined. [7] And God will destroy on this mountain the covering that is cast over all peoples, the veil that is spread over all nations. [8] God will swallow up death forever, and the Sovereign [[*or* Lord]] GOD will wipe away tears from all faces, and God will take away from all the earth the reproach of God's people; for GOD [[*or* the LORD]] has spoken.

[9] It will be said on that day, "This is our God, the one for whom we have waited, that we might be saved. This is the SOVEREIGN [[*or* LORD]] for whom we have waited; let us be glad and rejoice in God's salvation."

14 GOD [or The LORD] is my strength and my song,
and has become my salvation.
15 Hark, glad songs of victory
in the tents of the righteous:
"The right hand of GOD [or the LORD] does valiantly,
16   the right hand of GOD [or the LORD] is exalted,
the right hand of GOD [or the LORD] does valiantly!"
17 I shall not die, but I shall live,
and recount the deeds of GOD [or the LORD].
18 GOD [or The LORD] has chastened me sorely,
but has not given me over to death.
19 Open to me the gates of righteousness,
that I may enter through them
and give thanks to GOD [or the LORD].
20 This is the gate of GOD [or the LORD];
the righteous shall enter through it.
21 I thank you that you have answered me
and have become my salvation.
22 The stone which the builders rejected
has become the head of the corner.
23 This is GOD'S [or the LORD'S] doing;
it is marvelous in our eyes.
24 This is the day which GOD [or the LORD] has made;
let us rejoice and be glad in it.

Lesson 2 ～ 1 Corinthians 15:1–11

(If Isaiah 25:6–9 is read as the first lesson, Acts 10:34–43 should be read as Lesson 2.)

Paul recalls the tradition of the appearances of the risen Christ.

1 Now I would remind you, sisters and brothers, in what terms I preached to you the gospel, which you received, in which you stand, 2 by which you are saved, if you hold it fast—unless you believed in vain.

3 For I delivered to you as of first importance what I also received, that Christ died for our sins in accordance with the scriptures, 4 that Christ was buried, and was raised on the third day in accordance with the scriptures, 5 and that Christ appeared to Cephas, then to the twelve. 6 Then Christ appeared to more than five hundred followers at one time, most of whom are still alive, though some have fallen asleep. 7 Then Christ appeared to James, then to all the apostles. 8 Last of all, as to one untimely born, Christ

appeared also to me. ⁹ For I am the least of the apostles, unfit to be called an apostle, because I persecuted the church of God. ¹⁰ But by the grace of God I am what I am, and God's grace toward me was not in vain. On the contrary, I worked harder than any of them, though it was not I, but the grace of God which is with me. ¹¹ Whether then it was I or they, so we preach and so you believed.

Gospel ∼ John 20:1–18

The risen Christ appears to Mary Magdalene.

¹ Now on the first day of the week Mary Magdalene came to the tomb early, while it was still dark, and saw that the stone had been taken away from the tomb. ² So she ran, and went to Simon Peter and the other disciple, the one whom Jesus loved, and said to them, "They have taken the Sovereign [[or Lord]] out of the tomb, and we do not know where they have laid him." ³ Peter then came out with the other disciple, and they went toward the tomb. ⁴ They both ran, but the other disciple outran Peter, reached the tomb first, ⁵ and stooping to look in, saw the linen cloths lying there, but did not go in. ⁶ Then Simon Peter came, following after, and went into the tomb; Peter saw the linen cloths lying, ⁷ and the napkin, which had been on Jesus' head, not lying with the linen cloths but rolled up in a place by itself. ⁸ Then the other disciple, who reached the tomb first, also went in, and saw and believed; ⁹ for as yet they did not know the scripture, that Jesus must rise from the dead. ¹⁰ Then the disciples went back to their homes.

¹¹ But Mary stood weeping outside the tomb, and as she wept she stooped to look into the tomb; ¹² and she saw two angels in white, sitting where the body of Jesus had lain, one at the head and one at the feet. ¹³ They said to her, "Woman, why are you weeping?" She said to them, "Because they have taken away my Sovereign [[or Lord]], and I do not know where they have laid him." ¹⁴ Saying this, she turned round and saw Jesus standing, but she did not know that it was Jesus. ¹⁵ Jesus said to her, "Woman, why are you weeping? Whom do you seek?" Supposing Jesus to be the gardener, she answered, "Sir, if you have carried Jesus away, tell me where you have laid him, and I will take him away." ¹⁶ Jesus said to her, "Mary." She turned and responded in Hebrew, "Rabboni!" (which means Teacher). ¹⁷ Jesus said to her, "Do not hold me, for I have not yet ascended to God; but go to my friends and say to them, I am ascending to [God] my Father [and Mother*] and your Father [and Mother*], to my God and your God." ¹⁸ Mary Magdalene went and said to the disciples, "I have seen the Sovereign [[or Lord]]"; and she told them that Jesus had said these things to her.

---

*Addition to the text. See "Metaphor" and "God the Father and Mother" in the Appendix.

Gospel (alternate) ∽ Mark 16:1–8

Several women are appointed to tell the disciples they will see the risen Jesus.

¹ And when the sabbath was past, Mary Magdalene, and Mary the mother of James, and Salome, bought spices, so that they might go and anoint Jesus. ² And very early on the first day of the week they went to the tomb when the sun had risen. ³ And they were saying to one another, "Who will roll away the stone for us from the door of the tomb?" ⁴ And looking up, they saw that the stone was rolled back—it was very large. ⁵ And entering the tomb, they saw a youth sitting on the right side, dressed in a white robe; and they were amazed. ⁶ And the youth said to them, "Do not be amazed; you seek Jesus of Nazareth, who was crucified. Jesus has risen and is not here; see the place where they laid the body. ⁷ But go, tell the disciples and Peter that Jesus is going before you to Galilee; there you will see Jesus, as he told you." ⁸ And they went out and fled from the tomb; for trembling and astonishment had come upon them; and they said nothing to anyone, for they were afraid.

EASTER EVENING

(If the first lesson is read from the Old Testament, the lection from Acts should be read as Lesson 2.)

Lesson 1 ∼ Acts 5:29–32

Peter and the apostles bear witness to the risen Christ.

²⁹ But Peter and the apostles answered, "We must obey God rather than human beings. ³⁰ The God of our ancestors raised Jesus, whom you killed by hanging on a tree. ³¹ God exalted this Jesus at God's right hand as Leader and Savior, to give repentance to Israel and forgiveness of sins. ³² And we are witnesses to these things, and so is the Holy Spirit whom God has given to those who obey God."

Lesson 1 (alternate) ∼ Daniel 12:1–3

Daniel prophesies the events of the end time.

¹ At that time shall arise Michael, the great prince who has charge of your people. And there shall be a time of trouble, such as never has been since there was a nation till that time; but at that time your people shall be delivered, everyone whose name shall be found written in the book. ² And many of those who sleep in the dust of the earth shall awake, some to everlasting life, and some to shame and everlasting contempt. ³ And those who are wise shall shine like the brightness of the firmament; and those who turn many to righteousness, like the stars forever and ever.

Psalm 150

¹ Praise GOD [*or* the LORD]!
  Praise God in the sanctuary;
    praise God in the mighty firmament!
² Praise God for mighty deeds;
    praise God according to God's exceeding greatness!
³ Praise God with trumpet sound;
    praise God with lute and harp!
⁴ Praise God with timbrel and dance;
    praise God with strings and pipe!
⁵ Praise God with sounding cymbals;
    praise God with loud clashing cymbals!
⁶ Let everything that breathes praise GOD [*or* the LORD]!
  Praise GOD [*or* the LORD]!

Lesson 2 ~ 1 Corinthians 5:6–8

(If Daniel 12:1–3 is read as the first lesson, Acts 5:29–32 should be read as Lesson 2.)

Paul writes about the bread of the new passover.

⁶ Your boasting is not good. Do you not know that a little leaven leavens the whole lump? ⁷ Cleanse out the old leaven that you may be a new lump, as you really are unleavened. For Christ, our paschal lamb, has been sacrificed. ⁸ Let us, therefore, celebrate the festival, not with the old leaven, the leaven of malice and evil, but with the unleavened bread of sincerity and truth.

Gospel ~ Luke 24:13–49

Jesus meets two disciples on the road to Emmaus.

¹³ That very day two of the disciples were going to a village named Emmaus, about seven miles from Jerusalem, ¹⁴ and talking with each other about all these things that had happened. ¹⁵ While they were talking and discussing together, Jesus drew near and went with them. ¹⁶ But their eyes were kept from recognizing Jesus. ¹⁷ And Jesus said to them, "What is this conversation which you are holding with each other as you walk?" And they stood still, looking sad. ¹⁸ Then one of them, named Cleopas, answered, "Are you the only visitor to Jerusalem who does not know the things that have happened there in these days?" ¹⁹ And Jesus said to them, "What things?" And they said, "Concerning Jesus of Nazareth, who was a prophet mighty in deed and word before God and all the people, ²⁰ and how our chief priests and rulers delivered up this Jesus to be condemned to death, and crucified him. ²¹ But we had hoped that Jesus was the one to redeem Israel. Yes, and besides all this, it is now the third day since this happened. ²² Moreover, some women of our company amazed us. They were at the tomb early in the morning ²³ and did not find Jesus' body; and they came back saying that they had even seen a vision of angels, who said that Jesus was alive. ²⁴ Some of those who were with us went to the tomb, and found it just as the women had said; but Jesus they did not see." ²⁵ And Jesus said to them, "O foolish ones, and slow of heart to believe all that the prophets have spoken! ²⁶ Was it not necessary that the Christ should suffer these things and be glorified?" ²⁷ And beginning with Moses and all the prophets, Jesus interpreted to them in all the scriptures the things concerning the Christ.

²⁸ So they drew near to the village to which they were going. Jesus appeared to be going further, ²⁹ but they urged against it, saying, "Stay with us, for it is toward evening and the day is now far spent." So Jesus went in

to stay with them. [30] While at table with them, Jesus took the bread and blessed, and broke it, and gave it to them. [31] And their eyes were opened and they recognized Jesus, who then vanished out of their sight. [32] They said to each other, "Did not our hearts burn within us while Jesus talked to us on the road, and opened to us the scriptures?" [33] And they rose that same hour and returned to Jerusalem; and they found the eleven gathered together and those who were with them, [34] who said, "The Sovereign [[or Lord]] has risen indeed, and has appeared to Simon!" [35] Then they told what had happened on the road, and how Jesus was known to them in the breaking of the bread.

[36] As they were saying this, that very Jesus stood among them. [37] But they were startled and frightened, and supposed that they saw a spirit. [38] And Jesus said to them, "Why are you troubled, and why do questionings rise in your hearts? [39] See my hands and my feet, that it is I myself; handle me, and see; for a spirit has not flesh and bones as you see that I have." [41] And while they still disbelieved for joy, and wondered, Jesus said to them, "Have you anything here to eat?" [42] They gave Jesus a piece of broiled fish, [43] and Jesus took it and ate before them.

[44] Then Jesus said to them, "These are my words which I spoke to you, while I was still with you, that everything written about me in the law of Moses and the prophets and the psalms must be fulfilled." [45] Then Jesus opened their minds to understand the scriptures, [46] and said to them, "Thus it is written, that the Christ should suffer and on the third day rise from the dead, [47] and that repentance and forgiveness of sins should be preached in Christ's name to all nations, beginning from Jerusalem. [48] You are witnesses of these things. [49] And I am sending the promise of [God] my Father [and Mother*] upon you; but stay in the city until you are clothed with power from on high."

---

*Addition to the text. See "Metaphor" and "God the Father and Mother" in the Appendix.

EASTER 2

Lesson 1 ~ Acts 4:32–35

The author describes life in the early church.

32 Now the company of those who believed were of one heart and soul, and no one claimed personal ownership of any possessions, but they had everything in common. 33 And with great power the apostles gave their testimony to the resurrection of the Sovereign [*or* Lord] Jesus, and great grace was upon them all. 34 There was not a needy person among them, for as many as were possessors of lands or houses sold them, and brought the proceeds of what was sold 35 and laid it at the apostles' feet; and distribution was made to each as any had need.

Psalm 133

1 How good and pleasant it is
  when brothers and sisters dwell in unity!
2 It is like fragrant oil upon the head,
  running down upon the face,
 upon the face of Aaron,
  running down on the collar of the robes!
3 It is like the dew of Hermon,
  which falls on the mountains of Zion!
 For there GOD [*or* the LORD] has commanded the blessing,
  life forevermore.

Lesson 2 ~ 1 John 1:1–2:2

Eternal life is partnership with God and with one another.

[1] That which was from the beginning, which we have heard, which we have seen with our eyes, which we have looked upon and touched with our hands, concerning the word of life—[2] the life was made manifest, and we saw it, and testify to it, and proclaim to you the eternal life which was with God and was made manifest to us—[3] that which we have seen and heard we proclaim also to you, so that you may be partners with us; and our partnership is with [*God*] the Father [*and Mother**] and with God's Child° Jesus Christ. [4] And we are writing this that our joy may be complete.

[5] This is the message we have heard from Jesus Christ and proclaim to you, that God is light and in God is no shadow at all. [6] If we say we are partners with God while we walk in shadows, we lie and do not live according to the truth; [7] but if we walk in the light as God is in the light, we have partnership with one another, and the blood of Jesus, God's Child,° cleanses us from all sin. [8] If we say we have no sin, we deceive ourselves, and the truth is not in us. [9] If we confess our sins, God is faithful and just, and will forgive our sins and cleanse us from all unrighteousness. [10] If we say we have not sinned, we make God a liar, and God's word is not in us.

[2:1] My little children, I am writing this to you so that you may not sin; but if anyone does sin, we have an advocate with God,⊗ Jesus Christ the righteous, [2] who is the expiation for our sins, and not for ours only but also for the sins of the whole world.

---

*Addition to the text. See "Metaphor" and "God the Father and Mother" in the Appendix.
°RSV *his Son.* See Appendix.
⊗RSV *the Father.* See Appendix.

Gospel ~ John 20:19–31

The risen Christ appears to Thomas.

¹⁹ On the evening of that day, the first day of the week, the doors being shut where the disciples were, for fear of the religious authorities,ᵛ Jesus came and stood among them and said to them, "Peace be with you." ²⁰ Having said this, Jesus showed them Jesus' hands and side. Then the disciples were glad when they saw the Sovereign [[or Lord]]. ²¹ Jesus said to them again, "Peace be with you. As [God] the Father [and Mother*] has sent me, even so I send you." ²² Having said this, Jesus breathed on them, and said to them, "Receive the Holy Spirit. ²³ If you forgive the sins of any, they are forgiven; if you retain the sins of any, they are retained."

²⁴ Now Thomas, one of the twelve, called the Twin, was not with them when Jesus came. ²⁵ So the other disciples told him, "We have seen the Sovereign [[or Lord]]." But Thomas said to them, "Unless I see in Jesus' hands the print of the nails, and place my finger in the mark of the nails, and place my hand in Jesus' side, I will not believe."

²⁶ Eight days later, the disciples were again in the house, and Thomas was with them. The doors were shut, but Jesus came and stood among them, and said, "Peace be with you." ²⁷ Then Jesus said to Thomas, "Put your finger here, and see my hands; and put out your hand, and place it in my side; do not be faithless, but believing." ²⁸ Thomas answered, "My Sovereign [[or Lord]] and my God!" ²⁹ Jesus said to Thomas, "Have you believed because you have seen me? Blessed are those who have not seen and yet believe."

³⁰ Now Jesus did many other signs in the presence of the disciples, which are not written in this book; ³¹ but these are written that you may believe that Jesus is the Christ, the Child◇ of God, and that believing you may have life in Christ's name.

ᵛRSV *the Jews*. See Appendix.
*Addition to the text. See "Metaphor" and "God the Father and Mother" in the Appendix.
◇RSV *Son*. See Appendix.

128

EASTER 3

After healing a person who had been lame since birth, Peter addresses the people at the gate of the temple.

¹² Peter said, "People of Israel, why do you wonder at this, or why do you stare at us, as though by our own power or piety we had made this person walk? ¹³ The God of Abraham [*and Sarah**], of Isaac [*and Rebekah**], of Jacob, [*Leah, and Rachel**], the God of our ancestors, glorified God's servant Jesus, whom you delivered up and denied in the presence of Pilate, when he had decided to release Jesus. ¹⁴ But you denied the Holy and Righteous One, and asked for a murderer to be granted to you, ¹⁵ and killed the Author of life, whom God raised from the dead. To this we are witnesses. ¹⁶ And Jesus' name, by faith in that name, has made this person strong whom you see and know; and the faith which is through Jesus has given the person this perfect health in the presence of you all.

¹⁷ "And now, sisters and brothers, I know that you acted in ignorance, as did also your rulers. ¹⁸ But what God foretold by the mouth of all the prophets, that the Christ of God should suffer, God thus fulfilled. ¹⁹ Repent therefore, and turn again, that your sins may be blotted out, that times of refreshing may come from the presence of the Sovereign [[*or* Lord]]."

---

*Addition to the text. See "Addition of Women's Names to the Text" in the Appendix.

Psalm 4

¹ Answer me when I call, O God of my right!

    You gave me room when I was in distress.

    Be gracious to me, and hear my prayer.

² O people, how long shall my honor suffer shame?

    How long will you love vain words, and seek after lies?

³ But know that GOD [or the LORD] has set apart the godly;

    GOD [or the LORD] hears when I call.

⁴ Be angry, but sin not;

    commune with your own hearts on your beds, and be silent.

⁵ Offer right sacrifices,

    and put your trust in GOD [or the LORD].

⁶ There are many who say, "O that we might see some good!

    Lift up the light of your countenance upon us, O GOD [or LORD]!"

⁷ You have put more joy in my heart

    than they have when their grain and wine abound.

⁸ In peace I will both lie down and sleep;

    for you alone, O GOD [or LORD], make me dwell in safety.

Lesson 2 ~ 1 John 3:1–7

The love of God beckons us to a new life.

¹ See what love [*God*] the Father [*and Mother**] has given us, that we should be called children of God; and so we are. The reason the world does not know us is that it did not know Christ. ² Beloved, we are now God's children; it does not yet appear what we shall be, but we know that when Christ appears we shall be like Christ, for we shall see Christ just as Christ is. ³ And all who thus hope in Christ purify themselves just as Christ is pure. ⁴ Everyone who commits sin is guilty of lawlessness; sin is lawlessness. ⁵ You know that Christ, in whom there is no sin, appeared to take away sins. ⁶ No one who abides in Christ sins; no one who sins has either seen or known Christ. ⁷ Little children, let no one deceive you. The person who does right is righteous, as Christ is righteous.

---

*Addition to the text. See "Metaphor" and "God the Father and Mother" in the Appendix.

The risen Jesus appears to the disciples and sends them out to preach the gospel.

[35] Then they told what had happened on the road, and how Jesus was known to them in the breaking of the bread.

[36] As they were saying this, that very Jesus stood among them. [37] But they were startled and frightened, and supposed that they saw a spirit. [38] And Jesus said to them, "Why are you troubled, and why do questionings rise in your hearts? [39] See my hands and my feet, that it is I myself; handle me, and see; for a spirit has not flesh and bones as you see that I have." [41] And while they still disbelieved for joy, and wondered, Jesus said to them, "Have you anything here to eat?" [42] They gave Jesus a piece of broiled fish, [43] and Jesus took it and ate before them.

[44] Then Jesus said to them, "These are my words which I spoke to you, while I was still with you, that everything written about me in the law of Moses and the prophets and the psalms must be fulfilled." [45] Then Jesus opened their minds to understand the scriptures, [46] and said to them, "Thus it is written, that the Christ should suffer and on the third day rise from the dead, [47] and that repentance and forgiveness of sins should be preached in Christ's name to all nations, beginning from Jerusalem. [48] You are witnesses of these things."

EASTER 4

Lesson 1 ～ Acts 4:8–12

Peter speaks about the true source of the healing of the person who was born lame.

⁸ Then Peter, filled with the Holy Spirit, said to them, "Rulers of the people and elders, ⁹ if we are being examined today concerning a good deed done to one who was sick, by what means this person has been healed, ¹⁰ be it known to you all, and to all the people of Israel, that by the name of Jesus Christ of Nazareth, whom you crucified, whom God raised from the dead, by that name this person is standing before you well. ¹¹ This is the stone which was rejected by you builders, but which has become the head of the corner. ¹² And there is salvation in no one else, for there is no other name under heaven given among humankind by which we must be saved."

Psalm 23

¹ GOD [[*or* The LORD]] is my shepherd, I shall not want;
²   God makes me lie down in green pastures,
  and leads me beside still waters;
³   God restores my soul.
  God leads me in paths of righteousness
    for God's name's sake.
⁴ Even though I walk through the valley of the shadow of death,
    I fear no evil;
  for you are with me;
    your rod and your staff,
    they comfort me.
⁵ You prepare a table before me
    in the presence of my enemies;
  you anoint my head with oil,
    my cup overflows.
⁶ Surely goodness and mercy shall follow me
    all the days of my life;
  and I shall dwell in the house of GOD [[*or* the LORD]]
    forever.

Lesson 2 ~ 1 John 3:18–24

God's commandment is that we believe in Jesus Christ and love one another.

¹⁸ Little children, let us not love in word or speech but in deed and in truth.

¹⁹ By this we shall know that we are of the truth, and reassure our hearts before God ²⁰ whenever our hearts condemn us; for God is greater than our hearts, and knows everything. ²¹ Beloved, if our hearts do not condemn us, we have confidence before God; ²² and we receive from God whatever we ask, because we keep the commandments and do what pleases God. ²³ And this is God's commandment, that we should believe in the name of God's own Child◇ Jesus Christ and love one another, just as God has commanded us. ²⁴ All who keep the commandments abide in God, and God in them. And by this we know that God abides in us, by the Spirit which God has given us.

Gospel ~ John 10:11–18

John tells the parable of the good shepherd.

¹¹ I am the good shepherd. The good shepherd is willing to die for the sheep. ¹² A hireling who is not a shepherd, whose own the sheep are not, sees the wolf coming and leaves the sheep and flees; and the wolf snatches them and scatters them. ¹³ One who is a hireling flees, caring nothing for the sheep. ¹⁴ I am the good shepherd; I know my own and my own know me, ¹⁵ as God⊗ knows me and I know God;⊗ and I lay down my life for the sheep. ¹⁶ And I have other sheep, that are not of this fold; I must bring them also, and they will heed my voice. So there shall be one flock, one shepherd. ¹⁷ For this reason God⊗ loves me, because I lay down my life, that I may take it again. ¹⁸ No one takes it from me, but I lay it down of my own accord. I have power to lay it down, and I have power to take it again; this charge I have received from [*God*] my Father [*and Mother**].

◇RSV *of his Son.* See Appendix.
⊗RSV *the Father.* See Appendix.
*Addition to the text. See "Metaphor" and "God the Father and Mother" in the Appendix.

EASTER 5

Lesson 1 ~ Acts 8:26–40

Philip tells the good news of Jesus to an Ethiopian official.

²⁶ An angel said to Philip, "Rise and go toward the south to the road that goes down from Jerusalem to Gaza." This is a desert road. ²⁷ And Philip rose and went. And an Ethiopian, a eunuch, a minister of the Candace, queen of the Ethiopians, in charge of all her treasure, had come to Jerusalem to worship ²⁸ and was returning; seated in his chariot, the Ethiopian was reading the prophet Isaiah. ²⁹ And the Spirit said to Philip, "Go up and join this chariot." ³⁰ So Philip hurried over to the Ethiopian, and heard him reading Isaiah the prophet, and asked, "Do you understand what you are reading?" ³¹ And the Ethiopian replied, "How can I, unless someone guides me?" And he invited Philip to come up and sit with him. ³² Now the passage of the scripture which he was reading was this:

"As a sheep led to the slaughter
or a lamb before its shearer is dumb,
so this one does not say a word.
³³ In the humiliation of the silent one, justice was denied.
Who can describe the generation
of the one whose life is taken up from the earth?"

³⁴ And the Ethiopian eunuch said to Philip, "About whom, pray, does the prophet say this, about himself or about someone else?" ³⁵ Then Philip opened his mouth, and beginning with this scripture, told the Ethiopian the good news of Jesus. ³⁶ And as they went along the road they came to some water, and the eunuch said, "See, here is water! What is to prevent my being baptized?" ³⁸ And he commanded the chariot to stop, and they both went down into the water, Philip and the eunuch, and Philip baptized him. ³⁹ And when they came up out of the water, the Spirit of the Sovereign [*or* Lord] caught up Philip; and the Ethiopian eunuch saw him no more, and went on his way rejoicing. ⁴⁰ But Philip was found at Azotus, and passing on he preached the gospel to all the towns till he came to Caesarea.

25 From you comes my praise in the great congregation;
  my vows I will pay before those who fear God.
26 The afflicted shall eat and be satisfied;
  those who seek God shall praise GOD [[*or* the LORD]]!
  May your hearts live forever!
27 All the ends of the earth shall remember
  and turn to GOD [[*or* the LORD]];
 and all the families of the nations
  shall worship before God.
28 For dominion belongs to GOD [[*or* the LORD]],
  who rules over the nations.
29 Indeed, to God shall all the proud of the earth bow down;
  before God shall bow all who go down to the dust,
  and those who cannot keep themselves alive.
30 Posterity shall serve God;
  people shall tell of God [[*or* the Lord]] to the coming generation,
31 and proclaim God's deliverance to a people yet unborn,
  that God has wrought it.

Lesson 2 ~ 1 John 4:7–12

John unfolds the mystery and power of God's love.

7 Beloved, let us love one another; for love is of God, and whoever loves is born of God and knows God. 8 Whoever does not love does not know God; for God is love. 9 In this the love of God was made manifest among us, that God sent God's only Child◊ into the world, so that we might live through that Child. 10 In this is love, not that we loved God but that God loved us and sent God's own Child◊ to be the expiation for our sins. 11 Beloved, if God so loved us, we also ought to love one another. 12 No one has ever seen God; if we love one another, God abides in us and God's love is perfected in us.

◊RSV v. 9 *his only Son;* v. 10 *his Son.* See Appendix.

Gospel ~ John 15:1–8

Jesus tells the parable of the true vine.

¹ I am the true vine, and [*God*] my Father [*and Mother**] is the vine-dresser. ² Every branch of mine that bears no fruit, God takes away, and every branch that does bear fruit God prunes, that it may bear more fruit. ³ You are already made clean by the word which I have spoken to you. ⁴ Abide in me, and I in you. As the branch cannot bear fruit by itself, unless it abides in the vine, neither can you, unless you abide in me. ⁵ I am the vine, you are the branches. All who abide in me, and I in them, they are the ones who bear much fruit, for apart from me you can do nothing. ⁶ Anyone who does not abide in me is cast forth as a branch and withers; and the branches are gathered, thrown into the fire and burned. ⁷ If you abide in me, and my words abide in you, ask whatever you will, and it shall be done for you. ⁸ By this God⊗ is glorified, that you bear much fruit, and so prove to be my disciples.

---

*Addition to the text. See "Metaphor" and "God the Father and Mother" in the Appendix.
⊗RSV *my Father.* See Appendix.

EASTER 6

Lesson 1 ~ Acts 10:44–48

When Peter preaches at Caesarea, the Holy Spirit comes upon Jews and Gentiles alike.

⁴⁴ While Peter was still saying this, the Holy Spirit fell on all who heard the word. ⁴⁵ And the believers from among the Jews who came with Peter were amazed, because the gift of the Holy Spirit had been poured out even on the Gentiles. ⁴⁶ For they heard the Gentiles speaking in tongues and extolling God. Then Peter asked, ⁴⁷ "Can anyone forbid water for baptizing these people who have received the Holy Spirit just as we have?" ⁴⁸ And Peter commanded them to be baptized in the name of Jesus Christ. Then they asked Peter to remain for some days.

Psalm 98

¹ O sing a new song to GOD [*or* the LORD],
   who has done marvelous things,
  whose right hand and holy arm
   have gained the victory!
² GOD [*or* The LORD] has made known the victory,
   and has revealed God's vindication in the sight of the nations.
³ God has remembered God's steadfast love and faithfulness
   to the house of Israel.
  All the ends of the earth have seen
   the victory of our God.
⁴ Make a joyful noise to GOD [*or* the LORD], all the earth;
   break forth into joyous song and sing praises!
⁵ Sing praises to GOD [*or* the LORD] with the lyre,
   with the lyre and the sound of melody!
⁶ With trumpets and the sound of the horn
   make a joyful noise before the Ruler,□ the SOVEREIGN [*or* LORD]!
⁷ Let the sea roar, and all that fills it;
   the world and those who dwell in it!
⁸ Let the floods clap their hands;
   let the hills sing together for joy
⁹ before GOD [*or* the LORD], who comes
   to judge the earth,
  to judge the world with righteousness,
   and the nations with equity.

□RSV *King.* See Appendix.

Lesson 2 ∼ 1 John 5:1–6

We are children of God by the gift of God's Child, Jesus Christ.

¹ Everyone who believes that Jesus is the Christ is a child of God, and everyone who loves the parent loves the child. ² By this we know that we love the children of God, when we love God and obey God's commandments. ³ For this is the love of God, that we keep God's commandments, and they are not burdensome. ⁴ For whatever is born of God overcomes the world; and this is the victory that overcomes the world, our faith. ⁵ Who is it that overcomes the world but the person who believes that Jesus is the Child◇ of God?
⁶ This is the one who came by water and blood, Jesus Christ, not with the water only but with the water and the blood.

Gospel ∼ John 15:9–17

Jesus commands us to love one another.

⁹ As [*God*] the Father [*and Mother**] has loved me, so have I loved you; abide in my love. ¹⁰ If you keep my commandments, you will abide in my love, just as I have kept God's⊗ commandments and abide in God's love. ¹¹ These things I have spoken to you, that my joy may be in you, and that your joy may be full.
¹² This is my commandment, that you love one another as I have loved you. ¹³ Greater love has no one than this, that one lay down one's life for a friend. ¹⁴ You are my friends if you do what I command you. ¹⁵ No longer do I call you servants, for the servant does not know what the master is doing; but I have called you friends, for all that I have heard from God⊗ I have made known to you. ¹⁶ You did not choose me, but I chose you and appointed you that you should go and bear fruit and that your fruit should abide; so that whatever you ask [*God*] the Father [*and Mother**] in my name may be given to you. ¹⁷ This I command you, to love one another.

◇RSV *Son.* See Appendix.
*Addition to the text. See "Metaphor" and "God the Father and Mother" in the Appendix.
⊗RSV v. 10 *my Father's;* v. 15 *my Father.* See Appendix.

ASCENSION
(Or on Easter 7)

Lesson 1 ~ Acts 1:1-11

The risen Jesus is taken up into heaven.

¹ In the first book, O Theophilus, I have dealt with all that Jesus began to do and teach, ² until the day when Jesus was taken up, having given commandment through the Holy Spirit to the apostles whom Jesus had chosen. ³ After the passion Jesus was seen alive by the apostles through many proofs, appearing to them during forty days, and speaking of the realm☆ of God. ⁴ And while staying with the apostles, Jesus charged them not to depart from Jerusalem, but to wait for the promise of God,⊛ which, Jesus said, "you heard from me, ⁵ for John baptized with water, but before many days you shall be baptized with the Holy Spirit."

⁶ So when the apostles had come together, they asked Jesus, "Sovereign 〚*or* Lord〛, will you at this time restore the realm☆ to Israel?" ⁷ Jesus said, "It is not for you to know times or seasons which have been fixed by God's⊛ own authority. ⁸ But you shall receive power when the Holy Spirit has come upon you; and you shall be my witnesses in Jerusalem and in all Judea and Samaria and to the end of the earth." ⁹ And having said this, as the apostles were looking on, Jesus was lifted up and carried on a cloud out of their sight. ¹⁰ And while they were gazing into heaven as Jesus went, two figures stood by them in white robes, ¹¹ and said, "People of Galilee, why do you stand looking into heaven? This Jesus, who was taken up from you into heaven, will come in the same way as you saw Jesus go into heaven."

Psalm 47

¹ Clap your hands, all you people!
　　Shout to God with loud songs of joy!
² For GOD 〚*or* the LORD〛, the Most High, is terrible,
　　a great ruler⊡ over all the earth,
³ subduing all people under us,
　　and nations under our feet,
⁴ choosing our heritage for us,
　　the pride of Jacob whom God loves.

☆RSV *kingdom.* See Appendix.
⊛RSV v. 4 *the Father;* v. 7 *which the Father has fixed by his own authority.* See Appendix.
⊡RSV *king.* See Appendix.

⁵ God has gone up with a shout,
   the SOVEREIGN ⟦*or* LORD⟧ with the sound of a trumpet.
⁶ Sing praises to God, sing praises!
   Sing praises to our Ruler,▢ sing praises!
⁷ For God is the ruler▢ of all the earth;
   sing praises with a psalm!
⁸ God reigns over the nations,
   God sits on the holy throne.
⁹ The nobles of the nations gather
   as the people of the God of Abraham.
For the shields of the earth belong to God,
   who is highly exalted!

Lesson 2 ∼ Ephesians 1:15–23

The risen Christ is exalted as head over all.

¹⁵ For this reason, because I have heard of your faith in the Sovereign ⟦*or* Lord⟧ Jesus and your love toward all the saints, ¹⁶ I do not cease to give thanks for you, remembering you in my prayers, ¹⁷ that the God of our Sovereign ⟦*or* Lord⟧ Jesus Christ, the Father [*and Mother**] of glory, may give you a spirit of wisdom and of revelation in the knowledge of God, ¹⁸ having the eyes of your hearts enlightened, that you may know what is the hope to which you have been called, what are the riches of God's glorious inheritance in the saints, ¹⁹ and what is the immeasurable greatness of God's power in us who believe, according to the working of God's great might ²⁰ which was accomplished in Christ when God raised Christ from the dead and made Christ sit at God's right hand in the heavenly places, ²¹ far above all rule and authority and power and dominion, and above every name that is named, not only in this age but also in that which is to come; ²² and God has put all things under Christ's feet and has made Christ the head over all things for the church, ²³ which is Christ's body, the fullness of the one who fills all in all.

▢RSV v. 6 *King;* v. 7 *king.* See Appendix.
*Addition to the text. See "Metaphor" and "God the Father and Mother" in the Appendix.

Gospel ~ Luke 24:46–53

Jesus commissions the disciples and is parted from them.

⁴⁶ And Jesus said to them, "Thus it is written, that the Christ should suffer and on the third day rise from the dead, ⁴⁷ and that repentance and forgiveness of sins should be preached in Christ's name to all nations, beginning from Jerusalem. ⁴⁸ You are witnesses of these things. ⁴⁹ And I am sending the promise of [God] my Father [and Mother*] upon you; but stay in the city until you are clothed with power from on high."

⁵⁰ Then Jesus led them out as far as Bethany, and with uplifted hands blessed them. ⁵¹ While blessing them, Jesus parted from them, and was carried up into heaven. ⁵² And they returned to Jerusalem with great joy, ⁵³ and were continually in the temple blessing God.

Gospel (alternate) ~ Mark 16:9–16, 19–20

The risen Jesus appears first to Mary Magdalene and then to others, sending the disciples to preach the gospel.

⁹ Now having risen early on the first day of the week, Jesus appeared first to Mary Magdalene, from whom Jesus had cast out seven demons. ¹⁰ She went and told those who had been with Jesus, as they mourned and wept. ¹¹ But when they heard that Jesus was alive and had been seen by her, they would not believe it.

¹² After this Jesus appeared in another form to two of them, as they were walking into the country. ¹³ And they went back and told the rest, but they did not believe them.

¹⁴ Afterward Jesus appeared to the eleven themselves as they sat at table, and upbraided them for their unbelief and hardness of heart, because they had not believed those who saw Jesus after Jesus had risen. ¹⁵ And Jesus said to them, "Go into all the world and preach the gospel to the whole creation. ¹⁶ Whoever believes and is baptized will be saved; but whoever does not believe will be condemned."

¹⁹ So then the Sovereign [or Lord] Jesus, after speaking to them, was taken up into heaven, and sat down at the right hand of God. ²⁰ And they went forth and preached everywhere, while the Sovereign [or Lord] worked with them and confirmed the message by the signs that attended it. Amen.

---

*Addition to the text. See "Metaphor" and "God the Father and Mother" in the Appendix.

EASTER 7

Lesson 1 ~ Acts 1:15–17, 21–26

A new apostle is chosen to complete the number of the twelve.

¹⁵ In those days Peter stood up in the midst of the community—the company of persons was in all about a hundred and twenty—and said, ¹⁶ "Sisters and brothers, the scripture had to be fulfilled, which the Holy Spirit spoke beforehand by the mouth of David, concerning Judas who was guide to those who arrested Jesus. ¹⁷ For Judas was numbered among us, and was allotted his share in this ministry. ²¹ So one of those who have accompanied us during all the time that the Sovereign [or Lord] Jesus went in and out among us, ²² beginning from the baptism of John until the day when Jesus was taken up from us—one of those must become with us a witness of Jesus' resurrection." ²³ And they put forward two, Joseph called Barsabbas, who was surnamed Justus, and Matthias. ²⁴ And they prayed and said, "Sovereign [or Lord], who know the hearts of all, show which one of these two you have chosen ²⁵ to take the place in this ministry and apostleship from which Judas turned aside, to go to his own place." ²⁶ And they cast lots for the two, and the lot fell on Matthias, who was enrolled with the eleven apostles.

Psalm 1

¹ Blessed are those
   who walk not in the counsel of the wicked,
  nor stand in the way of sinners,
   nor sit in the seat of scoffers,
² but whose delight is in the law of GOD [or the LORD],
   and who meditate on that law day and night.
³ They are like a tree
   planted by streams of water,
  that yields its fruit in its season,
   and its leaf does not wither.
  In all that they do, they prosper.
⁴ The wicked are not so,
   but are like chaff which the wind drives away.
⁵ Therefore the wicked will not stand in the judgment,
   nor sinners in the congregation of the righteous;
⁶ for GOD [or the LORD] knows the way of the righteous,
   but the way of the wicked will perish.

Lesson 2 ~ 1 John 5:9–13

John reminds us of the testimony of God concerning God's own Child.

⁹ If we receive human testimony, the testimony of God is greater; for this is the testimony of God that God has borne witness to God's own Child.◇ ¹⁰ Those who believe in the Child◇ of God have the testimony within themselves. Those who do not believe God have made God a liar, by not believing in the testimony that God has borne to God's own Child.◇ ¹¹ And this is the testimony, that God gave us eternal life, and this life is in God's Child.◇ ¹² Whoever has that Child◇ has life; whoever does not have the Child◇ of God does not have life.

¹³ I write this to you who believe in the name of the Child◇ of God, that you may know that you have eternal life.

Gospel ~ John 17:11b–19

Jesus prays for the disciples.

¹¹ Holy [*God, my Mother and**] Father, keep them in your name, which you have given me, that they may be one, even as we are one. ¹² While I was with them, I kept them in your name, which you have given me; I have guarded them, and none of them is lost but the son of perdition, that the scripture might be fulfilled. ¹³ But now I am coming to you; and these things I speak in the world, that they may have my joy fulfilled in themselves. ¹⁴ I have given them your word; and the world has hated them because they are not of the world, even as I am not of the world. ¹⁵ I do not pray that you should take them out of the world, but that you should keep them from the evil one. ¹⁶ They are not of the world, even as I am not of the world. ¹⁷ Sanctify them in the truth; your word is truth. ¹⁸ As you sent me into the world, so I have sent them into the world. ¹⁹ And for their sake I consecrate myself, that they also may be consecrated in truth.

◇RSV vs. 9, 10b, 11 *his Son;* vs. 10a, 12, 13 *the Son.* See Appendix.
*Addition to the text. See "Metaphor" and "God the Father and Mother" in the Appendix.

PENTECOST

(If the first lesson is read from the Old Testament, the lection from Acts should be read as Lesson 2.)

Lesson 1 ~ Acts 2:1–21

Luke describes the day of Pentecost, when worshipers were filled with the Holy Spirit.

¹ When the day of Pentecost had come, they were all together in one place. ² And suddenly a sound came from heaven like the rush of a mighty wind, and it filled all the house where they were sitting. ³ And there appeared to them tongues as of fire, distributed and resting on each one of them. ⁴ And they were all filled with the Holy Spirit and began to speak in other tongues, as the Spirit gave them utterance.

⁵ Now there were dwelling in Jerusalem devout Jews from every nation under heaven. ⁶ And at this sound the multitude came together, and they were bewildered, because they heard them speaking each in their own language. ⁷ And they were amazed and wondered, saying, "Are not all these who are speaking Galileans? ⁸ And how is it that we hear, each of us in our own native language? ⁹ Parthians and Medes and Elamites and residents of Mesopotamia, Judea and Cappadocia, Pontus and Asia, ¹⁰ Phrygia and Pamphylia, Egypt and the parts of Libya belonging to Cyrene, and visitors from Rome, both Jews and proselytes, ¹¹ Cretans and Arabians, we hear them telling in our own tongues the mighty works of God." ¹² And all were amazed and perplexed, saying to one another, "What does this mean?" ¹³ But others mocking said, "They are filled with new wine."

¹⁴ But Peter, standing with the eleven, lifted up his voice and addressed them, "People of Judea and all who dwell in Jerusalem, let this be known to you, and give ear to my words. ¹⁵ For these people are not drunk, as you suppose, since it is only the third hour of the day; ¹⁶ but this is what was spoken by the prophet Joel:

¹⁷ 'And in the last days it shall be, God declares,
that I will pour out my Spirit upon all flesh,
and your sons and your daughters shall prophesy,
and the young shall see visions,
and the old shall dream dreams;
¹⁸ and in those days I will pour out my Spirit
on my servants, both men and women; and they shall prophesy.
¹⁹ And I will show wonders in the heaven above
and signs on the earth beneath,
blood, and fire, and vapor of smoke;

²⁰ the sun shall be turned into night
and the moon into blood,
before the day of the Sovereign [[or Lord]] comes,
the great and manifest day.
²¹ And it shall be that whoever calls on the name of the Sovereign [[or
Lord]] shall be saved.' "

Lesson 1 (alternate) ~ Ezekiel 37:1–14

Ezekiel sees a vision of the glorification of Israel.

¹ The hand of GOD [[or the LORD]] was upon me, and brought me out by
the Spirit of GOD [[or the LORD]], and set me down in the midst of the valley;
it was full of bones. ² And God led me round among them; and there were
very many upon the valley; and they were very dry. ³ And God said to me,
"O mortal,[○] can these bones live?" And I answered, "O Sovereign [[or Lord]]
GOD, you know." ⁴ Again God said to me, "Prophesy to these bones, and say
to them, O dry bones, hear the word of GOD [[or the LORD]]. ⁵ Thus says the
Sovereign [[or Lord]] GOD to these bones: I will cause breath to enter you,
and you shall live. ⁶ And I will lay sinews upon you, and will cause flesh to
come upon you, and cover you with skin, and put breath in you, and you shall
live; and you shall know that I am GOD [[or the LORD]]."

⁷ So I prophesied as I was commanded; and as I prophesied, there was a
noise and a rattling; and the bones came together, bone to its bone. ⁸ And
as I looked, there were sinews on them, and flesh had come upon them, and
skin had covered them; but there was no breath in them. ⁹ Then God said
to me, "Prophesy to the breath, prophesy, O mortal,[○] and say to the breath,
Thus says the Sovereign [[or Lord]] GOD: Come from the four winds, O
breath, and breathe upon these slain, that they may live." ¹⁰ So I prophesied
as God commanded me, and the breath came into them, and they lived, and
stood upon their feet, an exceedingly great host.

¹¹ Then God said to me, "O mortal,[○] these bones are the whole house of
Israel. They say, 'Our bones are dried up, and our hope is lost; we are clean
cut off.' ¹² Therefore prophesy, and say to them, Thus says the Sovereign [[or
Lord]] GOD: I will open your graves, and raise you from your graves, O my
people; and I will bring you home into the land of Israel. ¹³ And you shall
know that I am GOD [[or the LORD]], when I open your graves, and raise you
from your graves, O my people. ¹⁴ And I will put my Spirit within you, and
you shall live, and I will place you in your own land; then you shall know that
I, the SOVEREIGN [[or LORD]], have spoken, and I have done it, says the
SOVEREIGN [[or LORD]]."

[○]RSV vs. 3, 11 *Son of man;* v. 9 *son of man.* See Appendix.

²⁴ O GOD [*or* LORD], how manifold are your works!
In wisdom you have made them all;
the earth is full of your creatures.

²⁵ Yonder is the sea, great and wide,
which teems with things innumerable,
living things both small and great.

²⁶ There go the ships,
and Leviathan which you formed to sport in it.

²⁷ These all look to you,
to give them their food in due season.

²⁸ When you give to them, they gather it up;
when you open your hand, they are filled with good things.

²⁹ When you hide your face, they are dismayed;
when you take away their breath, they die
and return to their dust.

³⁰ When you send forth your Spirit, they are created;
and you renew the face of the ground.

³¹ May the glory of GOD [*or* the LORD] endure forever,
may GOD [*or* the LORD] rejoice in the works of God,

³² who looks on the earth and it trembles,
who touches the mountains and they smoke!

³³ I will sing to GOD [*or* the LORD] as long as I live;
I will sing praise to my God while I have being.

³⁴ May my meditation be pleasing to God,
in whom I rejoice.

Lesson 2 ～ Romans 8:22–27

(If Ezekiel 37:1–14 is read as the first lesson, Acts 2:1–21 should be read as Lesson 2.)

Paul tells the Romans that the Spirit is constantly at work on their behalf.

²² We know that the whole creation has been groaning in travail together until now; ²³ and not only the creation, but we ourselves, who have the firstfruits of the Spirit, groan inwardly as we wait for adoption as children of God, the redemption of our bodies. ²⁴ For in this hope we were saved. Now hope that is seen is not hope. For who hopes for what is already seen? ²⁵ But if we hope for what we do not see, we wait for it with patience.

²⁶ The Spirit helps us in our weakness; for we do not know how to pray as we ought, but that very Spirit intercedes for us with sighs too deep for words. ²⁷ And the one who searches human hearts knows what is the mind of the Spirit, because the Spirit intercedes for the saints according to the will of God.

Gospel ~ John 15:26–27; 16:4b–15

Jesus promises to send us the Spirit of truth.

²⁶ But when the Counselor comes, whom I shall send to you from God⊗ —even the Spirit of truth, who proceeds from [*God*] the Father [*and Mother**]—that Counselor will bear witness to me; ²⁷ and you also are witnesses, because you have been with me from the beginning.

¹⁶:⁴ I did not say these things to you from the beginning, because I was with you. ⁵ But now I am going to the one who sent me; yet none of you asks me, "Where are you going?" ⁶ But because I have said these things to you, sorrow has filled your hearts. ⁷ Nevertheless I tell you the truth: it is to your advantage that I go away, for if I do not go away, the Counselor will not come to you; but if I go, I will send the Counselor to you, ⁸ who, having come, will convince the world of sin and of righteousness and of judgment: ⁹ of sin, because they do not believe in me; ¹⁰ of righteousness, because I go to God,⊗ and you will see me no more; ¹¹ of judgment, because the ruler of this world is judged.

¹² I have yet many things to say to you, but you cannot bear them now. ¹³ When the Spirit of truth comes, that Spirit will guide you into all the truth; for the Spirit will not speak independently, but will speak only what the Spirit hears, and will declare to you the things that are to come. ¹⁴ The Spirit will glorify me by taking what is mine and declaring it to you. ¹⁵ All that [*God*] the [*Mother and**] Father has is mine; therefore I said that the Spirit will take what is mine and declare it to you.

⊗RSV *the Father*. See Appendix.
*Addition to the text. See "Metaphor" and "God the Father and Mother" in the Appendix.

TRINITY

Lesson 1 ~ Isaiah 6:1–8

Isaiah sees a vision.

¹ In the year that King Uzziah died I saw God [[*or* the Lord]] sitting upon a throne, high and lifted up, whose train filled the temple. ² Above God stood the seraphim; each had six wings: with two they covered their faces, and with two they covered their feet, and with two they flew. ³ And one called to another and said:

"Holy, holy, holy is the GOD [[*or* LORD]] of hosts;
the whole earth is full of God's glory."

⁴ And the foundations of the thresholds shook at the voice of the one who called, and the house was filled with smoke. ⁵ And I said: "Woe is me! For I am lost; for I am a person of unclean lips, and I dwell in the midst of a people of unclean lips; for my eyes have seen the Ruler,▯ the GOD [[*or* LORD]] of hosts!"

⁶ Then one of the seraphim flew to me, having in its hand a burning coal which it had taken with tongs from the altar. ⁷ And the seraph touched my mouth, and said: "This has touched your lips; your guilt is taken away, and your sin forgiven." ⁸ And I heard the voice of God [[*or* the Lord]] saying, "Whom shall I send, and who will go for us?" Then I said, "Here am I! Send me."

Psalm 29

¹ Ascribe to GOD [[*or* the LORD]], O heavenly beings,
ascribe to GOD [[*or* the LORD]] glory and strength.
² Ascribe to GOD [[*or* the LORD]] the glory of God's name;
worship GOD [[*or* the LORD]] in holy array.
³ The voice of GOD [[*or* the LORD]] is upon the waters;
the God of glory thunders,
GOD [[*or* the LORD]], upon many waters.
⁴ The voice of GOD [[*or* the LORD]] is powerful,
the voice of GOD [[*or* the LORD]] is full of majesty.
⁵ The voice of GOD [[*or* the LORD]] breaks the cedars,
GOD [[*or* the LORD]] breaks the cedars of Lebanon,
⁶ making Lebanon to skip like a calf,
and Sirion like a young wild ox.
⁷ The voice of GOD [[*or* the LORD]] flashes forth flames of fire.

▯RSV *King*. See Appendix.

⁸ The voice of GOD [or the LORD] shakes the wilderness,
   GOD [or the LORD] shakes the wilderness of Kadesh.
⁹ The voice of GOD [or the LORD] makes the oaks to whirl,
   and strips the forests bare;
   and in God's temple all cry, "Glory!"
¹⁰ GOD [or The LORD] sits enthroned over the flood;
   GOD [or the LORD] sits enthroned as ruler☐ forever.
¹¹ May GOD [or the LORD] give strength to the people!
   May GOD [or the LORD] bless the people with peace!

Lesson 2 ~ Romans 8:12–17

Paul writes to the Christians at Rome about the Spirit.

¹² So then, brothers and sisters, we are debtors, not to the flesh, to live according to the flesh— ¹³ for if you live according to the flesh you will die, but if by the Spirit you put to death the deeds of the body you will live. ¹⁴ For all who are led by the Spirit of God are daughters and sons of God. ¹⁵ For you did not receive the spirit of slavery to fall back into fear, but you have received the spirit of adoption as children of God. When we cry, "[*God! my Mother and**] Father!" ¹⁶ it is the Spirit bearing witness with our spirit that we are children of God, ¹⁷ and if children, then heirs, heirs of God and joint heirs with Christ, provided we suffer with Christ in order that we may also be glorified with Christ.

☐RSV *king.* See Appendix.
*Addition to the text. RSV *"Abba!"* See "Metaphor" and "God the Father and Mother" in the
  Appendix.

149

Gospel ~ John 3:1-17

Jesus tells Nicodemus about the work of the Spirit.

¹ Now there was a man of the Pharisees, named Nicodemus, a ruler of the Jews. ² Nicodemus came to Jesus by night and said, "Rabbi, we know that you are a teacher come from God; for no one can do these signs that you do, except by the power of God." ³ Jesus answered Nicodemus, "Truly, truly, I say to you, unless one is born anew,① one cannot see the realm☆ of God." ⁴ Nicodemus replied, "How can someone be born who is old? Can anyone enter the womb of one's mother a second time and be born?" ⁵ Jesus answered, "Truly, truly, I say to you, unless one is born of water and the Spirit, one cannot enter the realm☆ of God. ⁶ That which is born of the flesh is flesh, and that which is born of the Spirit is spirit. ⁷ Do not marvel that I said to you, 'You must be born anew.①' ⁸ The wind blows where it wills, and you hear the sound of it, but you do not know where it comes from or where it goes; so it is with everyone who is born of the Spirit." ⁹ Nicodemus said to Jesus, "How can this be?" ¹⁰ Jesus answered, "Are you a teacher of Israel, and yet you do not understand this? ¹¹ Truly, truly, I say to you, we speak of what we know, and bear witness to what we have seen; but you do not receive our testimony. ¹² If I have told you earthly things and you do not believe, how can you believe if I tell you heavenly things? ¹³ No one has ascended into heaven but the one who descended from heaven, the Human One.○ ¹⁴ And as Moses lifted up the serpent in the wilderness, so must the Human One○ be lifted up, ¹⁵ that whoever believes in that one may have eternal life."

¹⁶ For God so loved the world that God gave God's only Child,◇ that whoever believes in that Child should not perish but have eternal life. ¹⁷ For God sent that Child◇ into the world, not to condemn the world, but that through that Child the world might be saved.

---

①Or *from above.*
☆RSV *kingdom.* See Appendix.
○RSV *Son of man.* See Appendix.
◇RSV v. 16 *Son;* v. 17 *the Son.* See Appendix.

PENTECOST 2

Lesson 1 ~ 1 Samuel 16:1–13

Samuel anoints David to be king over Israel.

¹ GOD [*or* The LORD] said to Samuel, "How long will you grieve over Saul, seeing I have rejected him from being king over Israel? Fill your horn with oil, and go; I will send you to Jesse the Bethlehemite, for I have provided for myself a king among Jesse's sons." ² And Samuel said, "How can I go? If Saul hears it, he will kill me." And GOD [*or* the LORD] said, "Take a heifer with you, and say, 'I have come to sacrifice to GOD [*or* the LORD].' ³ And invite Jesse to the sacrifice, and I will show you what you shall do; and you shall anoint for me the one whom I name to you." ⁴ Samuel did what GOD [*or* the LORD] commanded, and came to Bethlehem. The elders of the city came to meet Samuel trembling, and said, "Do you come peaceably?" ⁵ And Samuel said, "Peaceably; I have come to sacrifice to GOD [*or* the LORD]; consecrate yourselves, and come with me to the sacrifice." And he consecrated Jesse and his sons, and invited them to the sacrifice.

⁶ When they came, Samuel looked on Eliab and thought, "Surely GOD'S [*or* the LORD'S] anointed is present." ⁷ But GOD [*or* the LORD] said to Samuel, "Do not look on Eliab's appearance or on the height of his stature, because I have rejected Eliab; for GOD [*or* the LORD] sees not as people see; people look on the outward appearance, but GOD [*or* the LORD] looks on the heart." ⁸ Then Jesse called Abinadab, and made Abinadab pass before Samuel. And Samuel said, "Neither has GOD [*or* the LORD] chosen this one." ⁹ Then Jesse made Shammah pass by. And Samuel said, "Neither has GOD [*or* the LORD] chosen this one." ¹⁰ And Jesse made seven of his sons pass before Samuel. And Samuel said to Jesse, "GOD [*or* The LORD] has not chosen these." ¹¹ And Samuel said to Jesse, "Are all your sons here?" And Jesse said, "There remains yet the youngest, but he is keeping the sheep." And Samuel said to Jesse, "Send and fetch him; for we will not sit down till he comes here." ¹² And Jesse sent, and brought David in. Now David was ruddy, and had beautiful eyes, and was handsome. And GOD [*or* the LORD] said, "Arise, anoint David; for this is the one." ¹³ Then Samuel took the horn of oil, and anointed David in the midst of his brothers; and the Spirit of GOD [*or* the LORD] came mightily upon David from that day forward. And Samuel rose up, and went to Ramah.

Psalm 20

¹ May GOD ⟦*or* the LORD⟧ answer you in the day of trouble!
   The name of the God of Jacob protect you!
² May God send you help from the sanctuary,
   and give you support from Zion,
³ remembering all your offerings,
   and regarding with favor your burnt sacrifices!
⁴ May God grant you your heart's desire,
   and fulfill all your plans!
⁵ May we shout for joy over your victory,
   and in the name of our God set up our banners!
 May GOD ⟦*or* the LORD⟧ fulfill all your petitions!
⁶ Now I know that GOD ⟦*or* the LORD⟧ will help God's anointed,
   and will answer the anointed one from God's holy heaven
   with mighty victories by God's right hand.
⁷ Some boast of chariots, and some of horses;
   but we boast of the name of the SOVEREIGN ⟦*or* LORD⟧ our God.
⁸ They will collapse and fall;
   but we shall rise and stand upright.
⁹ Give victory to the ruler,⬚ O GOD ⟦*or* LORD⟧;
   answer us when we call.

Lesson 2 ∼ 2 Corinthians 4:5–12

Paul speaks of the hiddenness of life in Christ.

⁵ For what we preach is not ourselves, but Jesus Christ as Sovereign ⟦*or* Lord⟧, with ourselves as your servants for Jesus' sake. ⁶ For it is the God who said, "Let light shine out of darkness," who has shone in our hearts to give the light of the knowledge of the glory of God in the face of Christ.

⁷ But we have this treasure in earthen vessels, to show that the transcendent power belongs to God and not to us. ⁸ We are afflicted in every way, but not crushed; perplexed, but not driven to despair; ⁹ persecuted, but not forsaken; struck down, but not destroyed; ¹⁰ always carrying in the body the death of Jesus, so that the life of Jesus may also be manifested in our bodies. ¹¹ For while we live we are always being given up to death for Jesus' sake, so that the life of Jesus may be manifested in our mortal flesh. ¹² So death is at work in us, but life in you.

⬚RSV *king.* See Appendix.

Gospel ～ Mark 2:23–3:6

Mark writes about Jesus' work on the sabbath.

²³ One sabbath Jesus was going through the grainfields; and as they made their way the disciples began to pluck heads of grain. ²⁴ And the Pharisees said to Jesus, "Look, why are they doing what is not lawful on the sabbath?" ²⁵ And Jesus said to them, "Have you never read what David did, when in need and hungry, he and those who were with him: ²⁶ how David entered the house of God, when Abiathar was high priest, and ate the bread of the Presence, which it is not lawful for any but the priests to eat, and also gave it to those who were with him?" ²⁷ And Jesus said to them, "The sabbath was made for the human being, not the human being for the sabbath; ²⁸ so the Human One° is sovereign [[*or* lord]] even of the sabbath."

³:¹ Again Jesus entered the synagogue, and a person was there who had a withered hand. ² And they watched, to see whether Jesus would heal on the sabbath, so that they might accuse him. ³ And Jesus said to the one who had the withered hand, "Come here." ⁴ And Jesus said to them, "Is it lawful on the sabbath to do good or to do harm, to save life or to kill?" But they were silent. ⁵ And looking around at them with anger, grieved at their hardness of heart, Jesus said to the person, "Stretch out your hand." The one with the withered hand stretched it out, and it was restored. ⁶ The Pharisees went out, and immediately held counsel with the Herodians against Jesus, how to destroy him.

°RSV *Son of man.* See Appendix.

PENTECOST 3

Lesson 1 ～ 1 Samuel 16:14–23

David becomes servant to Saul.

¹⁴ Now the Spirit of GOD [*or* the LORD] departed from Saul, and an evil spirit from GOD [*or* the LORD] tormented Saul. ¹⁵ And Saul's servants said to him, "An evil spirit from God is tormenting you. ¹⁶ Let our lord now command your servants, who are before you, to seek out someone who is skillful in playing the lyre; and when the evil spirit from God is upon you, that person will play it, and you will be well." ¹⁷ So Saul said to the servants, "Provide for me someone who can play well, and bring that person to me." ¹⁸ One of the young servants answered, "I have seen a son of Jesse the Bethlehemite, who is skillful in playing, brave, a warrior, prudent in speech, and of good presence; and GOD [*or* the LORD] is with him." ¹⁹ Therefore Saul sent messengers to Jesse, and said, "Send me David your son, who is with the sheep." ²⁰ And Jesse took a donkey laden with bread, and a skin of wine and a kid, and sent them by David his son to Saul. ²¹ And David came to Saul, and entered his service. And Saul loved him greatly, and David became Saul's armor-bearer. ²² And Saul sent to Jesse, saying, "Let David remain in my service, for he has found favor in my sight." ²³ And whenever the evil spirit from God was upon Saul, David took the lyre and played it with his hand; so Saul was refreshed, and was well, and the evil spirit departed from Saul.

Psalm 57

¹ Be merciful to me, O God, be merciful to me,
    for in you my soul takes refuge;
  in the shadow of your wings I will take refuge,
    till the storms of destruction pass by.
² I cry to God Most High,
    to God who fulfills God's purpose for me.
³ God will send from heaven and save me,
    putting to shame those who trample upon me.
  God will send forth God's steadfast love and faithfulness!
⁴ I lie in the midst of lions
    that greedily devour their human prey;
  their teeth are spears and arrows,
    their tongues sharp swords.
⁵ Be exalted, O God, above the heavens!
    Let your glory be over all the earth!

⁶ They set a net for my steps;
　　my soul was bowed down.
　They dug a pit in my way,
　　but they have fallen into it themselves.
⁷ My heart is steadfast, O God,
　　my heart is steadfast!
　I will sing and make melody!
⁸　　Awake, my soul!
　Awake, O harp and lyre!
　　I will awake the dawn!
⁹ I will give thanks to you, O God [or Lord], among the peoples;
　　I will sing praises to you among the nations.
¹⁰ For your steadfast love is great to the heavens,
　　your faithfulness to the clouds.
¹¹ Be exalted, O God, above the heavens!
　　Let your glory be over all the earth!

Lesson 2 ～ 2 Corinthians 4:13–5:1

Paul exhorts the Corinthians to look to the things that are not seen.

¹³ Since we have the same spirit of faith as the psalmist who wrote, "I believed, and so I spoke," we too believe, and so we speak, ¹⁴ knowing that the one who raised the Sovereign [or Lord] Jesus will raise us also with Jesus and will present us with you. ¹⁵ For it is all for your sake, so that as grace extends to more and more people it may increase thanksgiving, to the glory of God.

¹⁶ So we do not lose heart. Though our outer nature is wasting away, our inner nature is being renewed every day. ¹⁷ For this slight momentary affliction is preparing for us an eternal weight of glory beyond all comparison, ¹⁸ because we look not to the things that are seen but to the things that are unseen; for the things that are seen are transient, but the things that are unseen are eternal.

⁵:¹ For we know that if the earthly tent we live in is destroyed, we have a building from God, a house not made with hands, eternal in the heavens.

Jesus teaches that a house divided cannot stand.

²⁰ And the crowd came together again, so that they could not even eat.
²¹ And when Jesus' family heard it, they went out to seize him, for people
were saying, "He is beside himself." ²² And the scribes who came down from
Jerusalem said, "He is possessed by Beelzebul, and casts out the demons by
the prince of demons." ²³ And Jesus called them, and said to them in parables, "How can Satan cast out Satan? ²⁴ If a kingdom is divided against itself,
that kingdom cannot stand. ²⁵ And if a house is divided against itself, that
house will not be able to stand. ²⁶ And if Satan has risen up against Satan and
is divided, Satan cannot stand, but is coming to an end. ²⁷ But none can enter
the house of the strong and plunder their goods, without first binding the
strong; then indeed they may plunder the house.

²⁸ "Truly, I say to you, all sins will be forgiven human beings, and whatever
blasphemies they utter; ²⁹ but whoever blasphemes against the Holy Spirit
never has forgiveness, but is guilty of an eternal sin"—³⁰ for they had said,
"Jesus has an unclean spirit."

³¹ And Jesus' mother and brothers came; and standing outside they sent to
Jesus and called him. ³² And a crowd was sitting about Jesus; and they said,
"Your mother and your brothers are outside, asking for you." ³³ And Jesus
replied, "Who are my mother and my brothers?" ³⁴ And looking around on
those who sat about him, Jesus said, "Here are my mother and my brothers!
³⁵ Whoever does the will of God is my brother, and sister, and mother."

PENTECOST 4

David grieves for Saul and Jonathan.

¹ After the death of Saul, when David had returned from the slaughter of the Amalekites, David remained two days in Ziklag.

¹⁷ And David lamented with this lamentation over Saul and Jonathan his son, ¹⁸ and David said it should be taught to the people of Judah; behold, it is written in the Book of Jashar:

¹⁹ "Your glory, O Israel, is slain upon your high places!
    How are the mighty fallen!
²⁰ Tell it not in Gath,
        publish it not in the streets of Ashkelon;
    lest the daughters of the Philistines rejoice,
        lest the daughters of the Gentiles exult.
²¹ You mountains of Gilboa,
        let there be no dew or rain upon you,
        nor upsurging of the deep!
    For there the shield of the mighty was defiled,
        the shield of Saul, not anointed with oil.
²² From the blood of the slain,
        from the fat of the mighty,
    the bow of Jonathan turned not back,
        and the sword of Saul returned not empty.
²³ Saul and Jonathan, beloved and lovely!
        In life and in death they were not divided;
    they were swifter than eagles,
        they were stronger than lions.
²⁴ You daughters of Israel, weep over Saul,
        who clothed you daintily in scarlet,
        who put ornaments of gold upon your apparel.
²⁵ How are the mighty fallen
        in the midst of the battle!
    Jonathan lies slain upon your high places.
²⁶   I am distressed for you, my brother Jonathan;
    very pleasant have you been to me;
        your love to me was wonderful,
        passing the love of women.
²⁷ How are the mighty fallen,
        and the weapons of war perished!"

Psalm 46

¹ God is our refuge and strength,
   a very present help in trouble.
² Therefore we will not fear though the earth should change,
   though the mountains shake in the heart of the sea;
³ though its waters roar and foam,
   though the mountains tremble with its tumult.
⁴ There is a river whose streams make glad the city of God,
   the holy habitation of the Most High.
⁵ God is in the midst of it and it shall not be moved;
   God will help it right early.
⁶ The nations rage, the kingdoms totter;
   God speaks, the earth melts.
⁷ The GOD [or LORD] of hosts is with us;
   the God of Jacob is our refuge.
⁸ Come, behold the works of GOD [or the LORD],
   who has wrought desolations in the earth,
⁹ making wars cease to the end of the earth,
   breaking the bow, shattering the spear,
   and burning the chariots with fire!
¹⁰ "Be still, and know that I am God.
   I am exalted among the nations,
   I am exalted in the earth!"
¹¹ The GOD [or LORD] of hosts is with us;
   the God of Jacob is our refuge.

Lesson 2 ~ 2 Corinthians 5:6–10, 14–17

Paul writes that in Christ everything is made new.

⁶ So we are always of good courage; we know that while we are at home in the body we are away from the Sovereign [or Lord], ⁷ for we walk by faith, not by sight. ⁸ We are of good courage, and we would rather be away from the body and at home with the Sovereign [or Lord]. ⁹ So whether we are at home or away, we make it our aim to please the Sovereign [or Lord]. ¹⁰ For we must all appear before the judgment seat of Christ, so that each one may receive good or evil, according to what each has done in the body.

¹⁴ For the love of Christ controls us, because we are convinced that one has died for all; therefore all have died. ¹⁵ And Christ died for all, that those

who live might live no longer for themselves but for the one who for their sake died and was raised.

[16] From now on, therefore, we regard no one from a human point of view; even though we once regarded Christ from a human point of view, we regard Christ thus no longer. [17] Therefore, if anyone is in Christ, there is a new creation; the old has passed away—the new has come.

Gospel ~ Mark 4:26–34

Jesus teaches in parables about the realm of God.

[26] And Jesus said, "The realm☆ of God is as if someone should scatter seed upon the ground, [27] and should sleep and rise night and day, and the seed should sprout and grow, without the sower knowing how. [28] The earth produces of itself, first the blade, then the ear, then the full grain in the ear. [29] But when the grain is ripe, at once the one who has sown puts in the sickle, because the harvest has come."

[30] And Jesus said, "With what can we compare the realm☆ of God, or what parable shall we use for it? [31] It is like a grain of mustard seed, which, when sown upon the ground is the smallest of all the seeds on earth; [32] yet when it is sown it grows up and becomes the greatest of all shrubs, and puts forth large branches, so that the birds of the air can make nests in its shade."

[33] With many such parables Jesus spoke the word to them, as they were able to hear it; [34] he did not speak to them without a parable, but privately to his own disciples Jesus explained everything.

☆RSV *kingdom.* See Appendix.

PENTECOST 5

David reigns over Israel and Judah.

¹ Then all the tribes of Israel came to David at Hebron, and said, "We are your bone and flesh. ² In times past, when Saul was king over us, it was you that led out and brought in Israel; and GOD [[*or* the LORD]] said to you, 'You shall be shepherd of my people Israel, and you shall be prince over Israel.' " ³ So all the elders of Israel came to the king at Hebron; and King David made a covenant with them at Hebron before GOD [[*or* the LORD]], and they anointed David king over Israel. ⁴ David was thirty years old when he began to reign, and he reigned forty years. ⁵ At Hebron David reigned over Judah seven years and six months; and at Jerusalem he reigned over all Israel and Judah thirty-three years.

Psalm 48

¹ Great is GOD [[*or* the LORD]] and greatly to be praised
　　in the city of our God!
God's holy mountain, ² beautiful in elevation,
　　is the joy of all the earth,
Mount Zion, in the far north,
　　the city of the great Ruler.□
³ Within its citadels God
　　has proven to be a sure defense.
⁴ For the rulers□ assembled,
　　they came on together.
⁵ As soon as they saw it, they were astounded,
　　they were in panic, they took to flight;
⁶ trembling took hold of them there,
　　anguish as of a woman in travail.
⁷ By the east wind you shattered the ships of Tarshish.
⁸ As we have heard, so have we seen
　　in the city of the GOD [[*or* LORD]] of hosts,
　in the city of our God,
　　which God establishes forever.

[+]The NACCL reads 2 Sam. 5:1–12. See Appendix, p. 255.
□RSV v. 2 *King;* v. 4 *kings.* See Appendix.

⁹ We have thought on your steadfast love, O God,
    in the midst of your temple.
¹⁰ As your name, O God,
        so your praise reaches to the ends of the earth.
    Your right hand is filled with victory;
¹¹   let Mount Zion be glad!
    Let the daughters of Judah rejoice
        because of your judgments!
¹² Walk about Zion, go round about it,
        number its towers,
¹³ consider well its ramparts,
        go through its citadels;
    that you may tell the next generation
¹⁴   that this is God,
    our God forever and ever,
        who will be our guide forever.

Lesson 2 ~ 2 Corinthians 5:18–6:2

Paul speaks of the reconciliation of the world to God through Christ.

¹⁸ All this is from God, who through Christ reconciled us to God's self and gave us the ministry of reconciliation; ¹⁹ that is, God was in Christ reconciling the world to God's self, not counting their trespasses against them, and entrusting to us the message of reconciliation. ²⁰ So we are ambassadors for Christ, God making God's appeal through us. We beseech you on behalf of Christ, be reconciled to God. ²¹ For our sake God made to be sin the one who knew no sin, so that in this very one we might become the righteousness of God.

^{6:1} Working together with God, then, we entreat you not to accept the grace of God in vain. ² For God says,

"At the acceptable time I have listened to you,
and helped you on the day of salvation."

Now is the acceptable time; now is the day of salvation.

Mark tells of Jesus calming the sea.

35 On that day, when evening had come, Jesus said to the disciples, "Let us go across to the other side." 36 And leaving the crowd, they took Jesus with them, just as he was, in the boat. And other boats were there. 37 And a great storm of wind arose, and the waves beat into the boat, so that the boat was already filling. 38 And the disciples woke Jesus, who was asleep on a cushion in the stern, and they said, "Teacher, do you not care if we perish?" 39 And Jesus awoke and rebuked the wind, and said to the sea, "Peace! Be still!" And the wind ceased, and there was a great calm. 40 Jesus said to them, "Why are you afraid? Have you no faith?" 41 And they were filled with awe, and said to one another, "Who then is this, whom even the wind and the sea obey?"

PENTECOST 6

Lesson 1 ~ 2 Samuel 6:1–15

The ark of the covenant is brought to the city of David.

¹ David again gathered all the chosen of Israel, thirty thousand. ² And David arose and went with all the people who were with him from Baalejudah, to bring up from there the ark of God, which is called by the name of the GOD [*or* LORD] of hosts who sits enthroned on the cherubim. ³ And they carried the ark of God upon a new cart, and brought it out of the house of Abinadab which was on the hill; and Uzzah and Ahio, the sons of Abinadab, were driving the new cart ⁴ with the ark of God; and Ahio went before the ark. ⁵ And David and all the house of Israel were making merry before GOD [*or* the LORD] with all their might, with songs and lyres and harps and tambourines and castanets and cymbals.

⁶ And when they came to the threshing floor of Nacon, Uzzah put out his hand to the ark of God and took hold of it, for the oxen stumbled. ⁷ And the anger of GOD [*or* the LORD] was kindled against Uzzah; and God smote Uzzah there because he put forth his hand to the ark; and Uzzah died there beside the ark of God. ⁸ And David was angry because GOD [*or* the LORD] had broken forth upon Uzzah; and that place is called Perez-uzzah, to this day. ⁹ And David was afraid of GOD [*or* the LORD] that day; and David said, "How can the ark of GOD [*or* the LORD] come to me?" ¹⁰ So David was not willing to take the ark of GOD [*or* the LORD] into the city of David; but David took it aside to the house of Obed-edom the Gittite. ¹¹ And the ark of GOD [*or* the LORD] remained in the house of Obed-edom the Gittite three months; and GOD [*or* the LORD] blessed Obed-edom and all his household.

¹² And it was told King David, "GOD [*or* The LORD] has blessed the household of Obed-edom and all that belongs to him, because of the ark of God." So David went and brought up the ark of God from the house of Obed-edom to the city of David with rejoicing; ¹³ and when those who bore the ark of GOD [*or* the LORD] had gone six paces, David sacrificed an ox and a fatling. ¹⁴ And David danced before God with all his might; and David was girded with a linen ephod. ¹⁵ So David and all the house of Israel brought up the ark of GOD [*or* the LORD] with shouting, and with the sound of the horn.

163

¹ The earth is GOD'S 〚*or* the LORD'S〛 and the fullness thereof,
   the world and those who dwell therein;
² for God has founded it upon the seas,
   and established it upon the rivers.
³ Who shall ascend the hill of GOD 〚*or* the LORD〛?
   And who shall stand in God's holy place?
⁴ Those who have clean hands and a pure heart,
   who do not lift up their soul to what is false,
   and do not swear deceitfully.
⁵ They will receive blessing from GOD 〚*or* the LORD〛,
   and vindication from the God of their salvation.
⁶ Such is the generation of those who seek God,
   who seek the face of the God of Jacob.
⁷ Lift up your heads, O gates!
   and be lifted up, O ancient doors!
   that the Ruler□ of glory may come in.
⁸ Who is the Ruler□ of glory?
   GOD 〚*or* The LORD〛, strong and mighty,
   GOD 〚*or* the LORD〛, mighty in battle!
⁹ Lift up your heads, O gates!
   and be lifted up, O ancient doors!
   that the Ruler□ of glory may come in.
¹⁰ Who is this Ruler□ of glory?
   The GOD 〚*or* LORD〛 of hosts,
   that one is the Ruler□ of glory!

□RSV *King.* See Appendix.

Lesson 2 ～ 2 Corinthians 8:7–15

Paul urges the Corinthians to share out of their abundance.

⁷ Now as you excel in everything—in faith, in utterance, in knowledge, in all earnestness, and in your love for us—see that you excel in this gracious work also.

⁸ I say this not as a command, but to prove by the earnestness of others that your love also is genuine. ⁹ For you know the grace of our Sovereign [*or* Lord] Jesus Christ, who though rich, yet for your sake became poor, so that by the poverty of Christ you might become rich. ¹⁰ And in this matter I give my advice: it is best for you now to complete what a year ago you began not only to do but to desire, ¹¹ so that your readiness in desiring it may be matched by your completing it out of what you have. ¹² For if the readiness is there, it is acceptable according to what one has, not according to what one has not. ¹³ I do not mean that others should be eased and you burdened, ¹⁴ but that as a matter of equality your abundance at the present time should supply their want, so that their abundance may supply your want, that there may be equality. ¹⁵ As it is written, "The one who gathered much had nothing over, and the one who gathered little had no lack."

Jesus heals the daughter of Jairus and also the woman with the flow of blood.

21 And when Jesus had crossed again in the boat to the other side, a great crowd gathered around, and Jesus was beside the sea. 22 Then came one of the rulers of the synagogue, Jairus by name, who, seeing Jesus, fell at his feet, 23 and pleaded, "My little daughter is at the point of death. Come and lay your hands on her, so that she may be made well, and live." 24 And Jesus went with him.

And a great crowd followed and thronged about Jesus. 25 And there was a woman who had had a flow of blood for twelve years, 26 and who had suffered much under many physicians, and had spent all that she had, and was no better but rather grew worse. 27 Having heard the reports about Jesus, she came up in the crowd from behind, and touched Jesus' garment. 28 For she said, "If I touch even his garments, I shall be made well." 29 And immediately the hemorrhage ceased; and she felt in her body that she was healed of her disease. 30 And Jesus, perceiving in himself that power had gone forth from him, immediately turned about in the crowd, and said, "Who touched my garments?" 31 And the disciples said, "You see the crowd pressing around you, and yet you say 'Who touched me?'" 32 And Jesus looked around to see who had done it. 33 But the woman, knowing what had been done to her, came in fear and trembling and fell down before Jesus, and told the whole truth. 34 And Jesus said to her, "Daughter, your faith has made you well; go in peace, and be healed of your disease."

35 While Jesus was still speaking, there came from the ruler's house some who said, "Your daughter is dead. Why trouble the Teacher any further?" 36 But ignoring what they said, Jesus said to the ruler of the synagogue, "Do not fear, only believe." 37 And Jesus allowed no one to follow him except Peter and James and John the brother of James. 38 When they came to the house of the ruler of the synagogue, Jesus saw a tumult, and people weeping and wailing loudly. 39 And having entered, Jesus said to them, "Why do you make a tumult and weep? The child is not dead but sleeping." 40 And they laughed at him. But Jesus put them all outside, and took the child's father and mother and the disciples, and went in where the child was. 41 Taking her by the hand Jesus said to her, "Talitha cumi"; which means, "Little girl, I say to you, arise." 42 And immediately the girl got up and walked (for she was twelve years of age), and they were immediately overcome with amazement. 43 And Jesus strictly charged them that no one should know this, and told them to give her something to eat.

PENTECOST 7

Lesson 1 ～ 2 Samuel 7:1–17

David receives promises from God.

¹ Now when David the king dwelt in his house, and GOD [*or* the LORD] had given him rest from all his enemies round about, ² the king said to Nathan the prophet, "See now, I dwell in a house of cedar, but the ark of God dwells in a tent." ³ And Nathan said to the king, "Go, do all that is in your heart; for GOD [*or* the LORD] is with you."

⁴ But that same night the word of GOD [*or* the LORD] came to Nathan, ⁵ "Go and tell my servant David, 'Thus says the SOVEREIGN [*or* LORD]: Would you build me a house to dwell in? ⁶ I have not dwelt in a house since the day I brought up the people of Israel from Egypt to this day, but I have been moving about in a tent for my dwelling. ⁷ In all places where I have moved with all the people of Israel, did I speak a word with any of the judges of Israel, whom I commanded to shepherd my people Israel, saying, "Why have you not built me a house of cedar?" ' ⁸ Now therefore thus you shall say to my servant David, 'Thus says the GOD [*or* LORD] of hosts, I took you from the pasture, from following the sheep, that you should be prince over my people Israel; ⁹ and I have been with you wherever you went, and have cut off all your enemies from before you; and I will make for you a great name, like the name of the great ones of the earth. ¹⁰ And I will appoint a place for my people Israel, and will plant them, that they may dwell in their own place, and be disturbed no more; and the violent shall afflict them no more, as formerly, ¹¹ from the time that I appointed judges over my people Israel; and I will give you rest from all your enemies. Moreover GOD [*or* the LORD] declares to you that GOD [*or* the LORD] will make you a house. ¹² When your days are fulfilled and you lie down with your ancestors, I will raise up your offspring after you, who shall come forth from your body, and I will establish a kingdom for that offspring, ¹³ who shall build a house for my name, and I will establish the throne of that kingdom forever. ¹⁴ I will be parent to your child, and your child shall be my child. When your child commits iniquity, I will chasten that one with a rod of human discipline, with stripes of human hands; ¹⁵ but I will not take away my steadfast love as I took it from Saul, whom I put away from before you. ¹⁶ And your house and your kingdom shall be made sure forever before me; your throne shall be established forever.' "
¹⁷ In accordance with all these words, and in accordance with all this vision, Nathan spoke to David.

20 I have found David, my servant;
     with my holy oil I have anointed him;
21 so that my hand shall ever abide with David,
     my arm also shall strengthen him.
22 The enemy shall not outwit him,
     the wicked shall not humble him.
23 I will crush David's foes before him
     and strike down those who hate him.
24 My faithfulness and my steadfast love shall be with him,
     and in my name shall David's horn be exalted.
25 I will set his hand on the sea
     and his right hand on the rivers.
26 He shall cry to me, "You are my Parent,
     my God, and the Rock of my salvation."
27 And I will make him the firstborn,
     the highest of the kings of the earth.
28 My steadfast love I will keep for David forever,
     and my covenant will stand firm for him.
29 I will establish David's line forever
     and his throne as the days of the heavens.
30 If David's children forsake my law
     and do not walk according to my ordinances,
31 if they violate my statutes
     and do not keep my commandments,
32 then I will punish their transgression with the rod
     and their iniquity with scourges;
33 but I will not remove from David my steadfast love,
     or be false to my faithfulness.
34 I will not violate my covenant,
     or alter the word that went forth from my lips.
35 Once for all I have sworn by my holiness;
     I will not lie to David,
36 whose line shall endure forever,
     whose throne as long as the sun before me.
37 Like the moon it shall be established forever;
     it shall stand firm while the skies endure.

Lesson 2 ~ 2 Corinthians 12:1–10

Paul writes of God's all-sufficient grace.

¹ I must boast; there is nothing to be gained by it, but I will go on to visions and revelations of the Sovereign [[or Lord]]. ² I know someone in Christ who fourteen years ago was caught up to the third heaven—whether in the body or out of the body I do not know, God knows. ³ And I know that this person was caught up into Paradise—whether in the body or out of the body I do not know, God knows—⁴ and there heard things that cannot be told, which may not be uttered. ⁵ On behalf of this one I will boast, but on my own behalf I will not boast, except of my weaknesses. ⁶ Though if I wish to boast, I shall not be a fool, for I shall be speaking the truth. But I refrain from it, so that no one may think more of me than can be seen in me or heard from me. ⁷ And to keep me from being too elated by the abundance of revelations, a thorn was given me in the flesh, a messenger of Satan, to harass me, to keep me from being too elated. ⁸ Three times I besought the Sovereign [[or Lord]] about this, that it should leave me; ⁹ but the Sovereign [[or Lord]] said to me, "My grace is sufficient for you, for my power is made perfect in weakness." I will all the more gladly boast of my weaknesses, that the power of Christ may rest upon me. ¹⁰ For the sake of Christ, then, I am content with weaknesses, insults, hardships, persecutions, and calamities; for when I am weak, then I am strong.

Gospel ~ Mark 6:1–6

Jesus' neighbors are astonished and take offense at him.

¹ Jesus went away from there and came to his own country; and the disciples followed. ² And on the sabbath Jesus began to teach in the synagogue; and many who heard were astonished, saying, "Where did this man get all this? What is the wisdom given to him? What mighty works are wrought by his hands! ³ Is not this the carpenter, the son of Mary and brother of James and Joses and Judas and Simon, and are not his sisters here with us?" And they took offense at him. ⁴ And Jesus said to them, "A prophet is not without honor, except in the prophet's own country, and among the prophet's own kin, and in the prophet's own house." ⁵ And he could do no mighty work there, except to lay hands upon a few sick people and heal them. ⁶ And Jesus marveled because of their unbelief.

PENTECOST 8

Lesson 1 ~ 2 Samuel 7:18–29

David responds to promises from God.

¹⁸ Then King David went in and sat before GOD [*or* the LORD] and said, "Who am I, O Sovereign [*or* Lord] GOD, and what is my house, that you have brought me thus far? ¹⁹ And yet this was a small thing in your eyes, O Sovereign [*or* Lord] GOD; you have spoken also of your servant's house for a great while to come, and have shown me future generations, O Sovereign [*or* Lord] GOD! ²⁰ And what more can David say to you? For you know your servant, O Sovereign [*or* Lord] GOD! ²¹ Because of your promise, and according to your own heart, you have wrought all this greatness, to make your servant know it. ²² Therefore you are great, O SOVEREIGN [*or* LORD] God; for there is none like you, and there is no God besides you, according to all that we have heard with our ears. ²³ What other nation on earth is like your people Israel, whom God went to redeem to be God's people, making for God a name, and doing for them great and terrible things, by driving out before God's people a nation and its gods? ²⁴ And you established for yourself your people Israel to be your people forever; and you, O GOD [*or* LORD], became their God. ²⁵ And now, O SOVEREIGN [*or* LORD] God, confirm forever the word which you have spoken concerning your servant and concerning his house, and do as you have spoken; ²⁶ and your name will be magnified forever, saying, 'The GOD [*or* LORD] of hosts is God over Israel,' and the house of your servant David will be established before you. ²⁷ For you, O GOD [*or* LORD] of hosts, the God of Israel, have made this revelation to your servant, saying, 'I will build you a house'; therefore your servant has found courage to pray this prayer to you. ²⁸ And now, O Sovereign [*or* Lord] GOD, you are God, and your words are true, and you have promised this good thing to your servant; ²⁹ now therefore may it please you to bless the house of your servant, that it may continue forever before you; for you, O Sovereign [*or* Lord] GOD, have spoken, and with your blessing shall the house of your servant be blessed forever."

Psalm 132:11–18

¹¹ GOD [*or* The LORD] swore to David a sure oath
   and will not turn back from it:
"One from the fruit of your body
   I will set on your throne.

¹² If your children keep my covenant
  and my testimonies which I shall teach them,
their children also forever
  shall sit upon your throne."
¹³ For GOD [*or* the LORD] has chosen Zion,
  and has desired it for a habitation:
¹⁴ "This is my resting place forever;
  here I will dwell, for I have desired it.
¹⁵ I will abundantly bless its provisions;
  I will satisfy its poor with bread.
¹⁶ Its priests I will clothe with salvation,
  and its saints will shout for joy.
¹⁷ There I will make a horn to sprout for David;
  I have prepared a lamp for my anointed,
¹⁸ whose enemies I will clothe with shame;
  but upon my anointed the crown will shed its luster."

Lesson 2 ∼ Ephesians 1:1–10

The writer greets the saints who are faithful in Christ Jesus.

¹ Paul, an apostle of Christ Jesus by the will of God,
  To the saints who are also faithful in Christ Jesus:
² Grace to you and peace from God our Father [*and Mother**] and from the Sovereign [*or* Lord] Jesus Christ.
³ Blessed be God the Father [*and Mother**] of our Sovereign [*or* Lord] Jesus Christ, who has blessed us in Christ with every spiritual blessing in the heavenly places, ⁴ even as God chose us in Christ before the foundation of the world, that we should be holy and blameless before God, ⁵ who destined us in love to be God's children through Jesus Christ, according to the purpose of God's will, ⁶ to the praise of God's glorious grace freely bestowed on us in the Beloved, ⁷ in whom we have redemption by blood, the forgiveness of our trespasses, according to the riches of God's grace ⁸ lavished upon us. ⁹ For God has made known to us in all wisdom and insight the mystery of God's will, according to God's purpose set forth in Christ ¹⁰ as a plan for the fullness of time, to unite all things in Christ, things in heaven and things on earth.

---

*Addition to the text. RSV v. 2 *God our Father;* v. 3 *Blessed be the God and Father.* See "Metaphor" and "God the Father and Mother" in the Appendix.

Jesus sends out the twelve two by two.

⁷ Jesus called the twelve, and began to send them out two by two, and gave them authority over the unclean spirits. ⁸ He charged them to take nothing for their journey except a staff; no bread, no bag, no money in their belts; ⁹ but to wear sandals and not put on two tunics. ¹⁰ And Jesus said to them, "Where you enter a house, stay there until you leave the place. ¹¹ And if any place will not receive you and they refuse to hear you, when you leave, shake off the dust that is on your feet for a testimony against them." ¹² So they went out and preached that people should repent. ¹³ And they cast out many demons, and anointed with oil many that were sick and healed them.

PENTECOST 9

Lesson 1 ~ 2 Samuel 11:1–15

David takes Bathsheba and plots against her husband, Uriah.

[1] In the spring of the year, the time when kings go forth to battle, David sent Joab, and his servants with him, and all Israel; and they ravaged the Ammonites, and besieged Rabbah. But David remained at Jerusalem.

[2] It happened, late one afternoon, when David arose from his couch and was walking upon the roof of the king's house, that he saw from the roof a woman bathing; and the woman was very beautiful. [3] And David sent and inquired about the woman. And one said, "Is not this Bathsheba, the daughter of Eliam, the wife of Uriah the Hittite?" [4] So David sent messengers, and took her; and she came to him, and he lay with her. (Now she was carrying out her ritual purification.) Then she returned to her house. [5] And the woman conceived; and she sent and told David, "I am with child."

[6] So David sent word to Joab, "Send me Uriah the Hittite." And Joab sent Uriah to David. [7] When Uriah came to him, David asked how Joab was doing, and how the people fared, and how the war prospered. [8] Then David said to Uriah, "Go down to your house, and wash your feet." And Uriah went out of the king's house, and there followed him a present from the king. [9] But Uriah slept at the door of the king's house with all the servants of his lord, and did not go down to his house. [10] When they told David, "Uriah did not go down to his house," David said to Uriah, "Have you not come from a journey? Why did you not go down to your house?" [11] Uriah said to David, "The ark and Israel and Judah dwell in booths; and my lord Joab and the servants of my lord are camping in the open field; shall I then go to my house, to eat and to drink, and to lie with my wife? As you live, and as your soul lives, I will not do this thing." [12] Then David said to Uriah, "Remain here today also, and tomorrow I will let you depart." So Uriah remained in Jerusalem that day, and the next. [13] And David invited Uriah, who ate in his presence and drank, so that David made him drunk; and in the evening Uriah went out to lie on his couch with the servants of his lord, but did not go down to his house.

[14] In the morning David wrote a letter to Joab, and sent it by the hand of Uriah. [15] In the letter he wrote, "Set Uriah in the forefront of the hardest fighting, and then draw back from him, that he may be struck down, and die."

Psalm 53

¹ Fools say in their heart,
   "There is no God."
  They are corrupt, doing abominable iniquity;
   there is none that does good.
² God looks down from heaven
   upon humankind
  to see if there are any that are wise,
   that seek after God.
³ They have all fallen away;
   they are all alike depraved;
  there is none that does good,
   no, not one.
⁴ Have those who work evil no understanding,
   who eat up my people as they eat bread,
   and do not call upon God?
⁵ There they are, in great terror,
   in terror such as has not been!
  For God will scatter the bones of the ungodly;
   they will be put to shame, for God has rejected them.
⁶ O that deliverance for Israel would come from Zion!
   When God restores the fortunes of God's people,
   Jacob will rejoice and Israel be glad.

Lesson 2 ∼ Ephesians 2:11–22

The unity and peace of the household of God is in Christ.

¹¹ Therefore remember that at one time you Gentiles in the flesh, called the uncircumcision by what is called the circumcision, which is made in the flesh by hands—¹² remember that you were at that time separated from Christ, alienated from the commonwealth of Israel, and strangers to the covenants of promise, having no hope and without God in the world. ¹³ But now in Christ Jesus you who once were far off have been brought near in the blood of Christ. ¹⁴ For Christ is our peace, who has made us both one, and has broken down the dividing wall of hostility, ¹⁵ by abolishing in Christ's own flesh the law of commandments and ordinances, in order to create in Christ one new humanity in place of the two, so making peace, ¹⁶ and in order to reconcile us both to God in one body through the cross, thereby bringing the hostility to an end. ¹⁷ And Christ came and preached peace to you who were far off and peace to those who were near; ¹⁸ for through Christ

we both have access in one Spirit to [*God*] the [*Mother and**] Father. ¹⁹ So then you are no longer strangers and sojourners, but you are citizens together with the saints and members of the household of God, ²⁰ built upon the foundation of the apostles and prophets, Christ Jesus being the cornerstone, ²¹ in whom the whole structure is joined together and grows into a holy temple in the Sovereign [[*or* Lord]]; ²² in whom you also are built into it for a dwelling place of God in the Spirit.

Gospel ⁓ Mark 6:30–34

Large crowds keep following Jesus, who has compassion on them.

³⁰ The apostles returned to Jesus, and reported all that they had done and taught. ³¹ And Jesus said to them, "Come away by yourselves to a lonely place, and rest a while." For many were coming and going, and they had no leisure even to eat. ³² And they went away in the boat to a lonely place by themselves. ³³ Now many saw them going and knew them, and they ran there on foot from all the towns, and got there ahead of them. ³⁴ Going ashore, Jesus saw a great throng and had compassion on them, because they were like sheep without a shepherd; and Jesus began to teach them many things.

---

*Addition to the text. See "Metaphor" and "God the Father and Mother" in the Appendix.

PENTECOST 10

Lesson 1 ~ 2 Samuel 12:1–14

David is judged for taking Bathsheba and betraying Uriah.

¹ And GOD [[*or* the LORD]] sent Nathan to David. Nathan came to him and said, "There were two men in a certain city, the one rich and the other poor. ² The rich man had very many flocks and herds; ³ but the poor man had nothing but one little ewe lamb, which he had bought. And he brought it up, and it grew up with him and with his children; it used to eat of his morsel, and drink from his cup, and lie in his bosom, and it was like a daughter to him. ⁴ Now there came a traveler to the rich man, and he was unwilling to take one of his own flock or herd to prepare for the wayfarer who had come to him, but he took the poor man's lamb, and prepared it for the man who had come to him." ⁵ Then David's anger was greatly kindled against the man; and he said to Nathan, "As GOD [[*or* the LORD]] lives, the man who has done this deserves to die; ⁶ and he shall restore the lamb fourfold, because he did this thing, and because he had no pity."

⁷ Nathan said to David, "You are the man. Thus says the SOVEREIGN [[*or* LORD]], the God of Israel, 'I anointed you king over Israel, and I delivered you out of the hand of Saul; ⁸ and I gave you your master's house, and your master's wives into your bosom, and gave you the house of Israel and of Judah; and if this were too little, I would add to you as much more. ⁹ Why have you despised the word of GOD [[*or* the LORD]], to do what is evil in God's sight? You have smitten Uriah the Hittite with the sword, and have taken his wife to be your wife, and have slain him with the sword of the Ammonites. ¹⁰ Now therefore the sword shall never depart from your house, because you have despised me, and have taken the wife of Uriah the Hittite to be your wife.' ¹¹ Thus says the SOVEREIGN [[*or* LORD]], 'I will raise up evil against you out of your own house; and I will take your wives before your eyes, and give them to your neighbor, and he shall lie with your wives in the sight of this sun. ¹² For you did it secretly; but I will do this thing before all Israel, and before the sun.' " ¹³ David said to Nathan, "I have sinned against GOD [[*or* the LORD]]." And Nathan said to David, "GOD [[*or* The LORD]] also has put away your sin; you shall not die. ¹⁴ Nevertheless, because by this deed you have utterly scorned GOD [[*or* the LORD]], the child that is born to you shall die."

Psalm 32

¹ Blessed is the one whose transgression is forgiven,
  whose sin is covered.
² Blessed is the person to whom GOD [or the LORD] imputes no
    iniquity,
  and in whose spirit there is no deceit.
³ When I declared not my sin, my body wasted away
  through my groaning all day long.
⁴ For day and night your hand was heavy upon me;
  my strength was dried up as by the heat of summer.
⁵ I acknowledged my sin to you,
  and I did not hide my iniquity;
 I said, "I will confess my transgressions to GOD [or the LORD]";
  then you forgave the guilt of my sin.
⁶ Therefore let all who are godly
  offer prayer to you;
 at a time of distress, the rush of great waters
  shall not reach them.
⁷ You are a hiding place for me,
  you preserve me from trouble;
  you encompass me with deliverance.
⁸ I will instruct you and teach you
  the way you should go;
  I will counsel you with my eye upon you.
⁹ Be not like a horse or a mule, without understanding,
  which must be curbed with bit and bridle,
  else it will not keep with you.
¹⁰ Many are the pangs of the wicked;
  but steadfast love surrounds the one who trusts in GOD [or
    the LORD].
¹¹ Be glad in GOD [or the LORD], and rejoice, O righteous,
  and shout for joy, all you upright in heart!

Lesson 2 ～ Ephesians 3:14–21

The apostle prays for the church.

¹⁴ For this reason I bow my knees before [God] the Father [and Mother*],
¹⁵ from whom every family in heaven and on earth is named, ¹⁶ that according to the riches of God's glory God may grant you to be strengthened with

---

*Addition to the text. See "Metaphor" and "God the Father and Mother" in the Appendix.

177

might through God's Spirit in the inner person, [17] and that Christ may dwell in your hearts through faith; that you, being rooted and grounded in love, [18] may have power to comprehend with all the saints what is the breadth and length and height and depth, [19] and to know the love of Christ which surpasses knowledge, that you may be filled with all the fullness of God.

[20] Now to the one who by the power at work within us is able to do far more abundantly than all that we ask or think, [21] to God be glory in the church and in Christ Jesus to all generations, forever and ever. Amen.

Gospel ~ John 6:1–15

Jesus feeds the multitude.

[1] After this Jesus went to the other side of the Sea of Galilee, which is the Sea of Tiberias. [2] And a multitude followed, because they saw the signs which he did on those who were diseased. [3] Jesus went up on the mountain, and there sat down with the disciples. [4] Now the Passover, the Jewish feast, was at hand. [5] Looking up, then, and seeing that a multitude was approaching, Jesus said to Philip, "How are we to buy bread, so that these people may eat?" [6] This Jesus said to test Philip, for Jesus knew what he would do. [7] Philip answered, "Two hundred denarii would not buy enough bread for each of them to get a little." [8] One of the disciples, Andrew, Simon Peter's brother, said to Jesus, [9] "There is a child here who has five barley loaves and two fish; but what are they among so many?" [10] Jesus said, "Make the people sit down." Now there was much grass in the place; so the people sat down, in number about five thousand. [11] Jesus then took the loaves, and having given thanks, distributed them to those who were seated; so also the fish, as much as they wanted. [12] And when they had eaten their fill, Jesus told the disciples, "Gather up the fragments left over, that nothing may be lost." [13] So they gathered them up and filled twelve baskets with fragments from the five barley loaves, left by those who had eaten. [14] When the people saw the sign which Jesus had done, they said, "This is indeed the prophet who is to come into the world!"

[15] Perceiving then that they were about to come and take him by force to make him king, Jesus withdrew again to the mountain alone.

PENTECOST 11

Bathsheba gives birth to Solomon.

¹⁵ And GOD [*or* the LORD] struck the child that Uriah's wife bore to David, and it became sick. ¹⁶ David therefore besought God for the child; and he fasted, and went in and lay all night upon the ground. ¹⁷ And the elders of his house stood beside him, to raise him from the ground; but he would not, nor did he eat food with them. ¹⁸ On the seventh day the child died. And the servants of David feared to tell him that the child was dead; for they said, "While the child was yet alive, we spoke to the king, and he did not listen to us; how then can we say to him the child is dead? He may do himself some harm." ¹⁹ But when David saw that his servants were whispering together, he perceived that the child was dead; and David said to the servants, "Is the child dead?" They said, "It is dead." ²⁰ Then David arose from the earth, and washed, and anointed himself, and changed his clothes, and went into the house of GOD [*or* the LORD], and worshiped; David then went home; and when he asked, they set food before him, and he ate. ²¹ Then his servants said to him, "What is this thing that you have done? You fasted and wept for the child while it was alive; but when the child died, you arose and ate food." ²² David said, "While the child was still alive, I fasted and wept; for I said, 'Who knows whether GOD [*or* the LORD] will be gracious to me, that the child may live?' ²³ But now the child is dead; why should I fast? Can I bring it back again? I shall go to the child, but the child will not return to me."

²⁴ Then David comforted his wife, Bathsheba, and went in to her, and lay with her; and she bore a son, and David called his name Solomon. And GOD [*or* the LORD] loved Solomon.

[11] Come, O children, listen to me,
    I will teach you the fear of GOD [[*or* the LORD]].
[12] Which of you desires life,
    and covets many days to enjoy good?
[13] Keep your tongue from evil,
    and your lips from speaking deceit.
[14] Depart from evil, and do good;
    seek peace, and pursue it.
[15] The eyes of GOD [[*or* the LORD]] are toward the righteous,
    and God's ears toward their cry.
[16] The face of GOD [[*or* the LORD]] is against evildoers,
    to cut off the remembrance of them from the earth.
[17] When the righteous cry for help, GOD [[*or* the LORD]] hears,
    and delivers them out of all their troubles.
[18] GOD [[*or* The LORD]] is near to the brokenhearted,
    and saves the crushed in spirit.
[19] Many are the afflictions of the righteous,
    but GOD [[*or* the LORD]] delivers them from their pain.
[20] God keeps all their bones;
    not one of them is broken.
[21] Evil shall slay the wicked;
    and those who hate the righteous will be condemned.
[22] GOD [[*or* The LORD]] redeems the life of God's servants;
    none of those who take refuge in God will be condemned.

Lesson 2 ∼ Ephesians 4:1–6

The apostle urges the unity of the Spirit in the bond of peace.

[1] I therefore, a prisoner for the Sovereign [[*or* Lord]], beg you to lead a life worthy of the calling to which you have been called, [2] with all lowliness and meekness, with patience, forbearing one another in love, [3] eager to maintain the unity of the Spirit in the bond of peace. [4] There is one body and one Spirit, just as you were called to the one hope that belongs to your call, [5] one Sovereign [[*or* Lord]], one faith, one baptism, [6] one God, [*Mother**] and Father of us all, who is above all and through all and in all.

---

*Addition to the text. See "Metaphor" and "God the Father and Mother" in the Appendix.

Gospel ～ John 6:24–35

Jesus is the bread of life.

²⁴ So when the people saw that Jesus was not there, nor the disciples, they themselves got into the boats and went to Capernaum, seeking Jesus.

²⁵ When they found Jesus on the other side of the sea, they said to him, "Rabbi, when did you come here?" ²⁶ Jesus answered them, "Truly, truly, I say to you, you seek me, not because you saw signs, but because you ate your fill of the loaves. ²⁷ Do not labor for the food which perishes, but for the food which endures to eternal life, which the Human One° will give to you; for that one, God the Father [*and Mother**] has confirmed." ²⁸ Then they said to Jesus, "What must we do to be doing the works of God?" ²⁹ Jesus answered them, "This is the work of God, that you believe in the one whom God has sent." ³⁰ So they said to Jesus, "Then what sign do you do, that we may see, and believe you? What work do you perform? ³¹ Our ancestors ate the manna in the wilderness; as it is written, 'God gave them bread from heaven to eat.' " ³² Jesus then said to them, "Truly, truly, I say to you, it was not Moses who gave you the bread from heaven; God gives you the true bread from heaven. ³³ For the bread of God is that which comes down from heaven, and gives life to the world." ³⁴ They said to Jesus, "Give us this bread always."

³⁵ Jesus said to them, "I am the bread of life; whoever comes to me shall not hunger, and whoever believes in me shall never thirst."

°RSV *Son of man.* See Appendix.
*Addition to the text. See "Metaphor" and "God the Father and Mother" in the Appendix.

PENTECOST 12

Lesson 1 (alternate) ∼ 2 Samuel 14:4–17[+]

The woman of Tekoa argues with David on Absalom's behalf.

4 When the woman of Tekoa came to David, she fell on her face to the ground, and did obeisance, and said, "Help, O king." 5 And the king said to her, "What is your trouble?" She answered, "Alas, I am a widow; my husband is dead. 6 And your womanservant had two sons, and they quarreled with one another in the field; there was no one to part them, and one struck the other and killed him. 7 And now the whole family has risen against your woman-servant, and they say, 'Give up the man who struck his brother, that we may kill him for the life of his brother whom he slew'; and so they would destroy the heir also. Thus they would quench my coal which is left, and leave to my husband neither name nor remnant upon the face of the earth."

8 Then the king said to the woman, "Go to your house, and I will give orders concerning you." 9 And the woman of Tekoa said to the king, "On me be the guilt, my lord the king, and on my father's house; let the king and his throne be guiltless." 10 The king said, "Let whoever says anything to you be brought to me, and that person shall never touch you again." 11 Then she said, "Pray let the king invoke the SOVEREIGN [or the LORD] your God, that the avenger of blood slay no more, and my son be not destroyed." David said, "As GOD [or the LORD] lives, not one hair of your son shall fall to the ground."

12 Then the woman said, "Pray let your womanservant speak a word to my lord the king." David said, "Speak." 13 And the woman said, "Why then have you planned such a thing against the people of God? For in giving this decision the king convicts himself, inasmuch as the king does not bring Absalom, his banished one, home again. 14 We must all die, we are like water spilt on the ground, which cannot be gathered up again; but God will not take away the life of the one who devises means not to keep his banished one an outcast. 15 Now I have come to say this to my lord the king because the people have made me afraid; and your womanservant thought, 'I will speak to the king; it may be that the king will perform the request of his servant. 16 For the king will hear, and deliver his servant from the hand of the one who would destroy me and my son together from the heritage of God.' 17 And your womanservant thought, 'The word of my lord the king will set me at rest'; for my lord the king is like the angel of God to discern good and evil. The SOVEREIGN [or LORD] your God be with you!"

[+]Lection added. See Appendix, p. 255.

Lesson 1 ～ 2 Samuel 18:1, 5, 9–15

David's son Absalom is killed.

¹ Then David mustered the men who were with him, and set over them commanders of thousands and commanders of hundreds. ⁵ And the king ordered Joab and Abishai and Ittai, "Deal gently for my sake with the young Absalom." And all the people heard when the king gave orders to all the commanders about Absalom.

⁹ And Absalom chanced to meet the servants of David. Absalom was riding upon his mule, and the mule went under the thick branches of a great oak, and Absalom's head caught fast in the oak, and he was left hanging between heaven and earth, while the mule that was under him went on. ¹⁰ And someone saw it, and told Joab, "I saw Absalom hanging in an oak." ¹¹ Joab said to the one who told him, "What, you saw Absalom! Why then did you not strike him there to the ground? I would have been glad to give you ten pieces of silver and a belt." ¹² But the man said to Joab, "Even if I felt in my hand the weight of a thousand pieces of silver, I would not put forth my hand against the king's son; for in our hearing the king commanded you and Abishai and Ittai, 'For my sake protect the young Absalom.' ¹³ On the other hand, if I had dealt treacherously against Absalom's life (and there is nothing hidden from the king), then you yourself would have stood aloof." ¹⁴ Joab said, "I will not waste time like this with you." And Joab took three darts in his hand, and thrust them into the heart of Absalom, while he was still alive in the oak. ¹⁵ And ten young men, Joab's armor-bearers, surrounded Absalom and struck him, and killed Absalom.

Psalm 143:1–8

¹ Hear my prayer, O GOD [*or* LORD]; give ear to my supplications!
  In your faithfulness answer me, in your righteousness!
² Enter not into judgment with your servant;
  for no one living is righteous before you.
³ For the enemy has pursued me,
  has crushed my life to the ground,
    and has made me sit in darkness like those long dead.
⁴ Therefore my spirit faints within me;
  my heart within me is appalled.
⁵ I remember the days of old,
  I meditate on all that you have done;
    I muse on what your hands have wrought.

⁶ I stretch out my hands to you;
  my soul thirsts for you like a parched land.
⁷ Make haste to answer me, O GOD [[or LORD]]!
  My spirit fails!
 Hide not your face from me,
  lest I be like those who go down to the Pit.
⁸ Let me hear in the morning of your steadfast love,
  for in you I put my trust.
 Teach me the way I should go,
  for to you I lift up my soul.

Lesson 2 ∼ Ephesians 4:25–5:2

The apostle gives ethical instructions to the Ephesians.

²⁵ Therefore, putting away falsehood, let everyone speak the truth with their neighbor, for we are members one of another. ²⁶ Be angry but do not sin; do not let the sun go down on your anger, ²⁷ and give no opportunity to the devil. ²⁸ Let the thief no longer steal, but rather labor, doing honest manual work, in order to be able to give to those in need. ²⁹ Let no evil talk come out of your mouths, but only such as is good for edifying, as fits the occasion, that it may impart grace to those who hear. ³⁰ And do not grieve the Holy Spirit of God, in whom you were sealed for the day of redemption. ³¹ Let all bitterness and wrath and anger and clamor and slander be put away from you, with all malice, ³² and be kind to one another, tenderhearted, forgiving one another, as God in Christ forgave you.

⁵:¹ Therefore be imitators of God, as beloved children. ² And walk in love, as Christ loved us and gave up Christ's self for us, a fragrant offering and sacrifice to God.

Gospel (alternate) ∼ John 8:2–11[+]

Jesus defends a woman who has been abused.

² Early in the morning Jesus came again to the temple; all the people came to him, and he sat down and taught them. ³ The scribes and the Pharisees brought a woman who had been caught in adultery, and placing her in the midst ⁴ they said, "Teacher, this woman has been caught in the act of adultery. ⁵ Now in the law Moses commanded us to stone such. What do you say about her?" ⁶ This they said to test Jesus, that they might have

---

[+]Lection added. See Appendix, p. 255.

some charge to bring against him. Jesus bent down and wrote with his finger on the ground. ⁷ And as they continued to ask Jesus, he stood up and said to them, "Let the one who is without sin among you be the first to throw a stone at her." ⁸ And once more Jesus bent down and wrote with his finger on the ground. ⁹ But when they heard it, they went away, one by one, beginning with the eldest, and Jesus was left alone with the woman standing before him. ¹⁰ Jesus looked up and said to her, "Woman, where are they? Has no one condemned you?" ¹¹ She said, "No one, Sovereign [[or Lord]]." And Jesus said, "Neither do I condemn you; go, and do not sin again."

Gospel ∼ John 6:35, 41–51

Jesus is the bread of life.

³⁵ Jesus said to them, "I am the bread of life; whoever comes to me shall not hunger, and whoever believes in me shall never thirst."

⁴¹ The religious authorities∇ then murmured at Jesus for saying, "I am the bread which came down from heaven." ⁴² They said, "Is not this Jesus, the son of Joseph, whose father and mother we know? How does he now say, 'I have come down from heaven'?" ⁴³ Jesus answered them, "Do not murmur among yourselves. ⁴⁴ No one can come to me unless drawn by [God] the Father [and Mother*] who sent me; and I will raise that one at the last day. ⁴⁵ It is written in the prophets, 'And they shall all be taught by God.' Everyone who has heard and learned from God⊗ comes to me. ⁴⁶ Not that anyone has seen God⊗ except the one who is from God; that one has seen God.⊗ ⁴⁷ Truly, truly, I say to you, whoever believes has eternal life. ⁴⁸ I am the bread of life. ⁴⁹ Your ancestors ate the manna in the wilderness, and they died. ⁵⁰ This is the bread which comes down from heaven, that people may eat of it and not die. ⁵¹ I am the living bread which came down from heaven; anyone who eats of this bread will live forever; and the bread which I shall give for the life of the world is my flesh."

∇RSV *The Jews.* See Appendix.
*Addition to the text. See "Metaphor" and "God the Father and Mother" in the Appendix.
⊗RSV *the Father.* See Appendix.

PENTECOST 13

Lesson 1 ~ 2 Samuel 18:24–33

David receives the report of the death of Absalom.

²⁴ Now David was sitting between the two gates; and the sentry went up to the roof of the gate by the wall, and looking up, saw someone running alone. ²⁵ And the sentry called out and told the king. And the king said, "If the runner is alone, there are tidings." And the runner came apace, and drew near. ²⁶ And the sentry saw another runner, and the sentry called to the gate and said, "See, another runner who is alone!" The king said, "That runner also brings tidings." ²⁷ And the sentry said, "I think the running of the foremost is like the running of Ahimaaz the son of Zadok." And the king said, "He is a good man, and comes with good tidings."

²⁸ Then Ahimaaz cried out to the king, "All is well." And he bowed before the king with his face to the earth, and said, "Blessed be the SOVEREIGN [*or* LORD] your God, who has delivered up those who raised their hand against my lord the king." ²⁹ And the king said, "Is it well with the young Absalom?" Ahimaaz answered, "When Joab sent your servant, I saw a great tumult, but I do not know what it was." ³⁰ And the king said, "Turn aside, and stand here." So Ahimaaz turned aside, and stood still.

³¹ And the Cushite came; and the Cushite said, "Good tidings for my lord the king! For GOD [*or* the LORD] has delivered you this day from the power of all who rose up against you." ³² The king said to the Cushite, "Is it well with the young Absalom?" And the Cushite answered, "May the enemies of my lord the king, and all who rise up against you for evil, be like Absalom." ³³ And the king was deeply moved, and went up to the chamber over the gate, and wept; and as he went, David said, "O my son Absalom, my son, my son Absalom! Would I had died instead of you, O Absalom, my son, my son!"

Psalm 102:1–12

¹ Hear my prayer, O GOD [*or* LORD];
　　let my cry come to you!
² Do not hide your face from me
　　in the day of my distress!
　Incline your ear to me;
　　answer me speedily in the day when I call!
³ For my days pass away like smoke,
　　and my bones burn like a furnace.
⁴ My heart is smitten like grass, and withered;
　　I forget to eat my bread.

⁵ Because of my loud groaning
   my bones cleave to my flesh.
⁶ I am like a vulture of the wilderness,
   like an owl of the waste places;
⁷ I lie awake,
   I am like a lonely bird on the housetop.
⁸ All the day my enemies taunt me,
   those who deride me use my name for a curse.
⁹ For I eat ashes like bread,
   and mingle tears with my drink,
¹⁰ because of your indignation and anger;
   for you have taken me up and thrown me away.
¹¹ My days are like an evening shadow;
   I wither away like grass.
¹² But you, O GOD [or LORD], are enthroned forever;
   your name endures to all generations.

Lesson 2 ～ Ephesians 5:15–20

The apostle exhorts the Ephesians always to give thanks.

¹⁵ Look carefully then how you walk, not unwisely but wisely, ¹⁶ making the most of the time, because the days are evil. ¹⁷ Therefore do not be foolish, but understand what the will of the Sovereign [or Lord] is. ¹⁸ And do not get drunk with wine, for that is debauchery; but be filled with the Spirit, ¹⁹ addressing one another in psalms and hymns and spiritual songs, singing and making melody to the Sovereign [or Lord] with all your heart, ²⁰ always and for everything giving thanks in the name of our Sovereign [or Lord] Jesus Christ to God the Father [*and Mother**].

---

*Addition to the text. See "Metaphor" and "God the Father and Mother" in the Appendix.

Jesus teaches about the living bread.

⁵¹ "I am the living bread which came down from heaven; anyone who eats of this bread will live forever; and the bread which I shall give for the life of the world is my flesh."

⁵² The religious authorities▽ then disputed among themselves, saying, "How can this man give us his flesh to eat?" ⁵³ So Jesus said to them, "Truly, truly, I say to you, unless you eat the flesh and drink the blood of the Human One,○ you have no life in you; ⁵⁴ those who eat my flesh and drink my blood have eternal life, and I will raise them up at the last day. ⁵⁵ For my flesh is food indeed, and my blood is drink indeed. ⁵⁶ Those who eat of my flesh and drink of my blood abide in me, and I in them. ⁵⁷ As the living God⊗ sent me, and I live because of God,⊗ so whoever partakes of me will live because of me. ⁵⁸ This is the bread which came down from heaven, not such as our ancestors ate and died; whoever eats this bread will live forever."

▽RSV *The Jews.* See Appendix.
○RSV *Son of man.* See Appendix.
⊗RSV v. 57a *Father;* v. 57b *the Father.* See Appendix.

PENTECOST 14

Lesson 1 ~ 2 Samuel 23:1–7

David speaks a final word about the everlasting covenant with God.

¹ Now these are the last words of David:
The oracle of David, the son of Jesse,
    the oracle of the one who was raised on high,
the anointed of the God of Jacob,
    the sweet psalmist of Israel:
² "The Spirit of GOD [[*or* the LORD]] speaks by me,
    God's word is upon my tongue.
³ The God of Israel has spoken,
    the Rock of Israel has said to me:
When one rules justly over others,
    ruling in the fear of God,
⁴ God dawns on them like the morning light,
    like the sun shining forth upon a cloudless morning,
    like rain that makes grass to sprout from the earth.
⁵ Indeed, does not my house stand so with God?
    For God has made with me an everlasting covenant,
    ordered in all things and secure.
For will God not cause to prosper
    all my help and my desire?
⁶ But the godless are all like thorns that are thrown away;
    for they cannot be taken with the hand;
⁷ but the one who touches them
    is armed with iron and the shaft of a spear,
    and they are utterly consumed with fire."

Psalm 67

¹ May God be gracious to us and bless us
    and make God's face to shine upon us,
² that your way may be known upon earth,
    your saving power among all nations.
³ Let the people praise you, O God;
    let all the people praise you!
⁴ Let the nations be glad and sing for joy,
    for you judge the people with equity
    and guide the nations upon earth.

⁵ Let the people praise you, O God;
   let all the people praise you!
⁶ The earth has yielded its increase;
   God, our God, has blessed us.
⁷ God has blessed us;
   let all the ends of the earth fear God!

Lesson 2 ～ Ephesians 5:18b–6:4[+]

Christians are taught about the mutual responsibilities of God's people.

¹⁸ Be filled with the Spirit, ¹⁹ addressing one another in psalms and hymns and spiritual songs, singing and making melody to the Sovereign [*or* Lord] with all your heart, ²⁰ always and for everything giving thanks to God the Father [*and Mother**] in the name of our Sovereign [*or* Lord] Jesus Christ.

²¹ Be subject to one another out of reverence for Christ, ²² wives to your husbands as to the Sovereign [*or* Lord]. ²³ For the husband is the head of the wife as Christ is the head of the church, the body of Christ, of which Christ is Savior. ²⁴ In the same way that the church is subject to Christ in everything, so are wives to husbands. ²⁵ Husbands, love your wives, as Christ loved the church and gave up Christ's self on its behalf, ²⁶ so as to sanctify the church, having cleansed it by the washing of water with the word, ²⁷ in order to present it to Christ in splendor, without spot or wrinkle or any such thing, that the church might be holy and without blemish. ²⁸ In the same way husbands should love their wives as their own bodies. Anyone who loves his wife loves himself. ²⁹ None ever hates their own flesh, but nourishes and cherishes it, as Christ does the church, ³⁰ for we are members of Christ's body. ³¹ "For this reason a man shall leave his father and mother and be joined to his wife, and the two shall become one flesh." ³² This mystery is a profound one, and I am saying that it refers to Christ and the church; ³³ even so, let each one of you love your wife as yourself, and let the wife see that she also respects her husband.

^{6:1} Children, obey your parents in the Sovereign [*or* Lord], for this is right. ² "Honor your father and mother" (this is the first commandment with a promise), ³ "that it may be well with you and that you may live long on the earth." ⁴ Parents, do not provoke your children to anger, but bring them up in the guidance and instruction of the Sovereign [*or* Lord].

[+]NAACL reads Eph. 5:21–33. See Appendix, p. 255.
*Addition to the text. See "Metaphor" and "God the Father and Mother" in the Appendix.

Gospel ~ John 6:55–69

The author of the Gospel of John speaks about Jesus, the bread of life.

[55] "For my flesh is food indeed, and my blood is drink indeed. [56] Those who eat of my flesh and drink of my blood abide in me, and I in them. [57] As the living God⊗ sent me, and I live because of God,⊗ so whoever partakes of me will live because of me. [58] This is the bread which came down from heaven, not such as our ancestors ate and died; whoever eats this bread will live forever." [59] This Jesus said in the synagogue, while teaching at Capernaum.

[60] Many of the disciples, when they heard it, said, "This is a hard saying; who can listen to it?" [61] But Jesus, knowing that the disciples murmured at it, said to them, "Do you take offense at this? [62] Then what if you were to see the Human One° ascending back to heaven? [63] It is the spirit that gives life, the flesh is of no avail; the words that I have spoken to you are spirit and life. [64] But there are some of you that do not believe." For Jesus knew from the first who those were that did not believe, and who it was that would betray him. [65] And Jesus said, "This is why I told you that no one can come to me unless it is granted by [God] the Father [and Mother*]."

[66] After this many of the disciples drew back and no longer went about with him. [67] Jesus said to the twelve, "Do you also wish to go away?" [68] Simon Peter answered him, "To whom shall we go? You have the words of eternal life; [69] and we have believed, and have come to know, that you are the Holy One of God."

⊗RSV v. 57a *Father;* v. 57b *the Father.* See Appendix.
°RSV *Son of man.* See Appendix.
*Addition to the text. See "Metaphor" and "God the Father and Mother" in the Appendix.

PENTECOST 15

Lesson 1 ～ 1 Kings 2:1–4, 10–12

After David's death Solomon becomes king.

¹ When David's time to die drew near, he charged Solomon his son, saying, ² "I am about to go the way of all the earth. Be strong, and show yourself courageous, ³ and keep the charge of the SOVEREIGN 〚*or* LORD〛 your God, walking in God's ways and keeping God's statutes, commandments, ordinances, and testimonies, as it is written in the law of Moses, that you may prosper in all that you do and wherever you turn; ⁴ that the word which GOD 〚*or* the LORD〛 spoke concerning me may be established: 'If your descendants take heed to their way, to walk before me in faithfulness with all their heart and with all their soul, you shall not be without a descendant on the throne of Israel.' "

¹⁰ Then David slept with his ancestors, and was buried in the city of David. ¹¹ And the time that David reigned over Israel was forty years—seven years in Hebron, and thirty-three years in Jerusalem. ¹² So Solomon sat upon the throne of David his father; and Solomon's kingdom was firmly established.

Psalm 121

¹ I lift up my eyes to the hills.
    From whence does my help come?
² My help comes from GOD 〚*or* the LORD〛,
    who made heaven and earth.
³ God will not let your foot be moved;
    the one who keeps you will not slumber;
⁴ the one who keeps Israel
    will neither slumber nor sleep.
⁵ GOD 〚*or* The LORD〛 is your keeper;
    GOD 〚*or* the LORD〛 is your shade
    on your right hand.
⁶ The sun shall not smite you by day,
    nor the moon by night.
⁷ GOD 〚*or* The LORD〛 will keep you from all evil,
    and will keep your life.
⁸ GOD 〚*or* The LORD〛 will keep
    your going out and your coming in
    from this time forth and forevermore.

Lesson 2 ~ Ephesians 6:10–20

The armor of God is sufficient for the struggle.

¹⁰ Finally, be strong in the Sovereign [[*or* Lord]] and in the strength of the Sovereign's might. ¹¹ Put on the whole armor of God, that you may be able to stand against the wiles of the devil. ¹² For we are not contending against flesh and blood, but against the principalities, against the powers, against the world rulers of this present evil age, against the spiritual hosts of wickedness in the heavenly places. ¹³ Therefore take the whole armor of God, that you may be able to withstand in the evil day, and having done all, to stand. ¹⁴ Stand therefore, having girded your loins with truth, and having put on the breastplate of righteousness, ¹⁵ and having shod your feet with the equipment of the gospel of peace; ¹⁶ besides all these, taking the shield of faith, with which you can quench all the flaming darts of the evil one. ¹⁷ And take the helmet of salvation, and the sword of the Spirit, which is the word of God. ¹⁸ Pray at all times in the Spirit, with all prayer and supplication. To that end keep alert with all perseverance, making supplications for all the saints, ¹⁹ and also for me, that utterance may be given me in opening my mouth boldly to proclaim the mystery of the gospel, ²⁰ for which I am an ambassador in chains; that I may declare it boldly, as I ought to speak.

Gospel ~ Mark 7:1–8, 14–15, 21–23

Jesus teaches about the sources of defilement.

¹ Now when the Pharisees gathered together to Jesus, with some of the scribes, who had come from Jerusalem, ² they saw that some of Jesus' disciples ate with hands defiled, that is, unwashed. ³ (For the Pharisees, and all the Jews, do not eat unless they wash their hands, observing the tradition of the elders; ⁴ and when they come from the marketplace, they do not eat unless they purify themselves; and there are many other traditions which they observe, the washing of cups and pots and vessels of bronze.) ⁵ And the Pharisees and the scribes asked Jesus, "Why do your disciples not live according to the tradition of the elders, but eat with hands defiled?" ⁶ And Jesus said to them, "Well did Isaiah prophesy of you hypocrites, as it is written,

'This people honors me with their lips,
but their heart is far from me;
⁷ in vain do they worship me,
teaching human precepts as doctrines.'

⁸ You leave the commandment of God, and hold fast human tradition."

¹⁴ And Jesus called the people to him again, and said to them, "Hear me, all of you, and understand: ¹⁵ there is nothing outside a person which by going in can defile; but the things which come out are what defile. ²¹ For from within, out of the human heart, come evil thoughts, fornication, theft, murder, adultery, ²² coveting, wickedness, deceit, licentiousness, envy, slander, pride, foolishness. ²³ All these evil things come from within, and these are what defile."

PENTECOST 16

Lesson 1 ~ Ecclesiasticus (Sirach) 5:8–15

Sirach teaches that every facet of life must be lived attentively.

⁸ Do not depend on dishonest wealth,
    for it will not benefit you in the day of calamity.
⁹ Do not winnow with every wind,
    nor follow every path:
    the double-tongued sinner does that.
¹⁰ Be steadfast in your understanding,
    and let your speech be consistent.
¹¹ Be quick to hear,
    and be deliberate in answering.
¹² If you have understanding, answer your neighbor;
    but if not, put your hand on your mouth.
¹³ Glory and dishonor come from speaking,
    and the tongue is a person's downfall.
¹⁴ Do not be called a slanderer,
    and do not lie in ambush with your tongue;
for shame comes to the thief,
    and severe condemnation to the double-tongued.
¹⁵ In great or small matters do not act amiss,
    and do not become an enemy instead of a friend.

Lesson 1 (alternate) ~ Proverbs 2:1–8

Knowledge and fear of God are reflected in the way one lives, according to Proverbs.

¹ My child, if you receive my words
    and treasure up my commandments with you,
² making your ear attentive to wisdom
    and inclining your heart to understanding;
³ yes, if you cry out for insight
    and raise your voice for understanding,
⁴ if you seek it like silver
    and search for it as for hidden treasures;
⁵ then you will understand the fear of GOD [or the LORD]
    and find the knowledge of God.

⁶ For GOD [[*or* the LORD]] gives wisdom;
    from God's mouth come knowledge and understanding;
⁷ God stores up sound wisdom for the upright
    and is a shield to those who walk in integrity,
⁸ guarding the paths of justice
    and preserving the way of God's saints.

Psalm 119:129–136

¹²⁹ Your testimonies are wonderful;
    therefore my soul keeps them.
¹³⁰ The unfolding of your words gives light;
    it imparts understanding to those who are simple.
¹³¹ With open mouth I pant,
    because I long for your commandments.
¹³² Turn to me and be gracious to me,
    as is your wont toward those who love your name.
¹³³ Keep steady my steps according to your promise,
    and let no iniquity get dominion over me.
¹³⁴ Redeem me from human oppression,
    that I may keep your precepts.
¹³⁵ Make your face shine upon your servant,
    and teach me your statutes.
¹³⁶ My eyes shed streams of tears,
    because people do not keep your law.

Lesson 2 ~ James 1:17–27

James urges the church to be hearers and doers of the word.

¹⁷ Every good endowment and every perfect gift is from above, coming down from the God⊗ of lights with whom there is no variation or shadow due to change. ¹⁸ Of God's own will were we brought forth by the word of truth that we should be a kind of firstfruits of God's creatures.

¹⁹ Know this, my beloved brothers and sisters. Let everyone be quick to hear, slow to speak, slow to anger, ²⁰ for human anger does not work the righteousness of God. ²¹ Therefore put away all filthiness and rank growth of wickedness and receive with meekness the implanted word, which is able to save your souls.

⊗RSV *Father.*

196

²² But be doers of the word, and not hearers only, deceiving yourselves. ²³ For if any are hearers of the word and not doers, they are like those who observe their natural face in a mirror; ²⁴ for they observe themselves and go away and at once forget what they were like. ²⁵ But those who look into the perfect law, the law of liberty, and persevere, being no hearers that forget but doers that act, they shall be blessed in their doing.

²⁶ If any think they are religious, and do not bridle their tongue but deceive their heart, their religion is vain. ²⁷ Religion that is pure and undefiled before God⊛ is this: to visit orphans and widows in their affliction, and to keep oneself unstained from the world.

Gospel ∼ Mark 7:31–37

Jesus heals a person who is deaf and has a speech impediment.

³¹ Then Jesus returned from the region of Tyre, and went through Sidon to the Sea of Galilee, through the region of the Decapolis. ³² And they brought to him one who was deaf and had a speech impediment; and they besought Jesus to lay his hand upon that person. ³³ And taking the person aside from the multitude privately, Jesus put his fingers into the person's ears, and spat and touched the person's tongue; ³⁴ and looking up to heaven, Jesus sighed, and said, "Ephphatha," that is, "Be opened." ³⁵ And the person's ears were opened, the tongue was released, and the person spoke plainly. ³⁶ And Jesus charged them to tell no one; but the more he charged them, the more zealously they proclaimed it. ³⁷ And they were astonished beyond measure, saying, "Jesus has done all things well, even making those who are deaf to hear and those who are mute to speak."

⊛RSV *God and the Father.* See Appendix.

PENTECOST 17

Lesson 1 ~ Proverbs 22:1–2, 8–9

The just and the unjust are repaid in kind, according to Proverbs.

¹ A good name is to be chosen rather than great riches,
and favor is better than silver or gold.
² The rich and the poor meet together;
GOD [*or* the LORD] is the maker of them all.
⁸ Those who sow injustice will reap calamity,
and the rod of their fury will fail.
⁹ Those who have a bountiful eye will be blessed,
for they share their bread with the poor.

Psalm 125

¹ Those who trust in GOD [*or* the LORD] are like Mount Zion,
which cannot be moved, but abides forever.
² As the mountains are round about Jerusalem,
so GOD [*or* the LORD] is round about God's people,
from this time forth and forevermore.
³ For the scepter of wickedness shall not rest
upon the land allotted to the righteous,
lest the righteous put forth
their hands to do wrong.
⁴ Do good, O GOD [*or* LORD], to those who are good,
and to those who are upright in their hearts!
⁵ But those who turn aside upon their crooked ways
GOD [*or* the LORD] will lead away with evildoers!
Peace be in Israel!

James teaches that faith is expressed in works.

¹ My brothers and sisters, show no partiality as you hold the faith of our Sovereign ⟦*or* Lord⟧ Jesus Christ, the Sovereign ⟦*or* Lord⟧ of glory. ² For if someone with gold rings and in fine clothing comes into your assembly, and a poor person in shabby clothing also comes in, ³ and you pay attention to the one who wears the fine clothing and say, "Have a seat here, please," while you say to the poor person, "Stand there," or, "Sit at my feet," ⁴ have you not made distinctions among yourselves, and become judges with evil thoughts? ⁵ Listen, my beloved sisters and brothers. Has not God chosen those who are poor in the world to be rich in faith and heirs of the realm☆ which God has promised to those who love God?

⁸ If you really fulfill the royal law, according to the scripture, "You shall love your neighbor as yourself," you do well. ⁹ But if you show partiality, you commit sin, and are convicted by the law as transgressors. ¹⁰ For whoever keeps the whole law but fails in one point has become guilty of all of it.

¹⁴ What does it profit, my brothers and sisters, if someone claims to have faith but has not works? Can such faith save? ¹⁵ If a brother or sister is ill-clad and in lack of daily food, ¹⁶ and one of you says to them, "Go in peace, be warmed and filled," without giving them the things needed for the body, what does it profit? ¹⁷ So faith by itself, if it has no works, is dead.

☆RSV *kingdom.* See Appendix.

Peter confesses Jesus to be the Christ, and Jesus teaches about the cost of discipleship.

²⁷ And Jesus went on with the disciples, to the villages of Caesarea Philippi; and on the way he asked them, "Who do people say that I am?" ²⁸ And they said, "John the Baptist; and others say, Elijah; and others one of the prophets." ²⁹ And Jesus asked them, "But who do you say that I am?" Peter answered, "You are the Christ." ³⁰ And Jesus charged them to tell no one.

³¹ And Jesus began to teach them that the Human One° must suffer many things, and be rejected by the elders and the chief priests and the scribes, and be killed, and after three days rise again. ³² And Jesus said this plainly. And Peter took Jesus, and began to rebuke him. ³³ But turning and seeing the disciples, Jesus rebuked Peter, and said, "Get behind me, Satan! For you are not siding with God, but with humankind."

³⁴ And Jesus called the multitude with the disciples, and said to them, "If any would come after me, let them deny themselves and take up their cross and follow me. ³⁵ For those who would save their life will lose it; and those who lose their life for my sake and the gospel's will save it. ³⁶ For what advantage is it, to gain the whole world and forfeit one's life? ³⁷ For what shall one give in return for one's life? ³⁸ For any who are ashamed of me and of my words in this adulterous and sinful generation, of them will the Human One° also be ashamed, when the Human One° comes in the glory of God⊗ with the holy angels."

°RSV *Son of man.* See Appendix.
⊗RSV *his Father.* See Appendix.

PENTECOST 18

Lesson 1 ~ Job 28:20–28

God is the source of all wisdom.

[20] Whence then comes wisdom?
And where is the place of understanding?
[21] It is hid from the eyes of all living,
and concealed from the birds of the air.
[22] Abaddon and Death say,
"We have heard a rumor of it with our ears."
[23] God understands the way to it,
and knows its place.
[24] For God looks to the ends of the earth,
and sees everything under the heavens.
[25] When God gave to the wind its weight,
and meted out the waters by measure,
[26] and made a decree for the rain,
and a way for the lightning of the thunder;
[27] then God saw it and declared it,
established it, and searched it out.
[28] And God said to every human being,
"Behold, the fear of God, that is wisdom;
and to depart from evil is understanding."

Psalm 27:1–6

[1] GOD [or The LORD] is my light and my salvation;
whom shall I fear?
GOD [or The LORD] is the stronghold of my life;
of whom shall I be afraid?
[2] When evildoers assail me,
uttering slanders against me,
my adversaries and foes,
they shall stumble and fall.
[3] Though a host encamp against me,
my heart shall not fear;
though war arise against me,
yet I will be confident.

⁴ One thing have I asked of GOD ⟦*or* the LORD⟧,
  that will I seek after;
  that I may dwell in the house of GOD ⟦*or* the LORD⟧
    all the days of my life,
  to behold the beauty of GOD ⟦*or* the LORD⟧,
    and to inquire in God's temple.
⁵ For God will hide me in a shelter
    in the day of trouble,
  and will conceal me under the cover of God's tent.
    God will set me high upon a rock.
⁶ And now my head shall be lifted up
    above my enemies round about me;
  and I will offer in God's tent
    sacrifices with shouts of joy;
  I will sing and make melody to GOD ⟦*or* the LORD⟧.

Lesson 2 ~ James 3:13–18

James writes of wisdom that comes from above.

¹³ Who is wise and understanding among you? By a good life show your works in the meekness of wisdom. ¹⁴ But if you have bitter jealousy and selfish ambition in your hearts, do not boast and be false to the truth. ¹⁵ This wisdom is not such as comes down from above, but is earthly, unspiritual, devilish. ¹⁶ For where jealousy and selfish ambition exist, there will be disorder and every vile practice. ¹⁷ But the wisdom from above is first pure, then peaceable, gentle, open to reason, full of mercy and good fruits, without uncertainty or insincerity. ¹⁸ And the harvest of righteousness is sown in peace by those who make peace.

Gospel ~ Mark 9:30-37

Jesus teaches about the meaning of discipleship.

[30] They went on from there and passed through Galilee. And Jesus would not have anyone know it; [31] for he was teaching the disciples, saying to them, "The Human One° will be delivered into the hands of human beings, and will be killed by them; and having been killed, the Human One will rise after three days." [32] But they did not understand the saying, and they were afraid to ask Jesus.

[33] And they came to Capernaum; and having entered the house, Jesus asked them, "What were you discussing on the way?" [34] But they were silent; for on the way they had discussed with one another who was the greatest. [35] And Jesus sat down and called the twelve and said to them, "Anyone who would be first must be last of all and servant of all." [36] And Jesus took a child, and put the child in the midst of them; and taking the child in his arms, Jesus said to them, [37] "Whoever receives one such child in my name receives me; and whoever receives me, receives not me but the one who sent me."

°RSV *Son of man.* See Appendix.

PENTECOST 19

Lesson 1 ~ Job 42:1–6

Job repents in the presence of God.

¹ Then Job answered GOD [*or* the LORD]:
² "I know that you can do all things,
    and that no purpose of yours can be thwarted.
³ 'Who is this that hides counsel without knowledge?'
    Therefore I have uttered what I did not understand,
        things too wonderful for me, which I did not know.
⁴ 'Hear, and I will speak;
    I will question you, and you declare to me.'
⁵ I had heard of you by the hearing of the ear,
    but now my eye sees you;
⁶ therefore I despise myself,
    and repent in dust and ashes."

Psalm 27:7–14

⁷ Hear, O GOD [*or* LORD], when I cry aloud,
    be gracious to me and answer me!
⁸ You have said, "Seek my face."
    My heart says to you,
  "Your face, GOD [*or* LORD], do I seek."
⁹   Hide not your face from me.
  Turn not your servant away in anger,
    you who have been my help.
  Cast me not off, forsake me not,
    O God of my salvation!
¹⁰ For my father and my mother have forsaken me,
    but GOD [*or* the LORD] will take me up.
¹¹ Teach me your way, O GOD [*or* LORD];
    and lead me on a level path
    because of my enemies.
¹² Give me not up to the will of my adversaries;
    for false witnesses have risen against me,
    and they breathe out violence.
¹³ I believe that I shall see the goodness of GOD [*or* the LORD]
    in the land of the living!
¹⁴ Wait for GOD [*or* the LORD];
    be strong, and let your heart take courage;
    yes, wait for GOD [*or* the LORD]!

Lesson 2 ～ James 4:13–17; 5:7–11

James writes about suffering and patience and compassion.

¹³ Come now, you who say, "Today or tomorrow we will go into such and such a town and spend a year there and trade and get gain"; ¹⁴ whereas you do not know about tomorrow. What is your life? For you are a mist that appears for a little time and then vanishes. ¹⁵ Instead you ought to say, "If the Sovereign [*or* Lord] wills, we shall live and we shall do this or that." ¹⁶ As it is, you boast in your arrogance. All such boasting is evil. ¹⁷ It is sin for a person who knows what is right to fail to do it.

⁵:⁷ Be patient, therefore, my friends, until the coming of the Sovereign [*or* Lord]. Just as the farmer waits for the precious fruit of the earth, being patient over it until it receives the early and the late rain, ⁸ so you also be patient. Establish your hearts, for the coming of the Sovereign [*or* Lord] is at hand. ⁹ Do not grumble, sisters and brothers, against one another, that you may not be judged; behold, the Judge is standing at the gates. ¹⁰ As an example of suffering and patience, friends, take the prophets who spoke in the name of the Sovereign [*or* Lord]. ¹¹ We call those happy who were steadfast. You have heard of the steadfastness of Job, and you have seen the purpose of the Sovereign [*or* Lord], how the Sovereign [*or* Lord] is compassionate and merciful.

Jesus speaks of the inclusiveness of the gospel.

³⁸ John said to Jesus, "Teacher, we saw someone casting out demons in your name, and we forbade it, because the one who did it was not following us." ³⁹ But Jesus said, "Do not forbid such a person; for no one who does a mighty work in my name will be able soon after to speak evil of me. ⁴⁰ For whoever is not against us is for us. ⁴¹ For truly, I say to you, whoever gives you a cup of water to drink because you bear the name of Christ will by no means go unrewarded.

⁴² "Whoever causes one of these little ones who believe in me to sin, it would be better to have a great millstone hung around their neck and to be thrown into the sea. ⁴³ And if your hand causes you to sin, cut it off; it is better for you to enter life maimed than with two hands to go to hell, to the unquenchable fire. ⁴⁵ And if your foot causes you to sin, cut it off; it is better for you to enter life lame than with two feet to be thrown into hell. ⁴⁷ And if your eye causes you to sin, pluck it out; it is better for you to enter the realm☆ of God with one eye than with two eyes to be thrown into hell, ⁴⁸ where their worm does not die, and the fire is not quenched. ⁴⁹ For everyone will be salted with fire. ⁵⁰ Salt is good; but if the salt has lost its saltness, how will you season it? Have salt in yourselves, and be at peace with one another."

☆RSV *kingdom.* See Appendix.

PENTECOST 20

Lesson 1 ~ Genesis 2:18–24

God creates humankind.

[18] Then the SOVEREIGN [[*or* LORD]] God said, "It is not good that the human being should be alone; I will make a companion corresponding to the human being." [19] So out of the ground the SOVEREIGN [[*or* LORD]] God formed every beast of the field and every bird of the air, and brought them to the human being to see what they would be called; and whatever the human being called every living creature, that was its name. [20] The human being gave names to all cattle, and to the birds of the air, and to every beast of the field; but a companion corresponding to the human being was not found. [21] So the SOVEREIGN [[*or* LORD]] God caused a deep sleep to fall upon the human being, and took a rib out of the human being and closed up the place with flesh; [22] and the SOVEREIGN [[*or* LORD]] God made the rib taken from that human being into a woman and brought her to the man. [23] Then the man said,

> "This at last is bone of my bones
>   and flesh of my flesh;
> she shall be called Woman,
>   because she was taken out of Man."

[24] Therefore a man leaves his father and mother and cleaves to his wife, and they become one flesh.

Psalm 128

[1] Blessed is everyone who fears GOD [[*or* the LORD]],
    who walks in God's ways!
[2] You shall eat the fruit of the labor of your hands;
    you shall be happy, and it shall be well with you.
[3] Your beloved will be like a fruitful vine
    within your house;
  your children will be like olive shoots
    around your table.
[4] Thus shall the one be blessed
    who fears GOD [[*or* the LORD]].
[5] GOD [[*or* The LORD]] bless you from Zion!
    May you see the prosperity of Jerusalem
    all the days of your life!
[6] May you see your children's children!
    Peace be upon Israel!

Lesson 2 ~ Hebrews 1:1–4; 2:9–11

God speaks to us by the one through whom God created the world.

¹ In many and various ways God spoke of old to our forebears by the prophets; ² but in these last days God has spoken to us by a Child,◊ whom God appointed the heir of all things, through whom also God created the world. ³ This Child, by whose word of power the universe is upheld, reflects the glory of God and bears the very stamp of God's nature. Having made purification for sins, the Child sat down at the right hand of the Majesty on high, ⁴ having become as much superior to angels as the name the Child has obtained is more excellent than theirs.

2:9 But we see Jesus, who for a little while was made lower than the angels, crowned with glory and honor because of the suffering of death, so that by the grace of God Jesus might taste death for everyone.

¹⁰ For it was fitting that the one for whom and by whom all things exist, in bringing many sons and daughters to glory, should make the pioneer of their salvation perfect through suffering. ¹¹ For the one who sanctifies and those who are sanctified have all one origin. That is why Jesus is not ashamed to call them brothers and sisters.

◊RSV *Son.* See Appendix.

Jesus teaches about marriage and divorce, and later Jesus blesses the children.

² And Pharisees came up and in order to test Jesus asked, "Is it lawful for a husband to divorce his wife?" ³ He answered them, "What did Moses command you?" ⁴ They said, "Moses allowed a husband to write a certificate of divorce, and to put her away." ⁵ But Jesus said to them, "For your hardness of heart Moses wrote you this commandment. ⁶ But from the beginning of creation, 'God made them male and female.' ⁷ 'For this reason a man shall leave his father and mother and be joined to his wife, ⁸ and the two shall become one flesh.' So they are no longer two but one flesh. ⁹ What therefore God has joined together, let no one put asunder."

¹⁰ And in the house the disciples asked Jesus again about this matter. ¹¹ And Jesus said to them, "Whoever divorces his wife and marries another, commits adultery against her; ¹² and if she divorces her husband and marries another, she commits adultery."

¹³ And they were bringing children to Jesus, that he might touch them; and the disciples rebuked them. ¹⁴ But when Jesus saw it he was indignant, and said to them, "Let the children come to me, do not hinder them; for to such belongs the realm☆ of God. ¹⁵ Truly, I say to you, whoever does not receive the realm☆ of God like a child shall not enter it." ¹⁶ And Jesus took the children in his arms and blessed them, laying his hands upon them.

☆RSV *kingdom.* See Appendix.

PENTECOST 21

The woman and the man created by God learn the consequences of eating the forbidden fruit.

⁸ And they heard the sound of the SOVEREIGN [*or* LORD] God walking in the garden in the cool of the day, and the man and the woman hid themselves from the presence of the SOVEREIGN [*or* LORD] God among the trees of the garden. ⁹ But the SOVEREIGN [*or* LORD] God called to the man, and said to him, "Where are you?" ¹⁰ And he said, "I heard the sound of you in the garden, and I was afraid, because I was naked; and I hid myself." ¹¹ God said, "Who told you that you were naked? Have you eaten of the tree of which I commanded you not to eat?" ¹² The man said, "The woman whom you gave to be with me, she gave me fruit of the tree, and I ate." ¹³ Then the SOVEREIGN [*or* LORD] God said to the woman, "What is this that you have done?" The woman said, "The serpent beguiled me, and I ate." ¹⁴ The SOVEREIGN [*or* LORD] God said to the serpent,

"Because you have done this,
　cursed are you above all cattle,
　and above all wild animals;
upon your belly you will go,
　and dust you will eat
　all the days of your life.
¹⁵ I will put enmity between you and the woman,
　and between your seed and her seed;
they will bruise your head,
　and you will bruise their heel."
¹⁶ To the woman God said,
"I will greatly multiply your labor in childbearing;
　in labor you will bring forth children,
yet your desire will be for your husband,
　and he will rule over you."
¹⁷ And to Adam God said,
"Because you have listened to the voice of your mate,
　and have eaten of the tree
of which I commanded you,
　'You shall not eat of it,'
cursed is the ground because of you;
　in labor you will eat of it all the days of your life;
¹⁸ thorns and thistles it will bring forth to you;
　and you will eat the plants of the field.

¹⁹ In the sweat of your face
    you will eat bread
till you return to the ground,
    for out of it you were taken;
you are dust;
    and to dust you shall return."

Psalm 90:1–12

¹ God [[*or* Lord]], you have been our dwelling place
    in all generations.
² Before the mountains were brought forth,
    or ever you had formed the earth and the world,
    from everlasting to everlasting you are God.
³ You turn people back to the dust,
    and say, "Turn back, O mortals!"
⁴ For a thousand years in your sight
    are but as yesterday when it is past,
    or as a watch in the night.
⁵ You sweep people away; they are like a dream,
    like grass which is renewed in the morning:
⁶ in the morning it flourishes and is renewed;
    in the evening it fades and withers.
⁷ For we are consumed by your anger;
    by your wrath we are overwhelmed.
⁸ You have set our iniquities before you,
    our secret sins in the light of your countenance.
⁹ For all our days pass away under your wrath,
    our years come to an end like a sigh.
¹⁰ The years of our life are threescore and ten,
    or even by reason of strength fourscore;
yet their span is but toil and trouble;
    they are soon gone, and we fly away.
¹¹ Who considers the power of your anger,
    and your wrath according to the fear of you?
¹² So teach us to number our days
    that we may get a heart of wisdom.

Lesson 2 ～ Hebrews 4:1–3, 9–13

The sabbath rest which God has prepared is not easily attained.

¹ Therefore, while the promise of entering God's rest remains, let us fear lest any of you be judged to have failed to reach it. ² For good news came to us just as to them; but the message which they heard did not benefit them, because it did not meet with faith in the hearers. ³ For we who have believed enter that rest, as God has said,

> "As I swore in my wrath,
> 'They shall never enter my rest,' "

although God's works were finished from the foundation of the world. ⁹ So then, there remains a sabbath rest for the people of God; ¹⁰ for those who enter God's rest cease from their labors as God also did.

¹¹ Let us therefore strive to enter that rest, that no one fall by the same sort of disobedience. ¹² For the word of God is living and active, sharper than any two-edged sword, piercing to the division of soul and spirit, of joints and marrow, and discerning the thoughts and intentions of the heart. ¹³ And before God no creature is hidden, but all are open and laid bare to the eyes of the one with whom we have to do.

Gospel ～ Mark 10:17–30

Jesus teaches about wealth and eternal life.

¹⁷ And as Jesus was setting out on a journey, someone ran up and knelt before him, and asked, "Good Teacher, what must I do to inherit eternal life?" ¹⁸ And Jesus said, "Why do you call me good? No one is good but God alone. ¹⁹ You know the commandments: 'Do not kill, Do not commit adultery, Do not steal, Do not bear false witness, Do not defraud, Honor your father and mother.' " ²⁰ And the questioner said to Jesus, "Teacher, all these I have observed from my youth." ²¹ And Jesus looked upon the questioner with love and said, "You lack one thing; go, sell what you have, and give to the poor, and you will have treasure in heaven; and come, follow me." ²² Dismayed by this word, the person went away sorrowful because of having great possessions.

²³ And Jesus looked around and said to the disciples, "How hard it will be for those who have riches to enter the realm☆ of God!" ²⁴ And the disciples were amazed at Jesus' words. But Jesus said to them again, "Children, how hard it is to enter the realm☆ of God! ²⁵ It is easier for a camel to go through the eye of a needle than for a rich person to enter the realm☆ of God." ²⁶ And

---

☆RSV *kingdom.* See Appendix.

they were exceedingly astonished, and said to Jesus, "Then who can be saved?" 27 Jesus looked at the disciples and said, "With human beings it is impossible, but not with God; for all things are possible with God." 28 Peter began to say to Jesus, "Indeed, we have left everything and followed you." 29 Jesus said, "Truly, I say to you, there is no one who has left house or brothers or sisters or mother or father or children or lands, for my sake and for the gospel, 30 who will not receive a hundredfold now in this time, houses and brothers and sisters and mothers and children and lands, with persecutions, and in the age to come eternal life."

PENTECOST 22

Isaiah writes of the Suffering Servant.

⁷ The servant was oppressed, and was afflicted,
   yet did not say a word;
  like a lamb that is led to the slaughter,
    and like a ewe that before her shearers is dumb,
   the servant did not say a word.
⁸ By oppression and judgment the servant was taken away;
    and as for that one's generation, who considered
  that the servant was cut off out of the land of the living,
    stricken for the transgression of my people?
⁹ Although the servant had done no violence
    and had spoken no deceit,
  the servant was buried with the wicked,
    and with the rich in death.
¹⁰ Yet it was the will of GOD ⟦*or* the LORD⟧ to bruise
    and put to grief this one,
  who, after choosing to become an offering for sin,
    shall see offspring, and enjoy long life;
  the will of GOD ⟦*or* the LORD⟧ shall prosper in the servant's hand;
¹¹   my servant shall see the fruit of the soul's travail and be satisfied;
  by knowledge shall the righteous one, my servant,
    make many to be accounted righteous,
    and shall bear their iniquities.
¹² Therefore I will divide for this one a portion with the great,
    and my servant shall divide the spoil with the strong,
  because my servant poured out life and died,
    and was numbered with the transgressors,
  yet bore the sin of many,
    and made intercession for the transgressors.

¹⁷ How long, O God [or Lord], will you look on?
    Rescue me from their ravages,
    my life from the lions!
¹⁸ Then I will thank you in the great congregation;
    in the mighty throng I will praise you.
¹⁹ Let not those rejoice over me
    who are wrongfully my foes,
  and let not those wink the eye
    who hate me without cause.
²⁰ For they do not speak peace,
    but against those who are quiet in the land
    they conceive words of deceit.
²¹ They open wide their mouths against me;
    they say, "Aha, Aha!
    our eyes have seen it!"
²² You have seen, O GOD [or LORD]; be not silent!
    O God [or Lord], be not far from me!
²³ Bestir yourself, and awake for my right,
    for my cause, my God and my Sovereign [or Lord]!
²⁴ Vindicate me, O SOVEREIGN [or LORD], my God,
    according to your righteousness;
    and let them not rejoice over me!
²⁵ Let them not say to themselves,
    "Aha, we have our heart's desire!"
  Let them not say, "We have swallowed that one up."
²⁶ Let them be put to shame and confusion altogether
    who rejoice at my calamity!
  Let them be clothed with shame and dishonor
    who magnify themselves against me!
²⁷ Let those who desire my vindication
    shout for joy and be glad,
    and say evermore,
  "Great is GOD [or the LORD],
    who delights in the welfare of God's servant!"
²⁸ Then my tongue shall tell of your righteousness
    and of your praise all the day long.

Lesson 2 ～ Hebrews 4:14–16

Jesus, the great high priest, learns obedience through suffering.

[14] Since then we have a great high priest who has passed through the heavens, Jesus, the Child◇ of God, let us hold fast our confession. [15] For we have not a high priest who is unable to sympathize with our weaknesses, but one who in every respect has been tempted as we are, yet without sin. [16] Let us then with confidence draw near to the throne of grace, that we may receive mercy and find grace to help in time of need.

Gospel ～ Mark 10:35–45

Jesus answers James and John about greatness in the realm of God.

[35] And James and John, the sons of Zebedee, came forward to Jesus, and said, "Teacher, we want you to do for us whatever we ask of you." [36] And Jesus said to them, "What do you want me to do for you?" [37] And they said, "Grant us to sit, one at your right hand and one at your left, in your glory." [38] But Jesus said to them, "You do not know what you are asking. Are you able to drink the cup that I drink, or to be baptized with the baptism with which I am baptized?" [39] And they said to Jesus, "We are able." And Jesus said to them, "The cup that I drink you will drink; and with the baptism with which I am baptized, you will be baptized; [40] but to sit at my right hand or at my left is not mine to grant, but it is for those for whom it has been prepared." [41] And when the ten heard it, they began to be indignant at James and John. [42] And Jesus called them to him and said, "You know that those who are supposed to rule over the Gentiles lord it over them, and their great leaders exercise authority over them. [43] But it shall not be so among you; but whoever would be great among you must be your servant, [44] and whoever would be first among you must be slave of all. [45] For the Human One○ also came not to be served but to serve, and to give up life as a ransom for many."

◇RSV *Son.* See Appendix.
○RSV *Son of man.* See Appendix.

PENTECOST 23

Lesson 1 ～ Jeremiah 31:7–9

Jeremiah announces God's redemption of the remnant of Israel.

⁷ For thus says the SOVEREIGN [*or* LORD]:
"Sing aloud with gladness for Jacob,
    and raise shouts for the chief of the nations;
proclaim, give praise, and say,
    'GOD [*or* The LORD] has saved the people,
    the remnant of Israel.'
⁸ I will bring them from the north country,
    and gather them from the farthest parts of the earth,
among them those who are blind and those who are lame,
    the woman with child and the woman in travail, together;
a great company, they shall return here.
⁹ With weeping they shall come,
    and with consolations I will lead them back,
I will make them walk by brooks of water,
    in a straight path in which they shall not stumble;
for I am a father [*and a mother**] to Israel,
    and Ephraim is my firstborn."

Psalm 126

¹ When GOD [*or* the LORD] restored the fortunes of Zion,
    we were like those who dream.
² Then our mouth was filled with laughter,
    and our tongue with shouts of joy;
then they said among the nations,
    "GOD [*or* The LORD] has done great things for them."
³ GOD [*or* The LORD] has done great things for us;
    we are glad.
⁴ Restore our fortunes, O GOD [*or* LORD],
    like the watercourses in the Negeb!
⁵ May those who sow in tears
    reap with shouts of joy!
⁶ Those who go forth weeping,
    bearing the seed for sowing,
shall come home with shouts of joy,
    bringing their sheaves of grain.

---

*Addition to the text. See "Metaphor" and "God the Father and Mother" in the Appendix.

Lesson 2 ~ Hebrews 5:1–6

The author interprets the meaning of Jesus' high priesthood.

¹ For every high priest chosen from among human beings is appointed to act on their behalf in relation to God, to offer gifts and sacrifices for sins. ² A high priest can deal gently with the ignorant and wayward, since a high priest is also beset with weakness. ³ Because of this, high priests are bound to offer sacrifice for their own sins as well as for those of the people. ⁴ And one does not take the honor upon one's self, but is called by God, just as Aaron was.

⁵ So also Christ did not claim the exalted office of high priest, but was appointed to it by the one who said,

"You are my Child,◊
today I have begotten you";
⁶ as is said also in another place,
"You are a priest forever,
after the order of Melchizedek."

Gospel ~ Mark 10:46–52

Jesus heals the blind beggar Bartimaeus.

⁴⁶ And they came to Jericho; and as Jesus was leaving Jericho with the disciples and a great multitude, Bartimaeus, a blind beggar, the son of Timaeus, was sitting by the roadside. ⁴⁷ And hearing that it was Jesus of Nazareth, Bartimaeus began to cry out and say, "Jesus, Son of David, have mercy on me!" ⁴⁸ And many rebuked Bartimaeus, telling him to be silent; but he cried out all the more, "Son of David, have mercy on me!" ⁴⁹ And Jesus stopped and said, "Call him." And they called him, saying, "Take heart; rise, Jesus is calling you." ⁵⁰ And throwing off his mantle, Bartimaeus sprang up and came to Jesus. ⁵¹ And Jesus said to him, "What do you want me to do for you?" And he replied, "Teacher, let me receive my sight." ⁵² And Jesus said, "Go your way; your faith has made you well." And immediately Bartimaeus received his sight and followed Jesus on the way.

◊RSV *Son.* See Appendix.

218

PENTECOST 24

Lesson 1 ~ Deuteronomy 6:1–9

Moses teaches Israel the commandments of God.

¹ Now this is the commandment, the statutes and the ordinances which the SOVEREIGN [or LORD] your God commanded me to teach you, that you may do them in the land to which you are going over, to possess it; ² that you may fear the SOVEREIGN [or LORD] your God, you and your children and your children's children, by keeping all God's statutes and commandments, which I command you, all the days of your life; and that your days may be prolonged. ³ Hear therefore, O Israel, and be careful to do them; that it may go well with you, and that you may multiply greatly, as the SOVEREIGN [or LORD], the God of your ancestors, has promised you, in a land flowing with milk and honey.

⁴ Hear, O Israel: The SOVEREIGN [or LORD] is our God, the SOVEREIGN [or LORD] alone; ⁵ and you shall love the SOVEREIGN [or LORD] your God with all your heart, and with all your soul, and with all your might. ⁶ And these words which I command you this day shall be upon your heart; ⁷ and you shall teach them diligently to your children, and shall talk of them when you sit in your house, and when you walk by the way, and when you lie down, and when you rise. ⁸ And you shall bind them as a sign upon your hand, and they shall be as frontlets between your eyes. ⁹ And you shall write them on the doorposts of your house and on your gates.

Psalm 119:33–48

³³ Teach me, O GOD [or LORD], the way of your statutes;
   and I will keep it to the end.
³⁴ Give me understanding, that I may keep your law
   and observe it with my whole heart.
³⁵ Lead me in the path of your commandments,
   for I delight in it.
³⁶ Incline my heart to your testimonies,
   and not to gain!
³⁷ Turn my eyes from looking at vanities;
   and give me life in your ways.
³⁸ Confirm to your servant your promise,
   which is for those who fear you.
³⁹ Turn away the reproach which I dread;
   for your ordinances are good.

⁴⁰ I long for your precepts;
    in your righteousness give me life!
⁴¹ Let your steadfast love come to me, O GOD [[*or* LORD]],
    your salvation according to your promise;
⁴² then I shall have an answer for those who taunt me,
    for I trust in your word.
⁴³ And take not the word of truth utterly out of my mouth,
    for my hope is in your ordinances.
⁴⁴ I will keep your law continually,
    forever and ever;
⁴⁵ and I shall walk at liberty,
    for I have sought your precepts.
⁴⁶ I will also speak of your testimonies before rulers,□
    and shall not be put to shame;
⁴⁷ for I find my delight in your commandments,
    which I love.
⁴⁸ I revere your commandments, which I love,
    and I will meditate on your statutes.

Lesson 2 ～ Hebrews 7:23–28

Jesus' sacrifice is contrasted with sacrifices made by human high priests.

²³ The former priests were many in number, because they were prevented by death from continuing in office; ²⁴ but Jesus, who continues forever, holds the priesthood permanently, ²⁵ and so is able for all time to save those who draw near to God through Jesus, who always lives to make intercession for them.

²⁶ For it was fitting that we should have such a high priest, holy, blameless, unstained, separated from sinners, exalted above the heavens. ²⁷ Jesus has no need, like those high priests, to offer sacrifices daily, first for their own sins and then for those of the people; Jesus did this once for all, having offered up Jesus' own self. ²⁸ Indeed, the law appoints human beings in their weakness as high priests, but the word of the oath, which came later than the law, appoints a Child° who has been made perfect forever.

□RSV *kings.* See Appendix.
°RSV *Son.* See Appendix.

Jesus interprets the first and second commandments.

²⁸ One of the scribes came up and heard them disputing with one another, and seeing that Jesus answered them well, asked, "Which commandment is the first of all?" ²⁹ Jesus answered, "The first is, 'Hear, O Israel: The Sovereign [*or* Lord] our God, the Sovereign [*or* Lord] is one; ³⁰ and you shall love the Sovereign [*or* Lord] your God with all your heart, and with all your soul, and with all your mind, and with all your strength.' ³¹ The second is this, 'You shall love your neighbor as yourself.' There is no other commandment greater than these." ³² And the scribe said to Jesus, "You are right, Teacher; you have truly said that God is one, and there is no other but God; ³³ and to love God with all the heart, and with all the understanding, and with all the strength, and to love one's neighbor as oneself, is much more than all whole burnt offerings and sacrifices." ³⁴ And when Jesus saw that the scribe answered wisely, Jesus said to him, "You are not far from the realm☆ of God." And after that no one dared to ask Jesus any question.

☆RSV *kingdom.* See Appendix.

PENTECOST 25

Lesson 1 ~ 1 Kings 17:8–16

The widow from Zarephath ministers to Elijah.

⁸ Then the word of GOD [*or* the LORD] came to Elijah, ⁹ "Arise, go to Zarephath, which belongs to Sidon, and dwell there. I have commanded a widow there to feed you." ¹⁰ So Elijah arose and went to Zarephath; and when he came to the gate of the city, a widow was there gathering sticks; and Elijah called to her and said, "Bring me a little water in a vessel, that I may drink." ¹¹ And as she was going to bring it, he called to her and said, "Bring me a morsel of bread in your hand." ¹² And she said, "As the SOVER-EIGN [*or* LORD] your God lives, I have nothing baked, only a handful of meal in a jar and a little oil in a cruse; and now, I am gathering a couple of sticks, that I may go in and prepare it for myself and my child, that we may eat it, and die." ¹³ And Elijah said to her, "Fear not; go and do as you have said; but first make me a little cake of it and bring it to me, and afterward make for yourself and your child. ¹⁴ For thus says the SOVEREIGN [*or* LORD] the God of Israel, 'The jar of meal shall not be spent, and the cruse of oil shall not fail, until the day that GOD [*or* the LORD] sends rain upon the earth.'" ¹⁵ And she went and did as Elijah said; and she, and he, and her household ate for many days. ¹⁶ The jar of meal was not spent, neither did the cruse of oil fail, according to the word of GOD [*or* the LORD] which God spoke by Elijah.

Psalm 146

¹ Praise GOD [*or* the LORD]!
  Praise GOD [*or* the LORD], O my soul!
² I will praise GOD [*or* the LORD] as long as I live;
  I will sing praises to my God while I have being.
³ Put not your trust in rulers,
  in mortals, in whom there is no help.
⁴ When their breath departs they return to their earth;
  on that very day their plans perish.
⁵ Happy is the one whose help is the God of Jacob,
  whose hope is in God, the SOVEREIGN [*or* LORD],
⁶ who made heaven and earth,
  the sea, and all that is in them;
  who keeps faith forever;

7   who executes justice for the oppressed;
    who gives food to the hungry.
  GOD [or The LORD] sets the prisoners free;
8   GOD [or the LORD] opens the eyes of those who are blind.
  GOD [or The LORD] lifts up those who are bowed down;
    GOD [or the LORD] loves the righteous.
9 GOD [or The LORD] watches over the sojourners,
    and upholds the widow and the orphan,
    but brings the way of the wicked to ruin.
10 GOD [or The LORD] will reign forever,
    your God, O Zion, to all generations.
  Praise GOD [or the LORD]!

Lesson 2 ～ Hebrews 9:24–28

Christ, who will appear a second time, has offered a single sacrifice for sin.

24 For Christ has entered, not into a sanctuary made with hands, a copy of the true one, but into heaven itself, now to appear in the presence of God on our behalf. 25 Nor was it to offer Christ's self repeatedly, as the high priest enters the Holy Place yearly with the blood of another; 26 for then Christ would have had to suffer repeatedly since the foundation of the world. But as it is, Christ has appeared once for all at the end of the age to put away sin through Christ's sacrifice. 27 And just as it is appointed for human beings to die once, and after that comes judgment, 28 so Christ, having been offered once to bear the sins of many, will appear a second time, not to deal with sin but to save those who are eagerly waiting for Christ.

Gospel ～ Mark 12:38–44

Jesus praises a poor widow for her offering.

38 And in his teaching Jesus said, "Beware of the scribes, who like to go about in long robes, and to have salutations in the marketplaces 39 and the best seats in the synagogues and the places of honor at feasts, 40 who devour widows' houses and for a pretense make long prayers. They will receive the greater condemnation."

41 And Jesus sat down opposite the treasury, and watched the multitude putting money into the treasury. Many rich people put in large sums. 42 And a poor widow came, and put in two copper coins, which make a penny. 43 And Jesus called the disciples, and said to them, "Truly, I say to you, this poor widow has put in more than all those who are contributing to the treasury. 44 For they all contributed out of their abundance; but she out of her poverty has put in everything she had, her whole living."

PENTECOST 26

Lesson 1 ～ Daniel 7:9–14

One like a human being comes to the Ancient of Days.

⁹ As I looked,
   thrones were placed
      and one that was ancient of days sat down,
   whose raiment was white as snow,
      and whose hair was like pure wool;
   whose throne was fiery flames,
      its wheels were burning fire.
¹⁰ A stream of fire issued
      and came forth from before the ancient of days,
   who was served by a thousand thousands,
      and before whom stood ten thousand times ten thousand;
   the court sat in judgment,
      and the books were opened.

¹¹ I looked then because of the sound of the great words which the horn was speaking. And as I looked, the beast was slain, and its body destroyed and given over to be burned with fire. ¹² As for the rest of the beasts, their dominion was taken away, but their lives were prolonged for a season and a time.

¹³ I saw in the night visions,
   and behold, with the clouds of heaven
      there came one like a human being,°
   who came to the Ancient of Days
      and was presented before the Ancient of Days.
¹⁴ And to that one was given dominion
      and glory and sovereignty,☆
   that all peoples, nations, and languages
      should serve that one,
   whose dominion is an everlasting dominion,
      which shall not pass away,
   and whose realm☆ is one
      that shall not be destroyed.

°RSV *a son of man.* See Appendix.
☆RSV *kingdom.* See Appendix.

Psalm 145:8–13

⁸ GOD [*or* The LORD] is gracious and merciful,
    slow to anger and abounding in steadfast love.
⁹ GOD [*or* The LORD] is good to all,
    and has compassion over all that God has made.
¹⁰ All your works shall give thanks to you, O GOD [*or* LORD],
    and all your saints shall bless you!
¹¹ They shall speak of the glory of your realm,☆
    and tell of your power,
¹² to make known to humankind your mighty deeds,
    and the glorious splendor of your realm.☆
¹³ Your realm☆ is an everlasting realm,☆
    and your dominion endures throughout all generations.

Lesson 2 ～ Hebrews 10:11–18

Jesus the high priest offered a single sacrifice for sins.

¹¹ And every priest stands daily at services, offering repeatedly the same sacrifices, which can never take away sins. ¹² But this one, having offered for all time a single sacrifice for sins, sat down at the right hand of God, ¹³ then to wait until all enemies should be made a stool for Christ's feet. ¹⁴ For by a single offering Christ has perfected for all time those who are sanctified. ¹⁵ And the Holy Spirit also bears witness to us; for after saying,

¹⁶ "This is the covenant that I will make with them
    after those days, says the Sovereign [*or* Lord],
    I will put my laws on their hearts, and write them on their minds,"
¹⁷ then it is added,

    "I will remember their sins and their misdeeds no more."
¹⁸ Where there is forgiveness of these, there is no longer any offering for sin.

☆RSV *kingdom.* See Appendix.

Jesus speaks of the days when the Human One will come.

24 But in those days, after that tribulation, the sun will be darkened, and the moon will not give its light, 25 and the stars will be falling from heaven, and the powers in the heavens will be shaken. 26 And then they will see the Human One° coming in clouds with great power and glory. 27 And then the Human One will send out the angels, and gather the elect from the four winds, from the ends of the earth to the ends of heaven.

28 From the fig tree learn its lesson: as soon as its branch becomes tender and puts forth its leaves, you know that summer is near. 29 So also, when you see these things taking place, you know that the Human One is near, at the very gates. 30 Truly, I say to you, this generation will not pass away before all these things take place. 31 Heaven and earth will pass away, but my words will not pass away.

32 But of that day or that hour no one knows, not even the angels in heaven, nor the Child,◇ but only God.⊗

°RSV *Son of man.* See Appendix.
◇RSV *Son.* See Appendix.
⊗RSV *the Father.* See Appendix.

PENTECOST 27

Lesson 1 ~ Jeremiah 23:1–6

Jeremiah announces God's promise of a righteous ruler.

¹ "Woe to the shepherds who destroy and scatter the sheep of my pasture!" says the SOVEREIGN [*or* LORD]. ² Therefore thus says the SOVEREIGN [*or* LORD], the God of Israel, concerning the shepherds who care for my people: "You have scattered my flock, and have driven them away, and you have not attended to them. Behold, I will attend to you for your evil doings, says the SOVEREIGN [*or* LORD]. ³ Then I will gather the remnant of my flock out of all the countries where I have driven them, and I will bring them back to their fold, and they shall be fruitful and multiply. ⁴ I will set shepherds over them who will care for them, and they shall fear no more, nor be dismayed, neither shall any be missing, says the SOVEREIGN [*or* LORD].

⁵ "Behold, the days are coming, says the SOVEREIGN [*or* LORD], when I will raise up for David a righteous Branch, who shall reign as ruler⬚ and deal wisely, and shall execute justice and righteousness in the land. ⁶ In those days Judah will be saved, and Israel will dwell securely. And this is the name by which the Branch will be called: 'GOD [*or* The LORD] is our righteousness.' "

Psalm 93

¹ GOD [*or* The LORD] reigns, robed in majesty;
    GOD [*or* the LORD] is robed, and girded with strength.
  The world is established; it shall never be moved;
²   your throne is established from of old;
    you are from everlasting.
³ The floods have lifted up, O GOD [*or* LORD],
    the floods have lifted up their voice,
    the floods lift up their roaring.
⁴ Mightier than the thunders of many waters,
    mightier than the waves of the sea,
    GOD [*or* the LORD] on high is mighty!
⁵ Your decrees are very sure;
    holiness befits your house,
    O GOD [*or* LORD], forevermore.

⬚RSV *king.* See Appendix.

227

Lesson 2 ∼ Revelation 1:4b–8

John addresses the seven churches in the province of Asia.

⁴ Grace to you and peace from the one who is and who was and who is to come, and from the seven spirits who are before the throne, ⁵ and from Jesus Christ the faithful witness, the firstborn of the dead, and the ruler of kings on earth.

To the one who loves us and freed us from our sins by a blood sacrifice ⁶ and has made us a nation☆ and priests to God, Jesus' Father [*and Mother**], to whom be glory and dominion forever and ever. Amen. ⁷ That very one is coming with the clouds, and will be seen by every eye, by those who pierced that one, and on account of whom all tribes of the earth will wail. Even so. Amen.

⁸ "I am the Alpha and the Omega," says the Sovereign ⟦*or* Lord⟧ God, who is and who was and who is to come, the Almighty.

Gospel ∼ John 18:33–37

Pilate learns the nature of Jesus' authority.

³³ Pilate entered the praetorium again and called Jesus, and said, "Are you the King of the Jews?" ³⁴ Jesus answered, "Do you say this of your own accord, or did others say it to you about me?" ³⁵ Pilate answered, "Am I one of you?⊕ Your own nation and the chief priests have handed you over to me; what have you done?" ³⁶ Jesus answered, "My dominion☆ is not of this world; if my dominion☆ were of this world, my servants would fight, that I might not be handed over to the religious authorities;▽ but my dominion☆ is not from the world." ³⁷ Pilate said to Jesus, "So you are a king?" Jesus answered, "You say that I am a king. For this I was born, and for this I have come into the world, to bear witness to the truth. Everyone who is of the truth hears my voice."

☆RSV Rev. 1:6 *kingdom;* John 18:36 *kingship.* See Appendix.
*Addition to the text. RSV *priests to his God and Father.* See "Metaphor" and "God the Father and Mother" in the Appendix.
⊕RSV *"Am I a Jew?"*
▽RSV *the Jews.* See Appendix.

PRESENTATION—FEBRUARY 2

Lesson 1 ~ Malachi 3:1–4

The messenger goes before God to bring judgment to the people.

¹ I am sending my messenger to prepare the way before me, and God [*or* the Lord] whom you seek will suddenly come to the temple; the messenger of the covenant in whom you delight—that one is coming, says the GOD [*or* LORD] of hosts. ² But who can endure the day of that coming, and who can stand when the messenger appears?

For my messenger is like a refiner's fire and like launderers' bleach, ³ who will sit as a refiner and purifier of silver, and will purify the tribe of Levi and refine them like gold and silver, till they present right offerings to GOD [*or* the LORD]. ⁴ Then the offering of Judah and Jerusalem will be pleasing to GOD [*or* the LORD] as in the days of old and as in former years.

Psalm 84

¹ How lovely is your dwelling place,
  O GOD [*or* LORD] of hosts!
² My soul longs, even faints
  for the courts of GOD [*or* the LORD];
 my heart and flesh sing for joy
  to the living God.
³ Even the sparrow finds a home,
  and the swallow a nest for herself,
  where she may lay her young,
 at your altars, O GOD [*or* LORD] of hosts,
  my Ruler□ and my God.
⁴ Blessed are those who dwell in your house,
  ever singing your praise!
⁵ Blessed are those whose strength is in you,
  in whose heart are the highways to Zion.
⁶ As they go through the valley of Baca
  they make it a place of springs;
  the early rain also covers it with pools.
⁷ They go from strength to strength;
  the God of gods will be seen in Zion.
⁸ O SOVEREIGN [*or* LORD] God of hosts, hear my prayer;
  give ear, O God of Jacob!

□RSV *King.* See Appendix.

⁹ Behold our shield, O God;
   look upon the face of your anointed!
¹⁰ For a day in your courts is better
   than a thousand elsewhere.
  I would rather be a doorkeeper in the house of my God
   than dwell in the tents of wickedness.
¹¹ For the SOVEREIGN [*or* LORD] God is a sun and shield,
   who bestows favor and honor.
  No good thing does GOD [*or* the LORD] withhold
   from those who walk uprightly.
¹² O GOD [*or* LORD] of hosts,
   blessed is the one who trusts in you!

Psalm 24:7–10 (alternate)

⁷ Lift up your heads, O gates!
   and be lifted up, O ancient doors!
   that the Ruler☐ of glory may come in.
⁸ Who is the Ruler☐ of glory?
   GOD [*or* The LORD], strong and mighty,
   GOD [*or* the LORD], mighty in battle!
⁹ Lift up your heads, O gates!
   and be lifted up, O ancient doors!
   that the Ruler☐ of glory may come in.
¹⁰ Who is this Ruler☐ of glory?
   The GOD [*or* LORD] of hosts,
   that one is the Ruler☐ of glory!

☐RSV *King.* See Appendix.

230

Lesson 2 ∼ Hebrews 2:14–18

Jesus, by becoming a human being, delivers the people by making expiation for their sins.

¹⁴ Since therefore the children share in flesh and blood, Jesus likewise partook of the same nature in order to destroy through death the one who has the power of death, that is, the devil, ¹⁵ and to deliver all those who through fear of death were subject to lifelong bondage. ¹⁶ For surely it is not with angels that Jesus is concerned but with the descendants of Abraham [*and Sarah* *]. ¹⁷ Therefore Jesus had to be made like human beings in every respect, in order to become a merciful and faithful high priest in the service of God, to make expiation for the sins of the people. ¹⁸ For because Jesus also has suffered and been tempted, Jesus is able to help those who are tempted.

Gospel ∼ Luke 2:22–40

Mary and Joseph take the infant Jesus to the temple in Jerusalem, and the child is met there by Simeon and Anna.

²² And when the time came for their purification according to the law of Moses, they brought the child Jesus up to Jerusalem to be presented to God [*or* the Lord] ²³ (as it is written in the law of God [*or* the Lord], "Every male that opens the womb shall be called holy to God [*or* the Lord]"), ²⁴ and to offer a sacrifice according to what is said in the law of God [*or* the Lord], "a pair of turtledoves, or two young pigeons." ²⁵ Now there was a man in Jerusalem, whose name was Simeon, who was righteous and devout, looking for the consolation of Israel, and the Holy Spirit was upon him. ²⁶ And it had been revealed to Simeon by the Holy Spirit that he should not see death before he had seen the Christ of God [*or* the Lord]. ²⁷ And inspired by the Spirit, Simeon came into the temple; and when the parents brought in the child Jesus, to do for him according to the custom of the law, ²⁸ Simeon took the child in his arms and blessed God and said,

²⁹ "Sovereign [*or* Lord], now let your servant depart in peace,
    according to your word;
³⁰ for my eyes have seen your salvation
³¹ which you have prepared in the presence of all people,
³² a light for revelation to the Gentiles,
    and for glory to your people Israel."

---

*Addition to the text. See "Addition of Women's Names to the Text" in the Appendix.

³³ And the father and mother of Jesus marveled at what was said about their child; ³⁴ and Simeon blessed them and said to Mary, Jesus' mother,

"This child is set for the fall and rising of many in Israel,
and for a sign that is spoken against
³⁵ (and a sword will pierce through your own soul also),
that thoughts out of many hearts may be revealed."

³⁶ And there was a prophet, Anna, the daughter of Phanuel, of the tribe of Asher; she was of a great age, having lived with her husband seven years, ³⁷ and as a widow till she was eighty-four. She did not depart from the temple, worshiping with fasting and prayer night and day. ³⁸ And coming up at that very hour she gave thanks to God, and spoke about the child to all who were looking for the redemption of Jerusalem.

³⁹ And when Mary and Joseph had performed everything according to the law of God [*or* the Lord], they returned into Galilee, to their own city, Nazareth. ⁴⁰ And the child grew and became strong, filled with wisdom; and the favor of God was upon the child.

ANNUNCIATION—MARCH 25

Lesson 1 ~ Isaiah 7:10–14

Isaiah brings a word of assurance from God to Ahaz, ruler of Judah, in the face of a threat from the rulers of Syria.

[10] Again GOD [*or* the LORD] spoke to Ahaz, [11] "Ask a sign of the SOVEREIGN [*or* LORD] your God; let it be deep as Sheol or high as heaven." [12] But Ahaz said, "I will not ask, and I will not put GOD [*or* the LORD] to the test." [13] And Isaiah said, "Hear then, O house of David! Is it too little for you to weary human beings, that you weary my God also? [14] Therefore God [*or* the Lord] will give you a sign: a young woman shall conceive and bear a child, whom she shall call Immanuel."

Psalm 40:6–10[+]

[6] Sacrifice and offering you do not desire;
  but you have given me an open ear.
 Burnt offering and sin offering
  you have not required.
[7] Then I said, "I am coming;
  in the scroll of the book it is written of me;
[8] I delight to do your will, O my God;
  your law is within my heart."
[9] I have told the glad news of deliverance
  in the great congregation;
 I have not restrained my lips,
  as you know, O GOD [*or* LORD].
[10] I have not hid your saving help within my heart,
  I have spoken of your faithfulness and your salvation;
 I have not concealed your steadfast love and your faithfulness
  from the great congregation.

Lesson 2 ~ Hebrews 10:4–10

Jesus Christ, the high priest, is the single sacrifice for sins.

[4] For it is impossible that the blood of bulls and goats should take away sins.
 [5] Consequently, Christ, having come into the world, said,

"Sacrifices and offerings you have not desired,
 but a body you have prepared for me;

[+]Alternate Ps. 45 not included. See Appendix, p. 255.

⁶ in burnt offerings and sin offerings you have taken no pleasure.
⁷ Then I said, 'I have come to do your will, O God,'
  as it is written of me in the scroll of the book."

⁸ When Christ said above, "You have neither desired nor taken pleasure in sacrifices and offerings and burnt offerings and sin offerings" (these are offered according to the law), ⁹ then Christ added, "I have come to do your will." Christ abolishes the first in order to establish the second. ¹⁰ And by that will we have been sanctified through the offering of the body of Jesus Christ once for all.

Gospel ~ Luke 1:26–38

The angel Gabriel announces to Mary that she will bear the child of God.

²⁶ In the sixth month the angel Gabriel was sent from God to a city of Galilee named Nazareth, ²⁷ to a virgin betrothed to a man whose name was Joseph, of the house of David; and her name was Mary. ²⁸ And the angel came to her and said, "Hail, O favored one, God [[*or* the Lord]] is with you!" ²⁹ But she was greatly troubled at the saying, and considered in her mind what sort of greeting this might be. ³⁰ And the angel said to her, "Do not be afraid, Mary, for you have found favor with God. ³¹ You will conceive in your womb and bear a child, whose name you shall call Jesus.

³² This one will be great, and will be called the Child◇ of the Most
  High;
  and the Sovereign [[*or* Lord]] God will give to that Child the throne
    of David, the ancestor of the Child,
³³ to reign over the house of Jacob forever;
  and of that reign☆ there will be no end."

³⁴ And Mary said to the angel, "How shall this be, since I have no husband?" ³⁵ And the angel said to her,

  "The Holy Spirit will come upon you,
  and the power of the Most High will overshadow you;
  therefore the child to be born will be called holy,
  the Child◇ of God.

³⁶ And your kinswoman Elizabeth in her old age has also conceived a child; and this is the sixth month with her who was called barren. ³⁷ For with God nothing will be impossible." ³⁸ And Mary said, "I am the servant of God [[*or* the Lord]]; let it be to me according to your word." And the angel departed from her.

◇RSV *Son.* See Appendix.
☆RSV *his kingdom.* See Appendix.

VISITATION—MAY 31

Lesson 1 ~ 1 Samuel 2:1–10

Hannah offers a prayer to God.

¹ Hannah also prayed and said,
   "My heart exults in GOD [*or* the LORD];
      my strength is exalted in GOD [*or* the LORD].
   My mouth derides my enemies,
      because I rejoice in your salvation.
² There is none holy like GOD [*or* the LORD],
      there is none besides you;
      there is no rock like our God.
³ Talk no more so very proudly,
      let not arrogance come from your mouth;
   for GOD [*or* the LORD] is a God of knowledge,
      by whom actions are weighed.
⁴ The bows of the mighty are broken,
      but the feeble gird on strength.
⁵ Those who were full have hired themselves out for bread,
      but those who were hungry have ceased to hunger.
   The barren has borne seven,
      but she who has many children is forlorn.
⁶ It is GOD [*or* the LORD]. who kills and brings to life,
      who brings down to Sheol and raises up,
⁷ who makes poor and makes rich,
      who brings low and also exalts.
⁸ It is God who raises up the poor from the dust,
      and lifts the needy from the ash heap,
   to make them sit with nobles
      and inherit a seat of honor.
   For the pillars of the earth belong to GOD [*or* the LORD],
      and on them God has set the world.
⁹ God will guard the feet of the faithful ones;
      but the wicked shall be removed from sight;
      for not by might shall anyone prevail.
¹⁰ The adversaries of GOD [*or* the LORD] shall be broken to pieces;
      against them God will thunder in heaven.
   GOD [*or* The LORD] will judge the ends of the earth,
      giving strength to God's ruler,□
      and exalting the power of the anointed one."

□RSV *his king.* See Appendix.

Psalm 113

¹ Praise GOD [[*or* the LORD]]!
Praise, O servants of GOD [[*or* the LORD]],
praise the name of the SOVEREIGN [[*or* LORD]]!
² Blessed be the name of the SOVEREIGN [[*or* LORD]]
from this time forth and forevermore!
³ From the rising of the sun to its setting
the name of the SOVEREIGN [[*or* LORD]] is to be praised!
⁴ GOD [[*or* The LORD]] is high above all nations,
and God's glory above the heavens!
⁵ Who is like the SOVEREIGN [[*or* LORD]] our God,
who is seated on high,
⁶ who looks far down
upon the heavens and the earth?
⁷ God raises the poor from the dust,
and lifts the needy from the ash heap,
⁸ to make them sit with nobles,
with the nobles of God's people.
⁹ God gives the barren woman a home,
making her the joyous mother of children.
Praise GOD [[*or* the LORD]]!

Lesson 2 ∼ Romans 12:9–16b

Paul writes to the Christians at Rome about their relationships with one another.

⁹ Let love be genuine; hate what is evil, hold fast to what is good; ¹⁰ be affectionately devoted to one another; outdo one another in showing honor. ¹¹ Never flag in zeal, be aglow with the Spirit, serve the Sovereign [[*or* Lord]]. ¹² Rejoice in your hope, be patient in tribulation, be constant in prayer. ¹³ Contribute to the needs of the saints, practice hospitality.

¹⁴ Bless those who persecute you; bless and do not curse them. ¹⁵ Rejoice with those who rejoice, weep with those who weep. ¹⁶ Live in harmony with one another; do not be haughty, but associate with the lowly.

Mary greets Elizabeth and sings a song of praise to God.

³⁹ In those days Mary arose and went with haste into the hill country, to a city of Judah, ⁴⁰ and she entered the house of Zechariah and greeted Elizabeth. ⁴¹ And when Elizabeth heard the greeting of Mary, the baby leaped in her womb; and Elizabeth was filled with the Holy Spirit ⁴² and she exclaimed with a loud cry, "Blessed are you among women, and blessed is the fruit of your womb! ⁴³ And why is this granted me, that the mother of my Sovereign [or Lord] should come to me? ⁴⁴ For when the voice of your greeting came to my ears, the baby in my womb leaped for joy. ⁴⁵ And blessed is she who believed that there would be a fulfillment of what was spoken to her from God [or the Lord]." ⁴⁶ And Mary said,

"My soul magnifies the Sovereign [or Lord],
⁴⁷ and my spirit rejoices in God my Savior,
⁴⁸ who has regarded the low estate of God's servant.
For henceforth all generations will call me blessed;
⁴⁹ for the one who is mighty has done great things for me,
and holy is God's name.
⁵⁰ And God's mercy is on those who fear God
from generation to generation.
⁵¹ God has shown strength with God's arm,
and has scattered the proud in the imagination of their hearts,
⁵² God has put down the mighty from their thrones,
and exalted those of low degree;
⁵³ God has filled the hungry with good things,
and has sent the rich empty away.
⁵⁴ God has helped God's servant Israel,
in remembrance of God's mercy,
⁵⁵ as God spoke to our ancestors,
to Abraham [*and Sarah**] and to their posterity forever."

⁵⁶ And Mary remained with Elizabeth about three months, and returned to her home.

⁵⁷ Now the time came for Elizabeth to be delivered, and she gave birth to a son.

---

*Addition to the text. RSV *to Abraham and to his posterity.* See "Addition of Women's Names to the Text" in the Appendix.

HOLY CROSS—SEPTEMBER 14

Lesson 1 ~ Numbers 21:4b–9

Moses makes a bronze serpent to heal victims of the plague of fiery serpents.

⁴ The people became impatient on the way, ⁵ and they spoke against God and against Moses, "Why have you brought us up out of Egypt to die in the wilderness? For there is no food and no water, and we loathe this worthless food." ⁶ Then GOD [*or* the LORD] sent fiery serpents among the people, and they bit the people, so that many people of Israel died. ⁷ And the people came to Moses, and said, "We have sinned, for we have spoken against GOD [*or* the LORD] and against you; pray to GOD [*or* the LORD] to take away the serpents from us." So Moses prayed for the people. ⁸ And GOD [*or* the LORD] said to Moses, "Make a fiery serpent, and set it on a pole; and all who are bitten, when they see it, shall live." ⁹ So Moses made a bronze serpent, and set it on a pole; and anyone whom a serpent bit would look at the bronze serpent and live.

Psalm 98:1–5

¹ O sing a new song to GOD [*or* the LORD],
   who has done marvelous things,
whose right hand and holy arm
   have gained the victory!
² GOD [*or* The LORD] has made known the victory,
   and has revealed God's vindication in the sight of the nations.
³ God has remembered God's steadfast love and faithfulness
   to the house of Israel.
All the ends of the earth have seen
   the victory of our God.
⁴ Make a joyful noise to GOD [*or* the LORD], all the earth;
   break forth into joyous song and sing praises!
⁵ Sing praises to GOD [*or* the LORD] with the lyre,
   with the lyre and the sound of melody!

Psalm 78:1–2, 34–38 (alternate)

¹ Give ear, O my people, to my teaching;
　　incline your ears to the words of my mouth!
² I will open my mouth in a parable;
　　I will utter obscure sayings from of old.
³⁴ When God slew them, they sought for God;
　　they repented and sought God earnestly.
³⁵ They remembered that God was their rock,
　　the Most High God their redeemer.
³⁶ But they flattered God with their mouths;
　　they lied to God with their tongues.
³⁷ Their heart was not steadfast toward God;
　　they were not true to God's covenant.
³⁸ Yet God, being compassionate,
　　forgave their iniquity,
　　and did not destroy them.
　restraining God's anger often,
　　and not arousing all God's wrath.

Lesson 2 ～ 1 Corinthians 1:18–24

Paul writes to the Christians at Corinth about the wisdom of God.

¹⁸ For the word of the cross is folly to those who are perishing, but to us who are being saved it is the power of God. ¹⁹ For it is written,

"I will destroy the wisdom of the wise,
and the cleverness of the clever I will thwart."

²⁰ Where is the wise one? Where is the scribe? Where is the debater of this age? Has not God made foolish the wisdom of the world? ²¹ For since, in the wisdom of God, the world did not know God through wisdom, it pleased God through the folly of what we preach to save those who believe. ²² For Jews demand signs and Greeks seek wisdom, ²³ but we preach Christ crucified, a stumbling block to Jews and folly to Gentiles, ²⁴ but to those who are called, both Jews and Greeks, Christ the power of God and the wisdom of God.

Gospel ~ John 3:13–17

Those who believe in the Child of God will have eternal life.

¹³ "No one has ascended into heaven but the one who descended from heaven, the Human One.° ¹⁴ And as Moses lifted up the serpent in the wilderness, so must the Human One° be lifted up, ¹⁵ that whoever believes in that one may have eternal life."

¹⁶ For God so loved the world that God gave God's only Child,◊ that whoever believes in that Child should not perish but have eternal life. ¹⁷ For God sent that Child◊ into the world, not to condemn the world, but that through that Child the world might be saved.

°RSV *Son of man.* See Appendix.
◊RSV v. 16 *his only Son;* v. 17 *the Son.* See Appendix.

ALL SAINTS—NOVEMBER 1

(Or the first Sunday in November)

Lesson 1 ~ Revelation 21:1–6a

The seer envisions a new heaven and a new earth.

¹ Then I saw a new heaven and a new earth; for the first heaven and the first earth had passed away, and the sea was no more. ² And I saw the holy city, new Jerusalem, coming down out of heaven from God, prepared as a bride adorned for her husband; ³ and I heard a loud voice from the throne saying, "The dwelling of God is with human beings. God will dwell with them, and they shall be God's people, and God will indeed be with them. ⁴ God will wipe away every tear from their eyes, and death shall be no more, neither shall there be mourning nor crying nor pain anymore, for the former things have passed away."

⁵ And the one who sat upon the throne said, "See, I make all things new," to which was added, "Write this, for these words are trustworthy and true." ⁶ And the one who sat upon the throne said to me, "It is done! I am the Alpha and the Omega, the beginning and the end."

Psalm 24:1–6

¹ The earth is GOD'S [*or* the LORD'S] and the fullness thereof,
  the world and those who dwell therein;
² for God has founded it upon the seas,
  and established it upon the rivers.
³ Who shall ascend the hill of GOD [*or* the LORD]?
  And who shall stand in God's holy place?
⁴ Those who have clean hands and a pure heart,
  who do not lift up their soul to what is false,
  and do not swear deceitfully.
⁵ They will receive blessing from GOD [*or* the LORD],
  and vindication from the God of their salvation.
⁶ Such is the generation of those who seek God,
  who seek the face of the God of Jacob.

Lesson 2 ~ Colossians 1:9–14

The apostle prays for the Christians at Colossae.

⁹ And so, from the day we heard of it, we have not ceased to pray for you, asking that you may be filled with the knowledge of God's will in all spiritual wisdom and understanding, ¹⁰ to lead a life worthy of the Sovereign [or Lord], pleasing in everything, bearing fruit in every good work and increasing in the knowledge of God. ¹¹ May you be strengthened with all power, according to God's glorious might, for all endurance and patience with joy, ¹² giving thanks to [*God*] the [*Mother and**] Father, who has qualified us to share in the inheritance of the saints in light. ¹³ God has delivered us from the power of evil and transferred us to the dominion☆ of God's beloved Child,◇ ¹⁴ in whom we have redemption, the forgiveness of sins.

Gospel ~ John 11:32–44

Jesus raises Lazarus from the dead.

³² Then Mary, when she came and saw Jesus, fell at his feet, and said, "Sovereign [or Lord], if you had been here, my brother would not have died." ³³ When Jesus saw her weeping, and the Jews who came with her also weeping, he was indignant in spirit and troubled, ³⁴ and said, "Where have you laid Lazarus?" They answered, "Sovereign [or Lord], come and see." ³⁵ Jesus wept. ³⁶ So the Jews said, "See how Jesus loved him!" ³⁷ But some of them said, "Could not the one who opened the eyes of the person born blind have kept this one from dying?"

³⁸ Then Jesus, again indignant, came to the tomb; it was a cave, and a stone lay upon it. ³⁹ Jesus said, "Take away the stone." Martha, the sister of the one who had died, said to Jesus, "Sovereign [or Lord], by this time there will be an odor, for he has been dead four days." ⁴⁰ Jesus said to her, "Did I not tell you that if you would believe you would see the glory of God?" ⁴¹ So they took away the stone. And Jesus looked up and said, "[*God, my Mother and**] Father, I thank you that you have heard me. ⁴² I already knew that you hear me always, but I have said this on account of the people standing by, that they may believe that you sent me." ⁴³ Having said this, Jesus cried with a loud voice, "Lazarus, come out." ⁴⁴ The dead man came out, his hands and feet bound with bandages, and his face wrapped with a cloth. Jesus said to them, "Unbind him, and let him go."

---

*Addition to the text. See "Metaphor" and "God the Father and Mother" in the Appendix.
☆RSV *kingdom*. See Appendix.
◇RSV *Son*. See Appendix.

THANKSGIVING DAY

Lesson 1 ~ Joel 2:21–27

The prophet Joel praises God for the promise of an abundant harvest.

²¹ Fear not, O land;
    be glad and rejoice,
    for GOD [*or* the LORD] has done great things!
²² Fear not, you beasts of the field,
    for the pastures of the wilderness are green;
  the tree bears its fruit,
    the fig tree and vine give their full yield.
²³ Be glad, O children of Zion,
    and rejoice in the SOVEREIGN [*or* LORD], your God,
  who has given the early rain for your vindication,
    and has poured down for you abundant rain,
    the early and the latter rain, as before.
²⁴ The threshing floors shall be full of grain,
    the vats shall overflow with wine and oil.
²⁵ I will restore to you the years
    which the swarming locust has eaten,
  the hopper, the destroyer, and the cutter,
    my great army, which I sent among you.
²⁶ You shall eat in plenty and be satisfied,
    and praise the name of the SOVEREIGN [*or* LORD] your God,
  who has dealt wondrously with you.
And my people shall never again be put to shame.
²⁷ You shall know that I am in the midst of Israel,
    and that I, the SOVEREIGN [*or* LORD], am your God and there is
     none else.
And my people shall never again be put to shame.

Psalm 126

¹ When GOD ⟦*or* the LORD⟧ restored the fortunes of Zion,
  we were like those who dream.
² Then our mouth was filled with laughter,
    and our tongue with shouts of joy;
  then they said among the nations,
    "GOD ⟦*or* The LORD⟧ has done great things for them."
³ GOD ⟦*or* The LORD⟧ has done great things for us;
  we are glad.
⁴ Restore our fortunes, O GOD ⟦*or* LORD⟧,
  like the watercourses in the Negeb!
⁵ May those who sow in tears
  reap with shouts of joy!
⁶ Those who go forth weeping,
    bearing the seed for sowing,
  shall come home with shouts of joy,
    bringing their sheaves of grain.

Lesson 2 ~ 1 Timothy 2:1–7

The writer urges prayer for people in high places, in the name of God and the one mediator Christ Jesus.

¹ First of all, then, I urge that supplications, prayers, intercessions, and thanksgivings be made for all people, ² for rulers⬚ and all who are in high positions, that we may lead a quiet and peaceable life, godly and respectful in every way. ³ This is good, and it is acceptable in the sight of God our Savior, ⁴ who desires all people to be saved and to come to the knowledge of the truth. ⁵ For there is one God, and there is one mediator between God and humankind, Christ Jesus, ⁶ who sacrificed Christ's self as a ransom for all, the testimony to which was borne at the proper time. ⁷ For this I was appointed a preacher and apostle (I am telling the truth, I am not lying), a teacher of the Gentiles in faith and truth.

⬚RSV *kings.* See Appendix.

Gospel ∼ Matthew 6:25-33

Jesus teaches the disciples to trust in God.

²⁵ Therefore I tell you, do not be anxious about your life, what you shall eat or what you shall drink, nor about your body, what you shall put on. Is not life more than food, and the body more than clothing? ²⁶ Look at the birds of the air: they neither sow nor reap nor gather into barns, and yet [*God*] your heavenly Father [*and Mother**] feeds them. Are you not of more value than they? ²⁷ And which of you by being anxious can add one cubit to your span of life? ²⁸ And why are you anxious about clothing? Consider the lilies of the field, how they grow; they neither toil nor spin; ²⁹ yet I tell you, even Solomon in all his glory was not arrayed like one of these. ³⁰ But if God so clothes the grass of the field, which today is alive and tomorrow is thrown into the oven, will God not much more clothe you, O you of little faith? ³¹ Therefore do not be anxious, saying, "What shall we eat?" or "What shall we drink?" or "What shall we wear?" ³² For the Gentiles seek all these things; and [*God*] your heavenly [*Mother and**] Father knows that you need them all. ³³ But seek first God's realm☆ and God's righteousness, and all these things shall be yours as well.

---

*Addition to the text. See "Metaphor" and "God the Father and Mother" in the Appendix.
☆RSV *kingdom.* See Appendix.

Appendix

Metaphor

A metaphor is a figure of speech used to extend meaning through comparison of dissimilars. For example, "Life is a dream" is a metaphor. The character of dreams is ascribed to life, and the meaning of "life" is thus extended. "Dream" is used as a screen through which to view "life." Two dissimilars are juxtaposed.

The statement "God is Father" is also a metaphor. Two dissimilars, "Father" and "God," are juxtaposed, and so the meaning of "God" is extended. Although "God the Father" has been a powerful metaphor for communicating the nature of God, like any metaphor it can become worn. It may even be interpreted literally, that is, as describing exactly. The dissimilars become similar. The metaphor becomes a proposition.

Now, if one were to say "God is Mother," the power of the metaphor would be apparent. The image "God the Mother and Father" as a lens through which to view God elicits the response of a true metaphor, just as the statement "God is Father" once did. In this lectionary, "God the Father and Mother" is used as a formal equivalent of "the Father" or "God the Father." "God the Father" is clearly a metaphor, just as "God the Mother" is. God *is* not a father, any more than God *is* a mother, or than life *is* a dream. By reading and hearing "God the Father and Mother" we provide a metaphor for God that balances the more familiar *male* imagery for God with the less familiar *female* imagery.

There are many female images for God in the scriptures. For example, God as mother is found in the Old Testament, "Now I will cry out like a woman in travail" (Isa. 42:14), and "As one whom his mother comforts, so I will comfort you" (Isa. 66:13). In the New Testament, the parable of the woman seeking the lost coin (Luke 15:8–10) functions as a female image for God. Metaphors are figurative and open-ended. Their meanings vary from hearer to hearer, but they are not dispensable, for there is no other way by which to say directly what the metaphor communicates. A metaphor provides a new way of seeing.

247

(*)[*God*] the Father [*and Mother*] (RSV the Father; God the Father, God our Father; Abba)

One of the characteristics of the Christian faith is its emphasis on the personal nature of God. While God is also described in impersonal terms (rock, light, love), personal imagery prevails. "Father" is one such personal term. The Gospels record that when Jesus prayed he called God *"Abba"* ("Father," Mark 14:36), and frequently, especially in the Gospel of John, Jesus refers to God as Father. In the Old Testament, the term "Father" is used infrequently as a designation for God.

For Jesus, "Father" was a sacred word, pointing to the mysterious intimacy Jesus had with God (Matt. 11:27), and pointing to the intimate relationship his disciples also had with God (Matt. 23:9). Jesus' own use of the word "Father" in addressing God supported the church's claim that Jesus was the "Son."

The phrase used in this lectionary, "God the Father and Mother," is offered as a way of expressing the same intimacy, caring, and freedom that is found in Jesus' identification of God as *Abba.* Jesus' use of this term to refer to God was radically nontraditional. This warrants the use of nontraditional intimate language in contemporary reference to God. Thus the use of the phrase "God the Mother and Father" is a way to affirm the important Christian belief that Jesus is the Child of God. Just as we do not create our children, but give them birth out of our very selves, we believe that God did not create Jesus, but that God "gave birth to" or "begot" Jesus.

It is also the case that Christians rejected as pagan the view that God is father of the world. For Christians, God is Father in relation to the Son. Christians are brought into this relationship of God as "Father" because they are adopted as "sons" or "heirs" (Rom. 8:15, 23; Gal. 4:6; Eph. 1:5).

That Jesus called God "Father" is the basis for the church's thinking about Jesus Christ as one of the persons of the Trinity. The relationship described by the Father/Son imagery of the New Testament opened the way for the church later to identify the Son as of the same substance as the Father. And if God the Son proceeded from God the Father alone, the procession is both a male and a female action, a begetting *and* a birth. God is the *Mother and Father* of the Child who comes forth.

The image of God as Father has been misused to support the excessive authority of earthly fathers in a patriarchal social structure. The metaphor "God the Father and Mother" points to the close relationship between language about God and language about the human community. The mutuality and coequality of the persons of the Trinity is a model for human community and especially appropriate, therefore, for readings prepared for worship. Those who worship in the Christian church are struggling to bring about a community where there is "neither male nor female," but where all are "one in Christ Jesus" and "heirs according to promise" (Gal. 3:28–29). (See also Metaphor.)

(⊗)God (RSV my Father, the Father)

In the Gospel of John, and occasionally elsewhere, RSV "Father" is often rendered "God" where "Father" appears frequently in the lection.

Sovereign; God, the Sovereign; etc. (RSV Lord, Lord, etc.)

Sometime in the course of Israel's history the personal name of God, probably pronounced *Yahweh,* ceased to be spoken aloud for fear that it would be profaned, even though it continued to be written in the text of the scriptures. Thus, the practice was already established according to which the faith and piety of the community, shaped by the tradition of scripture itself, takes precedence over the written word in determining what is read for the divine name by the worshiping community. From that time on, the chief word read in place of the divine name was *Adonai*—an honorific title translated "Lord" or "my Lord."

In those places in the RSV where the underlying Hebrew text contains the divine name *(Yahweh),* and not simply the word *Adonai,* the typography is changed to Lord. Where the divine name is found in the original text, the Lectionary Committee prefers to render it as "God" or "the Sovereign." However, because of the deep commitment in the church to the word "Lord" in both Old and New Testaments, and because of a certain ambiguity about the extent to which "Lord" is heard as gender-specific, that term has been included in this lectionary text as an optional or alternative reading, set off in this manner: [*or* Lord]; [*or* the Lord].

In this lectionary the Hebrew word *Elohim* is rendered "God," as in the RSV. The word "God" is also usually used for masculine pronouns referring to the "Sovereign [*or* Lord]" or to "God."

Occasionally the divine name, Yahweh, is found in combination with the word for God *(Yahweh Elohim)* or with the word for Lord *(Adonai Yahweh).* These are rendered in the RSV as "the Lord God" and "the Lord God," respectively. In this lectionary the former is rendered as "the Sovereign [*or* Lord] God" and the latter as "the Sovereign [*or* Lord] God. The following chart summarizes these various renderings.

Hebrew Scriptures	RSV	Inclusive-Language Lectionary
Elohim	God	God
Adonai	Lord	God [*or* the Lord]; or the Sovereign [*or* Lord]
Yahweh	Lord	God [*or* the Lord]; or the Sovereign [*or* Lord]
Yahweh Elohim; or *Elohim Yahweh*	the Lord God	the Sovereign [*or* Lord] God
Adonai Yahweh; or *Yahweh Adonai*	the Lord God	the Sovereign [*or* Lord] God

In the Greek New Testament the most frequently used words for God are *Theos* ("God") and *Kyrios* ("Lord"). It is natural that *Kyrios* occurs so often for "God" in the New Testament, because that was the word by which the Greek version of the Old Testament rendered both *Yahweh* and *Adonai;* and it was the Greek version, not the original Hebrew, that was read by the New Testament authors. *Kyrios* was also taken over by the church as a primary way of designating Jesus: "Jesus is Lord."

Kyrios has a wide range of other meanings. It is used for the *owner* of possessions, for the *head* of a family, or for the *master* of a house or of slaves. In the vocative it often means "Sir." *Kyrios* is usually translated into English by "Lord" (in reference to God or Jesus) or "lord" (in reference to a man). In common usage, "lord" means a man with power and authority, such as a titled nobleman.

Because "Lord" is basically a gender-specific word (despite a certain ambiguity in contemporary usage), when used of either God or Christ it connotes, for some, a male being. Since the church believes that God transcends gender and that the risen Christ is one with God, in this lectionary *Kyrios,* occasionally rendered "God" or "Christ," usually has been translated as "Sovereign." (See chart below.) This word, like "Lord," means one supreme in power and authority, but it is inclusive—women as well as men are sovereigns. This translation follows the same principle used in rendering *Yahweh* and *Adonai* as "Sovereign" in the Old Testament lections, and the word "Lord" is included in the text as an alternative reading in the New Testament lections.

Greek New Testament	RSV	Inclusive-Language Lectionary
Kyrios	Lord	Sovereign [[*or* Lord]]
		Christ [[*or* the Lord]]
		God [[*or* the Lord]]

"Sovereign" has another advantage for the translator over "Lord." It is a word in contemporary usage in the political arena, and is not confined to religious usage, as is virtually the case with the word "Lord" in the United States. Not only are there living sovereigns in monarchical societies but nations as well are said to exercise sovereignty. The designation of Jesus Christ as *Kyrios* by the early church carried precisely such a political meaning: Jesus, not Caesar, was *Kyrios*. Christians believed that Jesus Christ is supreme over all earthly authorities. Hence, the status of the authority of the *Sovereign Jesus Christ* in relation to any national sovereignty is expressed in a contemporary idiom which brings to the fore the revolutionary significance of the statement *Kyrios Iēsous* (Jesus is Lord [Sovereign]) for the history of the church.

(°) Child, Child of God (RSV Son, Son of God)

"Son" is used as a designation of Jesus as the Messiah (e.g., Rom. 1:3; 5:10). At Jesus' baptism there was a voice from heaven: "This is my beloved Son" (Matt. 3:17). Jesus also refers to himself as "Son" (Matt. 11:27), though seldom except in the Gospel of John, where the self-designation is common.

A son is male, and of course the historical person, Jesus, was a man. But as the Gospels depict Jesus, his maleness is not said to have any significance for salvation. It is the fact that Jesus was *human* that is crucial, both for Jesus' designation as the Christ and for Jesus' work of salvation.

If the fact that Jesus was a male has no christological significance, then neither has the fact that Jesus was a *son* and not a *daughter.* Therefore, in this lectionary the formal equivalent "Child" or "Child of God" is used for "Son" when the latter has christological significance, and the masculine pronouns that refer to "Child" ("Son") are rendered as "Child." Thus, all hearers of the lectionary readings will be enabled to identify themselves with Jesus' *humanity.*

In traditional language, Jesus as "the Son" makes believers "sons" and therefore heirs. In this lectionary, Jesus as the Child of God makes believers—men and women—"children" of God and therefore heirs. When Jesus is called "Son of God" it is not Jesus' male character that is of primary importance but Jesus' intimate relationship with God (see Matt. 11:25–27). Other connotations of "sonship" are divine authority (see Matt. 28:18–20) and freedom (see Rom. 8:21).

While the word "child" may imply a minor, or childishness, in the New Testament it clearly refers to "adults" in more than half of its occurrences. For example, the word "child" or "children" is used for adult descendants (Acts 13:33; Rom. 9:8); or for adults who are "children" of a teacher or an apostle (1 Cor. 4:14; 2 Cor. 6:13); or for adult Christians (2 John 1, 4); or for adults who are "children of God" (John 11:52; Rom. 8:16). In these and many other passages, "child" or "children" connotes primarily a relationship, and more often of adults than of minors. The canon, therefore, itself provides the church with a substitute for the word "son" that is not gender-specific. The two meanings of the word "child" in the New Testament are also consistent with contemporary usage where the term "child" refers not only to minors but also to a relationship to parents without reference to age.

(○) The Human One (RSV the Son of Man)

The term "the Son of man" is found frequently in the Gospels, and almost nowhere else in the New Testament. Only Jesus uses the term (with a single exception), and the Gospel writers always intended the term to refer to Jesus. How do the Gospel authors interpret its meaning?

251

Much light would be shed on the meaning of the term if there were clear antecedents to its use in the Gospels, but any such antecedents are impossible to demonstrate. It cannot be shown that Jewish use of the term "Son of man" has influenced its use in the Gospels; in fact, the term does not appear to have functioned as a title prior to its application to Jesus by the church. Furthermore, its meaning varies in different contexts. The term, however, is subject to being misinterpreted as speaking about a male human being, a "son" of a "man." And so, in this lectionary, "the Human One" is used as a formal equivalent for "the Son of man." That formal equivalent is not derived from or dependent on any particular judgment as to the background of "the Son of man" in Judaism, and is not intended to prejudice in any way the ongoing discussion of that question. The Committee believes, however, that the title "the Human One" is open to the same nuances of interpretation allowed by the title "the Son of man." Many of these nuances are derived from the context in which the term is used rather than from the term itself.

In the Old Testament, Ezekiel is often addressed by God as "son of man," which is not a title, and connotes simply a "man." This lectionary renders this expression, "O mortal." In Dan. 7:13, an Aramaic expression is used which is translated "a son of man" in the RSV and "a human being" in this lectionary.

Gender-Specific Pronouns for God and Christ

Because English pronouns are inherently gender-specific, they are not used in this lectionary to refer either to God or to the preexistent or risen Christ.

(*) Realm of God (RSV Kingdom, Kingdom of God, Kingship)

The Greek word used frequently in the New Testament, and usually translated by the gender-specific word "kingdom," has generally been rendered in this lectionary as "realm," though it has also been translated by other terms as well. The Greek word refers either to the activity of God (i.e., God's "kingship" or "dominion" or "reign" or "rule") or to the state of affairs brought about by God (i.e., God's "kingdom" or "dominion" or "realm"). The Hebrew root usually translated "kingdom" in the RSV is occasionally rendered "kingdom" in this lectionary, but is usually rendered by other terms, primarily "realm."

(☐) Ruler, Monarch (RSV King)

The word "king" is used in the Bible both in reference to earthly royal figures and as a metaphor for God. In this lectionary "King" as a metaphor for God is rendered as "Ruler," "Sovereign," or occasionally "Monarch." The word "king" is retained in reference to specific earthly kings, such as David, and in stories and parables about kings.

(+) Teacher (RSV Master)

The Greek word used only by Luke in the New Testament and rendered "Master" in the RSV is translated in this lectionary by "Teacher." It had a wide variety of connotations, such as supervisor, administrator, or governor, but no specific religious connotations. It is used by Luke in passages where parallels in Matthew or Mark have "Sovereign," "Teacher," or "Rabbi."

Sisters and Brothers, Friends, Neighbors (RSV Brother, Brethren)

The contemporary use of such phrases as "sisters and brothers in Christ" to address members of the church is helpful in clarifying how the words "brother" and "brethren" are used in the Bible. In Hebrew and Greek usage, the same word could refer to a sibling, a more distant relative, a neighbor, or a member of one's community or race. Paul appears to reflect such a broad use of the word "brethren" in a phrase he uses in Rom. 9:3, where in the RSV "my brethren" is the equivalent of "my kinsmen by race" (in this lectionary the whole phrase appears as "my own people, my kinsfolk by race"). In Greek, "brother" was often used to refer to a friend, or one with whom one shares a common purpose, but not necessarily a blood relative.

In the New Testament, the plural form of the word "brother" appears to have been intended to include both women and men. For example, in Luke 21:16, "brothers" is certainly intended to mean "brothers and sisters"; and when Paul addressed Christians as "brethren" (e.g., Rom. 8:12; 1 Cor. 2:1) he was surely including women as well as men. In such cases of direct address, "brethren" has been rendered in this lectionary either as "sisters and brothers" ("brothers and sisters") or as "friends." In post-resurrection sayings attributed to Jesus, "brethren" is translated as "followers" (Matt. 28:10) or "friends" (John 20:17) to make clear that the reference is to the nascent church and not to Jesus' siblings.

(*) Addition of Women's Names to the Text

In a few instances, women's names have been added to the text in this lectionary. These names are included where generation or origin of the people is a major concern. The addition of these names is also consistent with the biblical tradition itself, where on occasion Sarah as well as Abraham is explicitly referred to as progenitor (cf. Isa. 51:1–2), or as one who along with Abraham trusted in God and God's promises (cf. Heb. 11:11). Women's names added to the text are placed in brackets and italicized. If the additional words involve a change in the verb form, the RSV rendering is in the footnotes.

(ᵛ) The Jews

The term "the Jews" occurs very frequently in the Gospel of John. Sometimes it refers in a straightforward, historical way to the ethnic people of whom Jesus was one and among whom Jesus lived out his life. Sometimes, however, it is used almost as a code word for religious leaders who misunderstand the true identity of Christ. When "the Jews" is used in the former sense in the lections from the Gospel of John, it remains unchanged in this lectionary. When it is used in the latter sense, it is rendered "the religious authorities" so as to minimize what could be perceived as a warrant for anti-Semitism in the Gospel of John.

Other Excluding Imagery: Darkness

The New Testament imagery of light versus darkness is often used to contrast good with evil. The equation of darkness with evil, or that which is done in secret and out of the light, has unfortunately led some persons and groups to condemn and reject anything that is black or any dark-hued person as evil or somehow condemned by God. This color symbolism has its equally inaccurate and unfortunate correlative in the equation of light with white—with what is true, good, and loved of God—for example, in the verse "Wash me, and I shall be whiter than snow" (Ps. 51:7). In this lectionary the word translated "whiter" in the RSV is rendered "cleaner." While the biblical context may be free from racist intent, the too-easy misconception that dark people are also condemned and to be avoided has led to the use in this lectionary of terminology other than "darkness" and "white" as metaphors for what is either condemned or loved by God.

Use of "They," "Them," "Themselves," "Their" as Singular Pronouns

In some cases, indefinite singular pronouns are rendered in this lectionary by "they," "them," "themselves," or "their." This usage is recognized as appropriate by the National Council of Teachers of English in its *Guidelines for Nonsexist Use of Language in NCTE Publications.* The *Oxford English Dictionary* says that "they" is "often used in reference to a singular noun made universal by *every, any,* or *no,* etc., or is applied to one of either sex (= 'he or she')." Those grammarians who oppose this usage follow common practice established by an 1850 Act of Parliament declaring that "he" is generic and legally includes "she." That declaration in turn was based on a rule invented in 1746 by John Kirby: the male gender is "more comprehensive" than the female. This lectionary follows the precedent of St. John Fisher (1535), who wrote that God "never forsaketh any creature unlesse they before have forsaken themselves," and William Shakespeare, who urged "everyone to rest themselves."

(⁺) **Changes in the Table of Readings and Psalms**

The mandate of the Inclusive-Language Lectionary Committee is to recast the language of the RSV in those places where male-biased or otherwise inappropriately exclusive language could be modified to reflect an inclusiveness of all persons. Consistent with the goal of this mandate, the Committee has determined that it is also appropriate to add certain lections about women that have not been included in the listing recommended by the North American Committee on Calendar and Lectionary. These alternate readings are:

In Year A

Easter 5, Lesson 2	Acts 17:1–12
Pentecost 25, Lesson 1	Wisd. of Sol. 6:12–16
Pentecost 26, Lesson 1	Prov. 31:10–13, 19–20, 30–31

In Year B

Epiphany 2, Lesson 2	Rom. 16:1–7
Lent 4, Lesson 1	Judges 4:4–9
Pentecost 12, Lesson 1	2 Sam. 14:4–17
Pentecost 12, Gospel	John 8:2–11

In Year C

Lent 3, Gospel	Luke 13:10–17
Easter 5, Lesson 1	Acts 16:11–15

Furthermore, where consistent with the mandate, the Committee has occasionally added or omitted some verses of a lection or substituted a reading. These alterations are:

In Year A

Pentecost 7, Lesson 1	Ex. 1:15–21
Pentecost 9, Gospel	Matt. 13:31–35
Annunciation	Alternate Ps. 45 not included

In Year B

Epiphany 2, Lesson 2	1 Cor. 6:12–15a, 19–20 (prescribed reading: ch. 6:12–20)
Pentecost 5, Lesson 2	2 Sam. 5:1–5 (prescribed reading: 5:1–12)
Pentecost 14, Lesson 2	Eph. 6:1–4 added
Annunciation	Alternate Ps. 45 not included

In Year C

Pentecost 16, Lesson 2	Heb. 13:8–16, 20–21 (prescribed reading: Philemon 1–20)
Annunciation	Alternate Ps. 45 not included

Index of Readings for Year B

*Based on the Lectionary prepared for trial use
by the North American Committee on
Calendar and Lectionary*

261